Janus-Faced Justice

Political Criminals in Imperial Japan

RICHARD H. MITCHELL

UNIVERSITY OF HAWAII PRESS
HONOLULU

Library of Congress Cataloging-in-Publication Data

Mitchell, Richard H.
  Janus-faced justice : political criminals in imperial Japan /
Richard H. Mitchell.
      p.   cm.
  Includes bibliographical references (p.   ) and index.
  ISBN 0-8248-1410-X
  1. Criminal justice, Administration of—Japan—History.
2. Political crimes and offenses—Japan—Prevention—History.
3. Political persecution—Japan—History. 4. Police—Japan—
Complaints against—History. 5. Political prisoners—Japan—
History. 6. Japan—Politics and government—1868-1912. 7. Japan—
Politics and government—1912-1945. I. Title.
HV9960.J3M57   1992
364.1'31'0952—dc20   91-41623
                                                          CIP

University of Hawaii Press books are printed on
acid-free paper and meet the guidelines for
permanence and durability of the Council
on Library Resources

Designed by Ken Miyamoto

For Okudaira Yasuhiro

Contents

Acknowledgments

I WISH to express my gratitude to those who have aided in the publication of this book. I am grateful to the American Philosophical Society for a research grant in 1986 and to the Center for International Studies, University of Missouri-St. Louis, for research funds. I am indebted to Lawrence W. Beer, William B. Cleary, Okudaira Yasuhiro, and Suzuki Yoshio for providing articles, books, and documents. I would like to thank Mary Hines for typing the manuscript. A special debt of gratitude is owed to Yoshiko for her double duty as research assistant and wife.

In the transliteration of Japanese names, the standard form is used, with the family name first. Macrons are used to mark long vowels except for common words found in collegiate dictionaries.

Introduction

JANUS IN ROMAN MYTH was the dual-faced guardian god of portals and patron of endings and beginnings. In this book, this duality describes two different situations in the system of justice in imperial Japan. First, it applies to the treatment of all criminal suspects, both regular and political, since those who passed through the portals of police stations were never certain which face they would encounter: lawless acts by police and procurators or the proper protection of individual rights under law. Second, this term neatly captures the state's criminal policy toward political criminal suspects (so-called thought criminals) during the 1930s and 1940s: either long-term prison confinement (for those who resisted pressures to reform) or reeducation and reintegration into society (for those who accepted state guidance).

While numerous publications excoriate the imperial Japanese state for repressive policies, a holistic understanding of the treatment of political criminals is lacking. This is especially odd in view of the long-running, intense debate on the nature of the "emperor system" and the contemporary controversy over alleged police brutality and forced confessions and charges that procurators improperly dominate the justice system. The reaction of historians to this current debate over justice is perhaps to wonder if the postwar reform of the prewar system of criminal justice failed to take hold because that reform aimed at strengthening guarantees of human rights for criminal suspects. Undoubtedly, some historians also recall the old saying that the more things change the more they remain the same. When, for example, government officials insist that changing the law to permit police to hold criminal suspects longer would solve problems of police abuse, this historian recalls a similar proposal made in the 1930s. Therefore, badly needed to properly understand the current heated debate is a long historical view of individual rights under the law.

This study focuses on the treatment of political criminal suspects and prisoners from 1868 to 1945, but the handling of regular criminal suspects and convicts is analyzed as well. Within the category of political criminals, the focus is on leftists, who were the most affected by the state's obsession to stamp out communism. Two themes are obvious: the degree of state repression in the handling of political criminals and concern for human rights *(jinken)*. The treatment of accused and convicted criminals is judged, using the measuring stick provided by the imperial state (i.e., did government officials follow the state's laws and regulations?); since the term *human rights* is too imprecise to use as an analytical tool, human rights is defined as *procedural rights* (i.e., individuals' rights under criminal procedure and the rights of prisoners based on the Meiji Constitution and the various laws and regulations).

Political crime is a slippery term, but it may be defined as any action "intended to disrupt or destroy the integrity of a governmental system."[1] Political offenses in one way or another strike at the roots of state power and "affect the structure or stability of the existing regime."[2] Actually, what makes a crime political is the legal response the criminal's action evokes from the state. "A common crime may be politically motivated or have a political object, but unless it is regarded as 'political' by authorities . . . the legal response to it will be the same as for other common crimes; there will be no 'special handling' of the case as is customary for true political crimes."[3]

While there is wide disagreement about which label to pin on the pre-1945 state, there is consensus that the state was repressive, lacking concern for human rights. The well-known historian Ienaga Saburō states: "The weak appreciation of civil rights was one cause of the Pacific War. . . . The abrogation of human rights kept pace with the intensified war. . . . This is the greatest issue of the war as far as domestic history is concerned. The failure within Japanese society was exported. . . . The mistreatment of local residents by our military during the Pacific War eternally blemished Japan's record as a civilized nation."[4] Lawrence Beer, a distinguished political scientist, writes: "The nadir for human rights came during the period of ultranationalist militarism in the wake of the Great Depression, 1930–1945."[5] The eminent political scientist Ishida Takeshi notes that during the war years "all human rights were sacrificed to the war effort. . . . Among scholars of law, the slogan 'Return to Gierke *(Zurück zu Gierke)*', introduced from Germany, was often used to emphasize the importance of traditional communal life in Japan; and the slogan 'Part from the Civil Code *(Abschied vom BGB)*' was invoked to get rid of the western concept of rights."[6] Beer and C. G. Weeramantry see a sharp break in the political order after Japan's defeat, with a human rights revolution after 1945 instigated by officials of the Allied Occupation aided by some supportive Japanese.[7] After looking at the attitudes and actions of government officials, lawyers, and others in connection with human rights (i.e., procedural rights), this study concludes that we must reassess the common view that the human rights movement began with the institutional reforms of the Occupation era.

Although nearly fifty years have passed since the collapse of imperial Japan, a lively debate continues on the subject of officially inspired brutality and torture. The highly emotional battle lines are firmly drawn, with defenders of the old government insisting that examples of torture represented individual actions and were not official Special Higher Police (Tokubetsu Kōtō Keisatsu or Tokkō) policy. Critics argue that torture was official policy and compare the Tokkō with the GPU (State Political Administration) or the Gestapo.[8] Typically, Ōno Tatsuzō brands the pre-1945 system "Torture and Brutal Killing by the Emperor System Police."[9] While torture was prohibited by law, he writes, it was encouraged in the emperor's name, an ideology above the law that permitted even the killing of suspects.[10] A popular two-volume history of Showa employs the subtitle "Severe Torture" in the section on the mass arrest of March 15, 1928. From this time, say the authors, the Tokkō gained a worldwide reputation as torturers. Moreover, the Tokkō trained personnel in torture techniques.[11] Yamabe Kentarō insists that torture was used not only by police to force confessions, but also by procurators. If a suspect repudiated the document produced by the police, the procurator could simply return him to the police for more persuasion.[12] These are but a sample of many similar statements found in books

published since 1945. Examples in English are also easy to come
by. "Those arrested were often subjected to police torture, and
some were tortured to death," writes Tsurumi Kazuko. "They
were given alternatives: If they announced that they had changed
their ideas . . . they could expect better treatment . . . and their
term of imprisonment might be shortened. But, if they refused
. . . they were bound to face either imprisonment for an indefinite
period or death."[13] Writing about the March 15, 1928, mass
arrest, Mikiso Hane states: "Torture was used freely during the
interrogation of these men."[14] Ralph Braibanti records: "Police
methods were often brutal. . . . the use of third degree tactics to
enforce confessions was common. In one instance the writer saw
the results of acid being poured over the eyes of prisoners, blind-
ing them for life."[15]

Despite such accounts, a nagging doubt remains, since many of
the postwar critics are angry victims of the old state's anticommunist program. Doubt is increased by scholarly theory about
"soft rule," which depicts force as frequently used in the West to
subjugate people, whereas in Japan obedience was secured
through persuasion rather than fear.[16] In normal circumstances,
"the Japanese policeman is sympathetic and succoring," writes
David Bayley. "An analogue of what the Japanese policeman
wants the offender to feel is the tearful relief of a child when confession of wrongdoing to his parents results in a gentle laugh and a
warm hug.[17] Bayley writes, of course, about the postwar police,
yet one must wonder if pre-1945 police practices were really so
very different, especially in light of the "soft rule" thesis. Therefore, a key purpose of this book is to investigate this subject of brutality and torture in a search for the historical truth.

This study raises many questions: How extensive were abuses
in procedures relating to arrest, detention, and trial? Did police
officials faithfully enforce the laws or did they encourage systematic brutality and torture? How common were forced confessions? Were criminal suspects killed during interrogation? What
bearing did normal police behavior have on the actions of the Special Higher Police (i.e., how were regular criminal suspects
treated)? How fair were preliminary judicial examinations and
regular trials? How extensive was judicial independence? How
humane were prison conditions? Were illegal practices blessed or
condemned by higher authorities? How did lawyers, bar associa-

tions, and legal scholars react to the state's handling of political criminals? What made some lawyers risk official censure and punishment to defend leftists? Why were some more successful than others? Did "rule-by-law," as many scholars contend, function fully? How pervasive in the system of justice was the Tokugawa legacy of suppression? Which label best fits pre-1945 Japan?

Realizing that a few examples prove nothing one way or another, this book presents many examples of the treatment of regular criminal and political criminal suspects, as well as convicts. Besides reviewing the justice system, this book offers the first extended treatment in English of Japan's embryonic gulag. Other matters, such as the origin of the substitute prison *(daiyō kangoku)*, which is central to the postwar public protest over police abuses, are investigated together with the beginning of concern for the human rights of criminal suspects and convicts. The book also deals with the sorely neglected subject of political trials and challenges common assumptions by reviewing the key trials of the 1920s; long-cherished views about the differences between the 1920s and the 1930s are also put to the test (e.g., that the Tokkō began to use their power improperly in 1932–1933). Next is an account of defense lawyers: the Radical Bar and the Civil Libertarians who were on the cutting edge of the human rights movement. Besides a reanalysis of the famous Tokyo trial of communist suspects, numerous cases of alleged police brutality are evaluated, and prison conditions are explored. Police actions are analyzed, based on police textbooks and other material. Secret Justice Ministry conferences and the public statements of high officials in the Home and Justice ministries are evaluated. *Tenkō* (conversion), a novel method of dealing with political criminal suspects and convicts, is explored together with the little-known *Keiji Hoshō Hō* (Criminal Compensation Law).

Since the Tokkō were, as former officers stress, merely an offshoot of the regular police, and since they received orders from procurators and followed "normal" police procedures, including being subject to the Criminal Procedure Code, Chapter 4 investigates brutality and torture in nonideological cases handled by regular police as a standard against which to measure Tokkō actions. Beginning with newspaper accounts, the investigation moves to the courtroom and the floor of the Diet and finally into the inner sanctum of the Justice Ministry via a confidential report done in February 1938 on police violations of human rights. This neglected document provides fresh insights into the thinking of justice officials. The chapter concludes with a look at police attitudes in connection with social status and ideological position, the failure of liberals to defend the legal rights of leftists, and police resistance to reform. Police actions and political trials during the Pacific War are the main focus of the next chapter. One section, however, which investigates conditions among the special prisoners held in preventive detention, may disrupt another long-cherished view. After drawing conclusions about the imperial state's treatment of political criminals, a cross-cultural perspective is made, comparing the Japanese case with that of other nations. Hannah Arendt's reason for comparing crimes is kept in mind: not to lump them together so they seem relative, but to look for their uniqueness. Finally, this study concludes that "a paternalistic police state" is the label that best fits pre-1945 Japan.

Among the widely ranging open sources and secret documents used are memoirs by leftists, most of whom were victims of state power. The question of reliability of accounts by angry victims quite naturally comes to mind. Therefore, accounts in memoirs were checked against statements in secret government documents, open government sources, books, articles, and newspapers, with attention given to the treatment of not only political criminal suspects but regular criminals as well. The conclusion is that in spite of disagreement on some details (e.g., was a particular policeman present at an interrogation or was electric torture used in one instance?) the description of brutality and torture in the memoirs is basically correct.

Janus-Faced Justice

1

Legacies

THE NEW MEIJI (1868–1912) government inherited from the Tokugawa (1603–1867) a transcendental administrative state in which superiors issued orders or delegated power to inferiors, unregulated by justiciable law. The outstanding trait of this political system was a lack of redress against authority. The dominant characteristic of the Tokugawa agrarian state's law was rule-by-status. This system extended equality of treatment appropriate to each person's status; there was no concept of individual rights independent of the family or the group. Confucianism did preach, however, that linked to loyalty toward superiors was the government's duty to act benevolently and responsibly. Given the Confucian ideals on which Tokugawa society was based, the Western concept of natural law would have seemed "unnatural law." Natural law assumed that people's rights were embedded in unchanging universal principles, which transcended the state and extended justice to all. Tokugawa law aimed at securing justice for the polity.[1]

Weakness and dissension impelled the Meiji regime to create a strong political police apparatus to suppress opponents. In May 1869, the government organized the Danjōdai, a police agency that mainly investigated political conspiracies. The Danjōdai was abolished in July 1871, but its duties were absorbed by the Shihōshō (Justice Ministry), which until early 1874 controlled the central police power.[2] Searching for a Western police force to copy, the Japanese picked the French model, a logical choice: it was famous, it was highly centralized, it performed a wide range of administrative functions (including preventive policing and political surveillance), and that model was already under study for the legal system and the courts. Kawaji Toshiyoshi, a member of the inspection team that went to Europe in 1872, recommended in his report that a European-style Home Ministry centralize all police functions (the Naimushō was established in November 1873) and that Tokyo be given a Keishichō (Metropolitan Police Board), financed by the central government with a chief directly responsible to the home minister. The board should emulate the broad range of administrative duties of the Paris model, including surveillance of political foes, and it should copy the French police power of using a large number of regulations to administer fines and limited jail sentences. The police should be split into two groups, he suggested: administrative (under the control of the Home Ministry) and judicial (under the supervision of the Justice Ministry). Roughly, the functional division was that the former were to maintain public order and the latter were to investigate offenses and aid judicial officials in prosecutions. This model was adopted in January 1874, with Kawaji as the chief of the Metropolitan Police Board.[3]

In this centralized structure, the Home Ministry held control of all personnel matters. Directly below the minister was the head of the Keihokyoku (Police Bureau; prior to April 1876 this bureau was called Keihoryō), who as the administrative officer acting in the minister's name issued orders to all prefectural forces except the Metropolitan Police Board. At the prefectural level, the centrally appointed governor in theory held police authority, but in fact the chief of the prefectural police was usually in charge. With some modifications, made primarily in order to use the strong Tokyo police force to suppress revolts by samurai and uprisings by commoners, this remained the basic police structure.[4]

One function of the new Metropolitan Police Board was to suppress political offenders in the capital. Nationwide the Police Bureau worked to prevent political crime, and in 1875 police were directed to control political offenses.[5] The political role of police is further illustrated by a Dajōkan (Great Council of State) decree, July 15, 1878, ordering police to attend meetings in rural areas at which various societies discussed political affairs; if such meetings seemed a threat to the government, they were to be disbanded.[6]

Authorities reacted to antigovernment movements by expanding the activities of National Affairs Police (Kokuji Keisatsu) (i.e., political police). Late in 1881, the new post of *keibuchō* (chief inspector) was created to more tightly control prefectural police. In connection with political cases, chief inspectors took orders from the Home Ministry. The Kōtō Keisatsu (Higher Police; the name change was made in July 1886), evolved directly out of the National Affairs Police, and like the former group they were a creature of the central administration. The new police officers, who specialized in political surveillance, were under the direct control of prefectural chief inspectors, and by late Meiji many prefectures had a separate administrative department for the Higher Police. Over the years these political policemen became the eyes and ears for a government eager to control political dissenters.[7]

Internal and external pressures forced the government to search for a unified legal structure. New laws were urgently needed so that coherent instructions could be issued to new provinces in need of guidelines for trials and execution of sentences. Externally, a new legal system was required to fit Japan into the world's capitalistic trading network and to shed the unequal treaties. A jury-rigged solution was modification and use of Chinese law while Western law was investigated. The first step was taken in late 1868 or early 1869, when Kumamoto legal scholars produced the *Kari Keiritsu* (Provisional Criminal Code). This was replaced in 1871 by the *Shinritsu Kōryō* (Essence of the New Code), the first substantial code. Later it was necessary to supplement it with the *Kaitei Ritsurei* (Statutes and Substatutes as Amended) of 1873. These Chinese-inspired codes were in force until 1882.[8]

Even though the essence of the Tokugawa legal system was transferred into the *Shinritsu Kōryō* and its supplementary regulations, the new code somewhat humanized the old penalties. Moreover, the government permitted copies of the code to be printed and sold by private bookstores.[9] Furthermore, the 1871 code provided safeguards for people on trial or in prison. Any government official who because of private malice or revenge imprisoned an innocent person or tortured such a person could be given a sentence ranging from one year in prison to death, depending upon the seriousness of the crime. Jailers who mistreated or injured a prisoner would be punished based on the resultant injury.[10]

Political Crime, Torture, Confession

One Tokugawa legacy was the idea of a political crime. Leaders of farmers protesting tax increases or gross injustices and demanding benevolent rule, to which they felt entitled, were often executed and stigmatized as "political criminals."[11] Intellectuals who criticized government policy, even in small gatherings or in unpublished manuscripts, ran a serious risk, since the Tokugawa wanted no public expression of private opinion on public matters. Government informers watched for anything new or challenging to the state's monopoly on setting moral standards: morals had a wide meaning, embracing politics, association, speech, publication, and sex. From the mid-eighteenth century, Edo authorities, to which the more important political cases were referred, established ever harsher punishments, expanding the definitions of illegal gatherings, conspiracy, and riot and after 1770 creating a system of rewards for informants. By the end of that century the legal structure to handle political crime was well in place.[12] Under the influence of Confucian thought, crimes of a political nature were fiercely punished, since they were regarded "as a violation of the basic human bonds and the Divine Order."[13] Thus, any political criticism, however mild, was equated with treason. In fact, all Japanese Confucian schools of thought saw political criticism as "a form of faction, and faction as a form of rebellion."[14] It is unsurprising, therefore, that the early Meiji leadership viewed a wide range of activities as political crimes. Indeed, even liberal intellectuals such as Fukuzawa Yukichi in the 1880s were still gravely concerned about the dangers of factionalism.[15]

Since death alone would not atone for a serious political crime, the new state followed the old example of exhibiting the decapitated head. "[T]he executioner would behead the criminal with a specially skillful cut in order to preserve the original shape of the head. It was then washed thoroughly and exhibited in a public place, normally on a stand at Shinagawa or Asakusa, to deter the public."[16] Between 1873 and 1878 (no figures for 1875) about eight-five heads were exhibited. Etō Shinpei, the first minister of justice, suffered this ignominious fate.[17]

Another Tokugawa legacy was the use of torture in criminal cases to secure confession. From 1742, however, torture was permitted only in homicide cases and specified felonies; special permission was required for other cases.[18] Usually, four degrees of torture were applied: flogging; piling heavy stone slabs on the suspect's thighs (the suspect knelt on sharp-edged strips of wood); tightly binding arms and legs (the legs pulled up to the chin and the arms pulled as high as the shoulder blades); and suspending the suspect (with the arms tightly bound behind the back).[19] Ishii Ryōnosuke characterizes the first three of the four stages as quasi torture and notes that only suspension was true *gōmon* (torture).[20] Like the Chinese, the Japanese attached great importance to confession in criminal proceedings; authorities usually felt a case was incomplete until a confession was secured, even though evidence clearly indicated guilt. Therefore, especially in grave offenses, a suspect was proclaimed guilty only on his confession.[21] Despite the use of torture blessed by the law, both the Chinese and the Japanese were sensitive to illegal uses of torture. Ch'ing dynasty authorities, for instance, carefully defined permissible behavior. "Limits were set on the amount of torture, the instruments to be used, and the parts of the body to be beaten. . . . officials were punished severely for violating the regulations."[22] The Japanese Confucianist Ogyū Sorai, in a memorial on social policy presented to the Shogunate in the early eighteenth century, complained that criminal suspects were being imprisoned for long periods, sometimes until they died, and that they were subject to severe interrogation. This, he wrote, was a "forbidden" and "evil practice" in violation of the codes.[23] Finally, it should be noted that torture, at least as officially recorded, was considerably restricted from the eighteenth century onward.[24]

Meiji authorities, too, regulated the use of torture in securing confessions. Under the *Kari Keiritsu* the following people were normally exempted: women for one hundred days after childbirth, persons of high rank, those under fifteen years of age and those over seventy, and the infirm. There was a provision for punishing a policeman who wrongfully arrested and tortured a personal enemy. The *Shinritsu Kōryō* imposed a tighter control over torture with heavier penalties for illegal actions by officials. In February 1873, the government restricted the use of tools for torture to the "interrogating stick" and the "abacus board." Thus, the government retained the first two of the Tokugawa four stages of torture. The abacus board had ten sharp-edged strips of wood on which the criminal suspect knelt. Flat stones, each weighing about a

hundred pounds (up to three for a stubborn resistance) were piled
on the suspect's thighs until the extreme pain forced a confession.
The *Kaitei Ritsurei,* like earlier regulations, demanded a confession
for conviction; this requirement of confession provided justifica-
tion for torture.[25] On September 28, 1879, the Justice Ministry
sent a notification to all courts, listing various kinds of proof for
use at trials; confession topped the list.[26]

By the mid-1870s, public criticism of torture was common. A
strong attack on torture as uncivilized and detrimental to getting
rid of the unequal treaties came from Tsuda Mamichi in the May
and June 1874 issues of the prestigious *Meiroku Zasshi,* the organ of
the Meirokusha (Meiji Six Society). Tsuda, who had studied
Western law in the Netherlands from 1862 to 1865, was a government official and a charter member of the Meirokusha. The society's journal, which began in early 1874 and lasted until late in
1875, had a remarkably high circulation of about 3,000 copies.[27]
Tsuda wrote in May: "No evil in the world is more wretched than
torture. . . . [P]ersons [are] forced to submit to false conviction
once torture is used! . . . [T]here is a tendency for them invari-
ably to admit the false charges even though they are not guilty.
. . . If we do not abolish torture, we cannot conclude equal treaties."[28] Tsuda's June article continued: "When it comes to
methods for administering criminal justice, we clearly differ from
them [Western nations]. For example, even if a crime has been
committed, their judicial officers cannot arrest persons without
evidence. With us, however, investigating officers are able to
arrest immediately upon suspicion even if there is no evidence.
. . . Torture is essential for us because . . . there can be no judge-
ment against a criminal without his confession."[29] Articles
sympathetic to Tsuda appeared in the leading newspaper, *Tokyo
Nichinichi,* in July 1874 and April 1875.[30]

Foreign criticism stimulated opinion makers and legal scholars,
who became extremely sensitive on this issue. Gustave E. Boissonade de Fontarabie, a French legal advisor outraged over physical torture, wrote a letter of protest to the justice minister.[31] On
April 17, 1875, as Boissonade walked by the Tokyo High Court
Building, "he was startled by a half-human, half-animal scream.
. . . [H]e walked quickly into the building. . . . Opening the
door, he was paralyzed with horror at the sight of a man seated on
a rigidly corrugated board holding a big stone slab on his lap,

screaming under the brutal torture."[32] Boissonade's letter was based on four points: natural law and justice, humanitarianism, national interest, and legality. All suspects, he wrote, should be presumed innocent; the use of torture during an investigation or trial was a violation of rights. Furthermore, a suspect had the right under natural law and justice to remain silent. Moreover, torture-induced confessions were unreliable. Finally, the unequal treaties would remain until torture was abolished.[33]

Boissonade's letter stimulated debate, and from mid-1876 judges were ordered to apply to the Justice Ministry for permission to employ torture. Moreover, judges were given instructions on evidence, informing them that confessions were no longer mandatory for conviction. This instruction reduced the use of torture except in special political cases, when authorities were eager for quick results. That political offenders were being tortured is suggested by an editorial in the *Tokyo Nichinichi* on December 26, 1877, calling for the deletion of the word *torture* from all legal regulations.[34] In June 1879, Ono Azusa, a foreign law expert serving the Genrōin (Chamber of Elders—the legislative organ of the government), appealed for the abolition of torture, because torture shamed the nation before the world and was a major obstacle to treaty revision.[35] Undoubtedly, Ono was speaking to the already converted: there were increasing calls for abolition from the press and government officials, and a year earlier at the conference of the International Law Association in Frankfurt the American scholar David Dudley Field and others had criticized torture. On October 8, 1879, the Great Council of State issued Decree No. 42, which abolished torture.[36]

The Growth of Rights Consciousness

It is not known when the term *kenri* (rights) was introduced into Japan, but it is clear that it was widely circulated in W. A. Martin's translation into Chinese of Henry Wheaton's *Elements of International Law* published in 1864. This use of rights, however, attached the concept to nations and not to individuals, an idea easily grasped by intellectuals; the rights of individuals continued to baffle most.[37]

Students in Europe discovered the Code Napoleon and other aspects of Western law. Tsuda Mamichi, for example, discovered civil law in the Netherlands and called it *minpō* (citizen's law). The

Meiji government ordered Mitsukuri Rinshō to begin translating
the French Penal Code in 1869 and the Code Napoleon in 1870.
Even though Mitsukuri was a precocious linguist, his work
required the invention of new legal terminology, and the translation of the Code Napoleon involved five codes, averaging more
than one thousand articles apiece.[38] For *rights*, Mitsukuri coined
the term *kenri* (power *plus* interest). In the Chinese and Japanese
classics, however, this was a vulgar concept, meaning something
like "thinking about making a profit," and the idea of making a
profit ran counter to Confucian norms.[39] Another vexing term
was *droits civils*, translated as *minken* (peoples' power *or* peoples'
authority). Mitsukuri relates: "[T]here was an argument over
what did I mean by saying that the people *(min)* have 'power'
(ken). Even though I tried to justify it as hard as I could, there was
an extremely furious argument. Fortunately, the chairman, Mr.
Etō [Shinpei] supported me and finally the matter was ended."[40]
These examples illustrate the difficulty the Meiji leadership had in
recognizing the concept of peoples' rights. Their response was to
introduce "rights" into the legal structure "only for those aspects
which could be utilized in the immediate problems of abolishing
feudal restraints, achieving political unity and nurturing capitalistic relationships, and accordingly, the statesmen could not espouse
the theory of natural ('heaven given') human rights *(tempu jinken
ron)*, which was fundamentally inappropriate for them."[41]

During the first flush of enthusiasm for Western ideas, human
rights was a much discussed subject. Fukuzawa Yukichi, the most
fully committed liberal, traced a domestic human rights tradition
back to the seventeenth-century peasant martyr Sakura Sōgorō.
This peasant leader, rebuffed in repeated attempts to gain tax
relief, broke the law by directly appealing to the shogun. The local
daimyo crucified Sakura and his wife and beheaded his four children. Fukuzawa praised Sakura for righteous, nonviolent actions
and for comprehending the basic principle of human rights. By
creating this view, Fukuzawa could argue that the principle was
not as foreign as the Meiji political leadership pretended.[42]

Itagaki Taisuke, after resigning from government, returned to
Tosa, where he established the Risshisha (Society for Fixing One's
Aim in Life) in April 1874. This political organization cham-
pioned natural rights, equality of all classes, self-government, and
the establishment of a national legislative assembly. The thirty

million people of Japan, stated the new group, "are all equally
endowed with certain definite rights, among which are those of
enjoying and defending life and liberty, acquiring and possessing
property, and obtaining a livelihood and pursuing happiness.
These rights are by Nature bestowed upon all men, and therefore,
cannot be taken away by the power of any man."[43] At the center of
the rights movement during the 1870s and 1880s was Ueki Emori,
who acted as a theorist for Itagaki and who published *Minken jiyū
ron* (An essay on freedom and popular rights) and many other
works explaining human rights and constitutionalism.[44] Another
theorist and political activist was Nakae Chōmin, who translated
Jean Jacques Rousseau's *Social Contract*. Nakae, who devoted his
professional life to the defense of freedom and people's rights,
wrote in April 1881: "In the countries of the East, the idea of liberty has never been especially prominent. In the past, when rulers . . . were dictatorial and arbitrary, there was no one to say
that they were endangering the people's liberty or infringing upon
their rights. No one until now was aware that man had been free
in his original state."[45] Nakae's translation of the first two books of
the *Social Contract* was serialized in a magazine from March 1882.
"Heaven," he wrote, "gave the right of liberty to us so that we
could be our own masters."[46] Ono Azusa entered the debate in an
article on natural rights and liberty published in 1875: "The rights
or liberty that men want to attain are rights based on common reason or justice. . . . The government has promulgated unfair laws,
which restrict popular rights and harm the people. These laws
have shown that the government is neglecting the common good
and popular rights. It is the people's right to resist the government
and end this evil."[47] In *Kokken hanron* (Outline of the national constitution), a private constitutional draft completed in September
1885, Ono called personal freedom the basic freedom and one that
must be defended from outside interference such as unreasonable
arrest.[48]

The Jiyū minken undō (Popular rights movement), which
embraced the politically explosive concept of heavenly endowed
human rights, emerged in the late 1870s. Liberal thinkers like
Nakae Chōmin, Baba Tatsui, and Ueki Emori battled in print
those with a more restricted view of human rights, like Katō
Hiroyuki, who drew upon Herbert Spencer's modification of
Darwinian theory on natural selection to illustrate that man was

born without the right of freedom.[49] Throughout the 1880s the rights issue was caught up in the political battles among the directive elite, with political power rights gradually overshadowing the original thrust for fundamental human rights.[50] A leading advocate of enlightenment for the common people, Fukuzawa Yukichi, deplored the concentration on political rights: "Recently, political discussions have been clamorous in regard to the give and take of public rights, in other words, political power. . . . But in order to protect or obtain the political power of the public, it is first important to secure one's own private rights. . . . In such an environment, discussing only political power cannot escape the criticism of putting the cart before the horse."[51] Out of forty-two privately drafted constitutions prepared during the 1880s, only two gave clear guarantees of fundamental human rights: the one done by Ueki Emori and the other by the Society for Fixing One's Aim in Life. Ueki's baldly stated that when the government violates either citizens' rights or the constitution it can be overthrown. Even Ueki, however, a few years later, as a member of the lower house of the Diet, lost his human rights zeal. He was not alone. Most of the former samurai leaders of the rights movement succumbed to class prejudices and the growing tide of Meiji nationalism—even the outstanding liberal Fukuzawa Yukichi.[52]

Rousseau, Locke, and Hobbes based political theory on the individual's inviolable rights, not on a given political order. The Western social contract idea held that people accept government authority in their own self-interest. Even Hobbes, who was highly authoritarian, argued that acceptance of government was conditional, that people could withdraw that consent, and that certain rights were inviolable. Few Meiji Japanese could stretch their minds to this extent. Even after accepting the idea that people had natural and inalienable rights, they concluded that since the state granted rights it could also curtail or nullify them; rights, therefore, only assume meaning when bestowed by the state.[53]

Western-style Laws

On July 17, 1880, the 430-article *Keihō* (Penal Code) was promulgated by Great Council of State Decree No. 36; it went into force on January 1, 1882. The *Chizai Hō* (Code of Criminal Instruction), Great Council of State Decree No. 37, became effective on the same date. The Penal Code, which was drafted by

Boissonade on the basis of the French Code Penale, was epoch-making in its total repudiation of traditional law. Article 1 classified crimes into three types—felonies, misdemeanors, and police offenses—thus limiting arbitrary sentences by judges. The next two articles clearly established the principle that a statutory norm must exist before an act could be considered a crime. Also, no person could be punished under an ex post facto law. Moreover, the new code was revolutionary in making the individual solely responsible for a crime and removing the old idea of collective criminal responsibility. Furthermore, by establishing the principle of equality before the law, the code swept away the legal remains of the Tokugawa rule-by-status system. Finally, a formal complaint was required before a proceeding could be commenced, and prosecutions were to start with a formal accusatory pleading. Political crimes were covered in the sections on Crimes Relating to State Affairs (Articles 121–135) and Crimes against the Imperial House (Articles 116–120). Under the former, for instance, Article 121 included insurrection, seditious acts, and civil war. Punishment for ringleaders was death or life imprisonment and for others either banishment for life, banishment for a limited period, servitude with or without heavy labor, or two to five years' imprisonment. Article 122 extended the same range of punishment to anyone who provided military supplies or helped in other ways to carry out an insurrection. Article 135 stated that anyone found guilty of a misdemeanor under the provisions of this part of the code would be placed under surveillance for six months to two years. Anyone who committed or attempted to commit a dangerous (injurious) act against the emperor or his family was subject to death (Articles 116 and 118); punishment for any disrespectful act was set at from three months to five years in prison and a fine of from twenty to two hundred yen; the same applied for a disrespectful act toward any emperor's mausoleum (Articles 117 and 119); anyone guilty of a misdemeanor under those articles would be placed under surveillance for a period of six months to two years (Article 120). (Ise Jingū, the shrine of the Sun Goddess, was not protected by this law, but this oversight was later corrected.) Those who escaped the death penalty under Articles 116–135 could expect banishment to Hokkaido with hard labor. Despite Japanese objections to special provisions to protect the imperial family, Boissonade convinced his colleagues, and these articles were retained. The new code contained provisions protecting criminal suspects from official violence. Article 278 stated that officials who did not follow the proper procedures for arrest or who illegally imprisoned an individual would be punished with from fifteen days to three months in prison and a fine of from two to fifty yen. Under Article 282 judges, procurators, and police officials who assaulted or injured suspects in forcing confessions would be punished with from four months to four years' imprisonment and a fine of from five to fifty yen. If an official caused a suspect's death, the penalty would depend upon the type of physical abuse or how the person was killed.[54]

On February 11, 1889, the Emperor Meiji promulgated the *Dai Nihon Teikoku Kenpō* (The Constitution of the Great Empire of Japan) on the anniversary of the accession of the legendary Emperor Jinmu. Implementation took place on November 29 of the following year.[55] The preamble to the new constitution and chapter two (Rights and Duties of Subjects) clearly reject Western ideas about limitations on the state imposed by social contracts and natural rights. The preamble reads: "We now declare to respect and protect the security of the rights and of the property of Our people, and to secure to them the complete enjoyment of the same, within the extent of the provisions of the present Constitution and of the law." The term "within the extent . . . of the law," or something similar, appears in fourteen of the fifteen articles in chapter two (Article 31 states that the emperor's powers override all articles in times of national emergency or war). Article 23 prohibits the arrest, detention, or punishment of any Japanese "unless according to the law"; Article 24 guarantees the right of trial according to law; Article 29 grants the right of public meetings and liberty of speech and publication.[56] It must be noted, however, that Article 29 was hostage to many regulations issued both before and after 1889.

The new constitution can be viewed as a glass half full or a glass half empty. In the first view, it is seen as an important milestone on the road to democratization. Conservative it was, but by incorporating the concept of rule-by-law, Itō Hirobumi and other drafters moved "far beyond the Tokugawa natural law theories of downward delegations of discretionary power to status officials who were responsible only to superiors. In this sense, to measure the Meiji formulation by modern democratic standards is rather like criticizing the Oregon Trail because it was an inadequate highway."[57] Viewed as a half empty glass, however, the "law" is seen as an implement of and not a limitation upon legislative and administrative power. Under the Meiji constitutional system the concept of natural laws was pushed into a dark corner, and administrative agencies were responsible mainly to themselves, with *kanson minpi* (putting government above people) as an all-pervasive attitude.[58] The distinguished legal scholar Hozumi Yatsuka viewed the relationship between the state and the individual as follows: "Sovereignty is sacred and inviolable. . . . The people must be absolutely obedient to it. . . . The subject gives absolute and unlimited obedience to the power of the state. . . . The rights and duties of the subject are the concern not of constitutional law but of administrative law."[59] While the constitution established an Administrative Court to review illegal administrative action, its jurisdiction was restricted, leaving most official actions unchallengeable.[60] In summary, the introduction of Western law was "accompanied by the authoritarian conception of law as an aggregate of legal rules imposed by sovereign authority rather than as an embodiment of reason and justice."[61] Thus, the new codes neatly reenforced Tokugawa ideas about no limits on law-making power and the lack of redress against authority; the blend of old and new maintained a transcendental administrative state.

The 1882 Code of Criminal Instruction was replaced by the *Keiji Soshō Hō* (Criminal Procedure Code), Law No. 96, promulgated October 7, 1890, and implemented on November 1, 1890. On paper, the code provided reasonable guarantees against procedural abuses. An arrest warrant was required except in the case of a flagrant offender (i.e., one caught in a criminal act or who had just committed a crime), and an accused person was to be brought before a judge within forty-eight hours or released. Every warrant required a statement of the nature of the alleged offense and a judge's signature (Articles 56, 58, 60, 73, 75). Article 94 ordered examining judges not to employ falsehoods or threats to force confessions.[62]

The Penal Code of 1880 was drastically changed by Law No. 45, 1907 (implemented October 1, 1908). Boissonade's idea of making the punishment exactly fit the crime had left little margin for judicial discretion. German legal science, however, was the inspiration behind the revision, in which a subjective punishment theory emerged. While parole had been recognized in the old code, the new one included suspension of the execution of sentence.[63] Specific provision was made to deter brutality and torture. Article 194 stated: "Every person exercising or assisting in judicial, prosecuting, or police functions who in abuse of his power has arrested or imprisoned a person shall be punished with penal servitude or imprisonment for not less than six months nor more than seven years." Article 195 said: "Every person exercising or assisting in judicial, prosecuting, or police functions who in the performance of his duties has committed an act of violence or cruelty against a criminally accused or other person shall be punished with penal servitude or imprisonment not exceeding three years."[64]

A few modifications were made in the Criminal Procedure Code by Law No. 75, 1922 (implemented on January 1, 1923). While suspension of the execution of judgment had been allowed since 1908 in cases involving a sentence of less than two years, there was no provision giving procurators a discretionary power of nonprosecution. The modified code changed this, permitting procurators to put more stress on rehabilitation for first-time offenders.[65]

The *Kangoku Hō* (Prison Law), Law No. 28, March 28, 1908, an important part of the penal reform package of late Meiji, reflected the views of progressive criminologists who focused on rehabilitation as much as on strict punishment. Officials were to inspect prison facilities periodically (Article 4); inmates were permitted to petition outside officials (Article 7); sanitary conditions were to be maintained (Article 24); adequate food was to be supplied (Article 34); necessary medical treatment was to be provided (Article 40); and better treatment was promised for repentant prisoners (Article 58).[66] This progressive law, however, contained a regressive feature in that it provided police with an opportunity to have easy and continual access to criminal suspects even up to the trial. Article 1, Section 3 reads: "The police jail may be substituted for a prison; provided that a convicted person sentenced to penal servitude or imprisonment shall not be detained therein continually for one month or more."[67] This unusual arrangement, which permitted criminal suspects to be held in police station jails in lieu of detention house cells, was enacted because of a shortage of detention house facilities. The government acknowledged the possibility of abuse of suspects' rights under this system but promised during the Diet debate on the law bill that police station jails would not be converted into *daiyō kangoku* (substitute prisons). Over the following years, however, this bargain was broken, as police jails were increasingly used as substitute prisons where police conducted long-term interrogations. Under this system it was easy for police to overstep their legal powers.[68]

Political Criminals

Samurai revolts, agrarian uprisings, and the Popular Rights Movement shook the post-Restoration regime. Saigō Takamori's rebellion (February–September 1877), for example, which involved a rebel force of about forty-two thousand and a government force of sixty thousand, seriously strained government resources. Thousands died in the Seinan War (Satsuma Rebellion), and afterwards the government executed 2,764 of Saigō's followers.[69]

Farmers demanding land reforms and rent reductions plagued the new regime. Feeding on such discontent, the Popular Rights Movement rapidly spread after Saigō's rebellion, with Itagaki stumping the countryside, denouncing "despotic" government. Yamagata Aritomo, a former war minister and chief of the General Staff Office in 1878, wrote Home Minister Itō Hirobumi in July 1879: "Itagaki's scheme . . . is to call for the people's rights, slander the government, abuse officials with reckless and groundless attacks . . . and spread unrest throughout the land. . . . [H]e hopes to unite the people and overthrow the government at an opportune moment. Therefore, every day we delay, the evil poison will spread farther and penetrate the minds of the young and produce, inevitably, incalculable harm."[70] In a memorial presented to the emperor in December 1879, Yamagata wrote: "When we consider the tendencies of popular sentiments today, the people have no respect for the government nor do they submit to its law. . . . The people . . . seem to be rebellious and grow more and more suspicious. . . . A careful study . . . shows that at home the people are alienated from the government."[71] Itagaki and other antigovernment leaders were not considering armed insurrection; indeed, Saigō's crushing defeat had removed that option and, undoubtedly, Yamagata, who had played a key role in removing Saigō, well understood this. What worried Yamagata was not guns and swords but the spreading of antigovernment words in which the opposition appeared to be winning a propaganda war to capture the people's hearts. The government's harsh treatment of opponents during the 1880s is better understood if we keep Yamagata's views in mind, especially since he became home minister in December 1883, a position he held for more than six years. While Yamagata believed that force alone would not eliminate the causes of popular discontent, he was ever willing to continue a harsh punishment policy.

The Fukushima Incident (November 1882), which was symptomatic of the radicalization of the democratic movement, resulted from a confrontation between a highly repressive governor and local Jiyūtō (Liberal Party) members. Kōno Hiromi and five other defendants were charged with conspiracy to overthrow the government (Kōno was sentenced to seven years and the others to six). Many accounts of brutality and torture by police emerged during and after this trial. Defendant Igarashi Takehide displayed marks on his body to the court. One newspaper account told about a prisoner kept standing without food night and day who was kicked until blood flowed. Haneda Kiyomizu, caught up in a general arrest during this incident and charged with insulting an official, died of pneumonia after prolonged standing outdoors.[72]

In May 1884, local Liberal Party leaders in Gunma prefecture led several thousand farmers against a moneylender and the police. Some of those apprehended died under torture. Murakami Taiji, for example, was beaten to death.[73] In the Kabasan Incident (September 1884), Kōno Hiroshi, Hiromi's nephew, led fifteen men against the government. To depoliticize the affair and offset the negative publicity resulting from the Fukushima Incident, the authorities prosecuted the rebels for armed robbery, even though they admitted to treason. Found guilty of armed robbery and murder, seven rebels were sentenced to death; five (including Kōno) got indefinite prison terms.[74]

The Chichibu Incident (November 1884), the largest armed farmer uprising, occurred when appeals for economic relief went unanswered. Tashiro Eisuke, a former samurai and prominent village leader, led an attack on moneylenders and government offices, destroying the paper debt record. Reinforced by other protestors to a strength of about five thousand men, they marched on Ōmiya, the county seat. Nearly two hundred fifty leaders were charged with instigation of violence, robbery, and fomenting rebellion. Tashiro and seven others were sentenced to hang, and most of the others got prison sentences of five to eight years.[75]

Two other antigovernment plots worried Home Minister Yamagata: the Nagoya (Iida) Incident (December 1884) and the Shizuoka Incident (June 1886). The former plan to overthrow the government by armed force was squelched before it was under way as was the latter, which was a plot to assassinate various government leaders. After the Nagoya Incident, Okunomiya Kenshi got a life term, and several others were sentenced to prison for terms ranging from nine to fifteen years. More than a hundred were arrested in connection with the Shizuoka Incident, and twenty-four were imprisoned; the longest sentences (given to five people) were fifteen years.[76]

During this turbulent era, the prison system was deluged by waves of political prisoners. The Satsuma Rebellion alone produced 43,000 people sentenced with 27,000 confined or put at hard labor. This flood of *kokujihan* (state affairs crime) offenders set the government to thinking about a new type prison. By December 1877 Home Ministry officials were planning for a *shūjikan* (gather-and-control prison) in Tokyo (Kosuge Prison) and one in Miyagi prefecture.[77]

Some officials saw that the penal system might supply a labor force for the exploitation of empty Hokkaido. This northern island, which embraced roughly one-quarter of Japan, was regarded by most people as a remote, cold, and inhospitable place.[78] When thinking about *naichi* (Japan proper), people mentally excluded the northern island. The government, however, was intent on developing Hokkaido's resources, but by the late 1870s early ambitious plans were failing for lack of a labor force to construct a road network, the key to opening up the island's interior.[79] Sometime after the Satsuma Rebellion, the government asked Kuroda Kiyotaka, director of the Hokkaido development project, to formulate a plan to hold the war's captives on the island. This idea of building prisons in Hokkaido was discussed at the Genrōin in 1878 and again in 1879. Home Minister Itō Hirobumi wrote Sanjō Sanetomi, head of the Great Council of State, asking his advice. There were, noted Itō, 24,000 prisoners with sentences of from twelve to fifteen years. Hokkaido seemed the best place for them in spite of extremely cold weather. The prisoners could, said

Itō, pay their debt by engaging in agriculture and mining. By 1880 Itō was certain that Hokkaido was the solution to over-crowded prisons in Japan proper and the labor shortage in Hokkaido. Writing to Kuroda in February, he noted the plan's merits: dangerous elements would be removed from Honshu, prison overcrowding would be lessened, and Hokkaido could be developed with cheap labor. In April of the next year, Home Minister Matsukata Masayoshi notified Sanjō that there were more than 4,000 *kokujihan* prisoners sentenced to terms ranging from five years to life. Since the new prisons of Kosuge and Miyagi were full, it would be best to transfer these people to Hokkaido to do development work. No more prisons should be constructed in Japan proper, he felt; from a financial point of view it made more sense to build them in Hokkaido.[80]

Kabato, which officially opened on September 2, 1881, got its first batch of forty long-term prisoners from Kosuge the previous April. The opening of Kabato, the headquarters for the Hokkaido network, was followed by the opening of Sorachi Prison in July 1882, Kushiro in 1885, Abashiri in August 1890, and Tokachi in March 1895. Generally, authorities used Kabato for political prisoners, Sorachi for regular criminals, and Kushiro for former Military Police (Kenpei) personnel; but there were exceptions, and Sorachi got its share of political offenders from the Fukushima, Gunma, Kabasan, Shizuoka, and Nagoya incidents. The best known were Kōno Hiromi, Kobayashi Tokutarō, Koinuma Ku-hachirō, and Koike Isamu. Others, like Okunomiya Kenshi, Hisano Kotarō, and Tsukahara Kuwakichi, were sent to Kabato. While road-building crews worked out of these three prisons, Sorachi inmates also dug coal from the Horonai Mine; at Kushiro, inmates excavated sulfur. Abashiri got its start as one of the work camps for gangs out from Kushiro, but as prison populations rose it became permanent. Tokachi's background was similar. Shortly before Abashiri became a regular prison site the total prison population in Hokkaido was 8,000 (Kabato, 1,700; Sorachi, 1,200; Kushiro, 1,200; various work camps, 3,900). While far from Hokkaido, the prison at Miike in Kyushu was established for reasons similar to the creation of Sorachi: a shortage of labor to work a coal field. From 1889 Mitsui Mining operated the mine, but prisoners continued to provide the labor.[81]

That the government was intent on formulating a prison labor policy is indicated by Kaneko Kentarō's seventy-day tour of Hokkaido in the summer of 1885. Kaneko, then a secretary for the Great Council of State, became one of Itō Hirobumi's three closest assistants after December 22, 1885, when Itō became the nation's first prime minister.[82] Kaneko's report noted that all prisoners with sentences of ten years or more went to Hokkaido, and he strongly urged using them for road construction, since regular laborers had to be paid forty sen per day whereas prisoners were paid only eighteen. Moreover, even if they died, he wrote, that fact, too, would merely reduce expenses.[83] Finally, Kaneko, who was a graduate of Harvard Law School (1878), pointed out: "Even if prisoners die from the hard labor, they are bad people to begin with, and the result differs from the disastrous scene of ordinary laborers dying and leaving behind wives and children."[84] Tokyo quickly acted on Kaneko's recommendations. Iwamura Michitoshi, appointed governor of Hokkaido in January 1886, ordered the warden of Kabato to start road construction in April, and in May 1887, at a conference held in Sapporo, officials from all parts of the island were presented with a comprehensive road development scheme. The key to this ambitious plan's success was cheap prison labor, which was to be mobilized to develop a road network, linking inaccessible agricultural and mining areas with the major cities and seaports.[85]

In September 1881, reasonably enlightened *Kangoku Soku* (Prison Rules) were introduced nationwide. One provision ordered trustees not to use prisoners for personal purposes or to treat them cruelly. From the start, however, full enforcement of these regulations was nearly impossible; the dilapidated condition of many of the prefectural prisons and the inferior caliber of the guards worked against more humane conditions.[86] As late as 1889, "the typical prison for almost all prefectures became the temporary dumping grounds for low ranking government clerks or quasi or complete incompetents from the police bureau."[87] Thus, enlightened rules notwithstanding, conditions deteriorated. Military Police were assigned first to Kosuge (1883) and later to Miike (1889). In 1884 guards at Kabato and Sorachi were permitted to carry pistols, and the wardens were given limited judicial rights.[88] In August 1885 Home Minister Yamagata Aritomo pointed out to governors that the number of prisoners was increasing. Some prison officials, he wrote, had forgotten the primary purpose of a prison. "Of course, the prison must try to rehabilitate prisoners, but also it should obligate them to do intolerable disciplinary punishment and make them learn how fearful imprisonment is in order to stop them from repeating their crimes. This is the prison's main principle."[89] Given such encouragement, officials put reformist ideas on a back shelf and emphasized punishment and brute force to maintain discipline. Home Ministry official Onoda Motohiro, for example, explained in a pamphlet that hard labor which would cause prisoners the most pain was the best suited for disciplinary purposes. Falling in with this idea, Governor Utsumi Tadakatsu (Hyōgo) ordered the adoption of the "penal rock" policy (January 1887); the neighboring Osaka quickly followed suit. Under the rock policy, prisoners were forced to carry heavy rocks (25–125 pounds), usually during the last two hours of the workday.[90]

Hokkaido prisoners worked under hazardous conditions. The Horonai Coal Mine, using prison labor hired from Sorachi, began operations in 1883. Normally, 800 to 1,000 men worked the mine, but always at least 20 percent were disabled with injuries. Even though more than half the prisoners were in their twenties and thirties, 265 died from bad working conditions and malaria in 1889 and 941 died between 1886 and 1897; this was the highest death rate among the Hokkaido prisons, despite the fact that prisoners stopped mining coal in 1890. Conditions at Kushiro were harsh. All prisoners wore a ball and chain on one leg. Those who attempted to escape, if not killed, had a light chain run through an ear lobe and attached to the leg iron. No writing or reading material was permitted. The banker Yasuda Zenjirō held the contract for prison labor to work the sulfur mine near Kushiro. This hell pit was operated with prison labor from January 1886 until November 1888. Out of 300 working the mine the first six months, 42 died and 145 became ill. Sulfurous gas caused blindness among many.[91]

All Hokkaido prisons sent out road-building gangs. Indeed, Kushiro Prison was established not only because of the proximity to the sulfur mine, but also as a base from which to extend roads to Abashiri and Tokachi. After the sulfur mine closed, all prisoners switched over to road making. Still, working conditions were bad; prisoners suffered from a shortage of proper equipment and from very long working hours; rising at 3:00 A.M. and completing work at 7:00 P.M. was not unusual. Road gangs working out of Abashiri Prison were pushed hard, sometimes working from 1:00 A.M. by torchlight. During one six-month period, 914 of 1,015 road builders were ill and 186 died from disease or overwork or were killed trying to escape. The bodies were left unburied where they fell. Once the major roads were laid, the state began turning prison labor to work within the walls; the hiring-out system was abolished in 1895. Only at Miike did Hokkaido-style labor policies continue.[92]

Political prisoners in the Hokkaido prison system received uncivilized treatment. At the very least, their legal rights under the Penal Code were violated. Judges who sentenced political prisoners to ten or twelve years at hard labor were ordering a term of penal servitude, not a death sentence. However, government prison policy in Hokkaido during the 1880s and 1890s in effect overturned court sentences: prisoners were worked to death. The government easily accepted Kaneko Kentarō's view that it was of no consequence if prisoners died from overwork. Hiramatsu Yoshirō writes that the assignment of Military Police to several prisons in the 1880s left an indelible mark on Japan's penal history. Perhaps, but that is a minor matter when compared to prison policy in Hokkaido and the Miike Prison in Kyushu.

Harsh prison conditions did not go unnoticed. The "penal rock" policy, for instance, was criticized by the Osaka Municipal Assembly in May 1887, and in August the Osaka Bar Association asked that it be stopped. Within a few months both Osaka and Hyōgo abolished this practice.[93] Hara Taneaki, who was hired in 1888 by the Home Ministry to escort four hundred prisoners to Kushiro, found conditions at the sulfur mine so terrible that he wrote to Kiyoura Keigo, head of the Police Bureau, urging the withdrawal of prison labor. Supported by the prison warden as well, Hara got the Home Ministry to break its contract with Yasuda Zenjirō: the sulfur mine was closed.[94] Kiyoura's support is not surprising, since pressure was building for a change in prison policy. One of the objects behind reform efforts was treaty revision (the revised treaties went into effect in 1899), but there were humanitarian considerations as well. The timing was propitious in that Hokkaido's desperate need for road-building gangs had passed. A national center was opened in 1890 to train prison officers, and in 1893 an examination system was introduced for

guards. By the turn of the century, the trend in penal management
was toward reform and vocational training and away from the old
system of harsh discipline and labor for profit. In 1900 the Imperial Diet legislated to defray all prison expenses from the national
treasury, and in March 1903 the Justice Ministry took over all
prisons. The old gather-and-control prison, represented by Kosuge, Miyagi, and the Hokkaido facilities, became obsolete.[95]

The government used the promulgation of the Meiji Constitution in February 1889 to pardon some political criminals and the
death of the empress dowager Eishō in January 1897 to pardon
many more. Imperial Ordinance No. 7, January 31, 1897, freed
nationwide 9,997 of which 2,495 in Hokkaido returned to Japan
proper, leaving Abashiri Prison so empty that it was temporarily
closed.[96] Probably, the government proclaimed the *Taisharei*
(Great Amnesty) because of the greatly changed political and
social situation. The government was firmly entrenched, the
opposition had the floor of the Diet for a protest platform, and
prison reform was in progress. Furthermore, as a healing gesture
this mass release earned the government praise and popularity.

Not all political offenders built roads and mined coal and sulfur
in Hokkaido's embryonic gulag. Those convicted of minor offenses ended up in places like Ishikawajima Prison near Tokyo.
These lesser offenders were caught by special laws, outside the formal codes, designed to tightly control publication, speech, and
gatherings. The maximum penalties were three years (periodical
publishing), three years (Libel Law, 1875), and five years (Public
Gatherings Ordinance, 1882). One source lists 118 journalists
imprisoned from 1875 to 1881, of which 30 were sentenced to one
year or longer.[97] Another source has 198 newspapermen serving
time in prison from 1883 to 1887.[98]

Hoshi Tooru, a journalist, lawyer, and Liberal Party activist,
was arrested in March 1888 and given twenty-two months in Ishikawajima Prison for illegal printing. Hoshi recalled that one unit
of the prison was filled with Liberal Party members; it was almost
as if the party executive committee was holding a meeting.
Kataoka Kenkichi and Hoshi acted as representatives for the
political offenders. Harsh prison regulations (e.g., having to ask
permission to lie down) were particularly hard on ill prisoners.
Living conditions were painful during wintertime and guards
often violent. Since Hoshi's sentence was without labor, however,

he was able to read books and write to his wife. Fate smiled on Hoshi, in the form of an amnesty connected with the constitutional celebration in February 1889.[99]

Fukuda Hideko, who was tried in May 1887 for plotting with Ōi Kentarō to aid a Korean revolutionary movement, was convicted and sentenced to eighteen months for violating the *Bakuhatsubutsu Torishimari Bassoku* (Explosives Control Penal Regulations), Great Council of State, Decree No. 32, 1884. Because of this sensational case and her later books, Fukuda became well known as the first Meiji woman jailed for a political offense. Like Hoshi, she benefited from the 1889 amnesty. (So did Ōi, even though sentenced to six years.) Fukuda served time in Tsu City, Mie prefecture, where she voluntarily joined other prisoners making kimono and other garments, reading only during the final two hours of each workday. Although imprisoned, Fukuda was intellectually productive during this time; she was fortunate to have a sympathetic prison warden.[100]

Additional light is shed on prison conditions by Baba Tatsui, a leader in the Popular Rights Movement, who was arrested on October 16, 1885, for inquiring about the purchase of explosives to be used in a mining venture. Brought to preliminary trial, he was acquitted and released on June 2, 1886, on a technicality in the wording of the Explosives Control Penal Regulations: he had merely inquired and had not attempted to purchase explosives. It is not known if Baba contemplated a violent use of the explosives, but it is known that his health was undermined by six months in jail. Baba's "In a Japanese Cage" appeared in a Washington, D.C., newspaper on June 25, 1887. The article, subtitled "The Horrors of Life in a Prison in Tokio," exposed in graphic detail the inadequacy of sanitation, diet, and hospital facilities. Prison officials, he wrote, were tyrannical and sadistic.[101]

Late Meiji produced socialist and anarchist political activists and the first large-scale labor violence. The government's primary response to maintain the social order was to tighten police surveillance of suspected radicals and to enact new restrictive legislation. A key control device was the *Chian Keisatsu Hō* (Public Peace Police Law), promulgated March 10, 1900, Law No. 36, by the second Yamagata Aritomo cabinet. This law aimed at the control of organizations connected with political affairs and at firmly checking the expanding labor movement; Article 17, while not

explicitly outlawing union organizing activities or strikes, was
worded in a manner that allowed government officials to interpret
such activities as illegal. The maximum term of imprisonment
under this law was one year.[102] The Christian humanist Katayama Sen wrote: "The law provides carefully clauses that will
enable police authorities to stop, to punish and to fine working
men who speak or agitate for wages, and hours of labour."[103]
Partly blocked on the labor front, Katayama and other reformers
tried the political route by forming the Shakai Minshu Tō (Social
Democratic Party) in May 1901. Even though the platform of the
new party was more democratic than socialist, the supposedly liberal Itō Hirobumi cabinet ordered its dissolution.[104]

Other useful police regulations were *Ikeizai Sokketsu Rei* (Summary Trial Regulations for Police Offenses), Great Council of
State Decree No. 31, September 24, 1885; *Gyōsei Shikkō Hō*
(Administrative Enabling Law), Law No. 84, June 2, 1900;
Keisatsuhan Shobatsu Rei (Regulations for the Punishment of Police
Offenses), Home Ministry No. 16, September 29, 1908. The 1885
regulation empowered the chief of each police station, or his dep-
uty, summarily to convict people for minor crimes committed
within the station's jurisdiction. Even though a prisoner could
appeal the chief's judicial decision and demand a formal trial, at
which time the prisoner was supposed to be released from jail, the
application for a trial had to be filled within a specific time with
the police station. The maximum sentence was twenty-nine days
in jail. Under the 1900 law police could arrest a suspect without a
judicial warrant, if that person appeared as though he might dis-
turb public peace; police also could take anyone into protective
custody. People arrested under this provision (Article 1) were to be
held no longer than sunset of the following day. Police chiefs using
the 1908 law could order detention for loitering without a fixed
residence or a job or for interfering with another person's work.[105]

While fines were light and jail time short, these regulations were
used effectively against the government's political foes as well as
against individuals in the various movements for social reform;
and in so doing police badly abused their power to arrest. Indeed,
the 1900 law proved so useful that a police textbook writer said
that it was as precious as an "heirloom sword."[106] According to
the Penal Code, police were to pass suspects on to the procurator,
who normally had ten days to make his case. However, the police

frequently detained suspects illegally (under the 1900 law detention only until sunset the next day was legal) for long periods and used various methods, including torture, to force confessions. The 1885 regulations could be used to harass "socialists." Police tricks and outright violations of the law were common. For example, suspects might not be told about their right to a formal trial or, even if suspects appealed within the prescribed time, police might tear up the applications. Besides this, the 1900 law contained vague phrases like "apprehension about damage to public peace," which permitted an easy application of the law to socialists. Police led socialists out the back entrance just before sundown of the day following their arrest and then rearrested them and brought them into the station via the front entrance or took them to another station. Hence, a contemporary criminal lawyer likened the 1900 law to a knife in the hands of a lunatic.[107]

Even apologists concede that the 1900 Administrative Enabling Law was improperly used. They add, however, that the government tried in June and July 1900 to educate overzealous policemen by issuing directives on the proper use of the law; in June 1916 the Home Ministry tried again in Naimu, Secret, No. 1425 ("Matters in Connection with the Administrative Enabling Law") issued to each prefecture, which requested that serious consideration be given to the proper use of the law. These Home Ministry orders had little effect.[108]

This illegal use of the law reflects a general abuse of authority well entrenched within the police structure; it is not surprising, given the viewpoint of Kawaji Toshiyoshi, the father of the modern police system, who regarded the state as an extended family: the government was the parent, the people were the children, and the policemen were the nurses of the children.[109] The paternalistic authoritarianism of Yamagata Aritomo and others who built the modern force contributed to police attitudes of superiority and omnipotence and indirectly encouraged police to exceed legal bounds. Furthermore, the attitude of police toward the people was, by and large, one of contempt and arrogance. Especially among lower-ranking policemen there were those who acted without common sense and needlessly suppressed people; their actions in turn stimulated antipolice feeling.[110]

By late Meiji, the government was paying special attention to anarchists, socialists, and others influenced by imported ideologies. At the center of this watch on potential political offenders was the Peace Section, Police Bureau, Home Ministry. *Shakaishugisha Enkaku* (Development of the Socialists), a secret police report, of which volume one ends at July 1908, illustrates that socialists were carefully watched. Socialists, stated the report, while small in numbers were influencing the intellectual world by propagandizing in publications and in speech at meetings. They held unacceptable, unhealthy thoughts and on more than one occasion narrowly missed violating the law. Four hundred sixty resident socialists were identified, of whom ninety-eight were regarded as active propagandists. Volume two of this series covered from August 1908 to July 1909, and the final volume, August 1909 to June 1911.[111] By this time, police had become more knowledgeable about socialists: "Among those we have been calling socialists are some who are anarchists, communists, socialists, and people who are calling for land redistribution. . . . Since there is the possibility of making errors if we continue to simply class them as socialists, we have decided to call all of them *tokubetsu yō shisatsunin* (people requiring special surveillance)."[112] Perhaps this growing police sophistication was connected with the introduction of special police into the Peace Section, Police Bureau, in 1911 to oversee efforts to control "socialists."[113]

People on police lists often were followed by uniformed officers or detectives. Authorities were especially attentive to radicals like Kōtoku Shūsui. The years 1908 and 1909 were bad ones for Kōtoku, with stepped-up police surveillance reflecting Prime Minister Katsura Tarō's hatred of and worry about spreading socialism. "Wherever he went there was the inevitable 'tail.' By the summer of 1908 surveillance turned into open harassment. Police detectives were now continuously posted outside of the Kōtoku home and sake shop. Customers who did not care for the indignities of police interrogation ceased coming; overnight the shop's trade virtually ceased." This surveillance occurred in Kōtoku's hometown of Kōchi, but returning to Tokyo was no escape: "Early in June 1909 police officials set up a tent in a field across from the Heiminsha and anyone coming to visit Kōtoku was ushered behind its red and white curtain and interrogated. Four policemen constantly watched the exits of the building and anyone coming out was followed."[114] Procurator Koyama Matsukichi, who was on the prosecution team at the 1910 trial of Kōtoku and others, read all of the surveillance record and concluded: "It was like being in detention. If Kōtoku left the place, the plainclothes police followed, and even if he entered a toilet, the tail would peek in at the window."[115] As for police treatment of Kōtoku and others, Koyama says that it was "rough" and that a police spy may have led those arrested in the Red Flag Incident into a police trap.[116]

Koyama, who was an associate procurator at the Tokyo District Court, recalled: "I often called Kōtoku in and investigated him as well as Ishikawa Sanshirō and others. Then I prosecuted them one after another. . . . The chief procurator . . . was Kobayashi Yoshirō, who told me that no matter what happened I was to prosecute them as rapidly as possible. . . . However, there were many cases at that time in which I was not sure if the verdict would be guilty, since at that time the public did not exactly understand what socialism was really like. Unless they used very violent language or writings, the court [Judge Imamura Kyōtarō handled these socialist cases] would not pronounce them guilty."[117] Besides being an indication of the Justice Ministry's eagerness to place a legal noose over the heads of socialists, this account illustrates the independence of the judiciary.

An outstanding example of police brutality is linked to the Red Flag Incident, which grew out of a celebration held for Yamaguchi Koken's release from prison in June 1908. Well-wishers sang revolutionary songs and carried red flags down the street; among those hauled off to a police station were Ōsugi Sakae and Arahata Kanson. "Stripped naked, both men were dragged by their feet along the corridors, were kicked, beaten, and stamped on, the police only ultimately relenting when Arahata had been beaten into unconsciousness."[118] For their flag carrying and singing, nine people were sentenced to terms of up to two and one-half years. According to a report in a socialist newspaper, police openly bragged that they considered themselves unbound by the constitution when it came to socialists.[119]

Increasingly harsh government measures against leftists culminated in the High Treason Incident of 1910 and the sensational secret trial of Kōtoku Shūsui and twenty-five others. Kōtoku and eleven others were found guilty of violating Article 73 of the Penal Code ("Every person who had committed, or has attempted to commit, a dangerous . . . act against . . . the Emperor . . . shall be condemned to death."). Although no attack was made on the emperor, the court accepted the prosecution argument that the defendants had "attempted to commit" such an act and were therefore guilty. They were hanged on January 24, 1911.[120]

One significant reaction to the High Treason Incident was the creation of the Tokubetsu Kōtō Keisatsu (Special Higher Police; known by the acronym Tokkō). In 1912 the first independent Tokkō sections were placed in the Metropolitan Police Board and the Osaka Prefectural Headquarters. While the direct organization of the Tokkō dates from 1912, its roots extend back to the earlier Meiji political police and more indirectly into the Tokugawa. Over the years the Tokkō developed into the most important and prestigious police branch, expanding into each prefectural government, but the Higher Police (created in 1886) continued to function, with a special emphasis on crimes connected with elections, regulating meetings and associations, watching mass movements, and keeping a sharp eye on people requiring special surveillance. In the beginning, however, the Tokkō was merely to reinforce the Higher Police so it could better cope with anarchism and socialism. Therefore, its main task was the investigation and control of social movements and the suppression of radicals spreading dangerous foreign ideas.[121]

Ōsugi, who became the most famous Japanese anarchist after Kōtoku's death, was a favorite police surveillance target. Police records suggest that shadowing began sometime in December 1910; it continued until Ōsugi's murder in 1923. Many of Ōsugi's tails were in uniform, and sometimes friendly feelings developed. That this was not always the case, however, is illustrated by the fact that Ōsugi was jailed for three months for striking a uniformed policeman whom he mistakenly thought was watching him. Ōsugi spent ten days in protective custody during August 1918. This was, he sarcastically wrote, an act of kindness during the Rice Riots, because police were worried that he might mistakenly be killed by soldiers brought in under martial law to help police quell the disturbances.[122]

An upsurge in leftist political activity after World War I forced authorities to modify surveillance techniques and focus more on groups. *Shisō dantai jōkyō* (Condition of thought groups), first issued in January 1921, is but one example of the Tokkō's new approach. This report identified 123 "thought groups," of which

53 needed special attention. It is clear from this document that the Police Bureau, Home Ministry, was drawing on prefectural police units to compile a monthly report on the activities of leftists and the condition of thought groups.[123] Among the thought groups identified in the January 1921 report as needing special attention was the Shinjinkai (New Man Society) founded in 1918 and consisting mainly of students and former students of Tokyo Imperial University. The members of this group burned with revolutionary zeal; they rejected the capitalistic and authoritarian power structure in favor of a new, more just society. An undated Home Ministry document marks fourteen members as persons under surveillance, and another source reports that a detective from the Metropolitan Police Board watched the group's headquarters continuously.[124]

Treatment of those jailed for minor political offenses after 1900 was similar to the treatment accorded our earlier examples. "For Kōtoku Shūsui," writes his biographer, "the five months spent in Sugamo Prison [for a Press Law violation in January 1905] constituted a period of intensive reading and introspection. For over a year he had been faced with constant duties. . . . Once before, as a student of [Nakae] Chōmin's, he had disassociated himself from the political arena for a period of quiet introspective reflection. So now he once more disassociated himself from the events of the previous year in order to read and think."[125] Kōtoku's variegated reading and research schedule is reflected in a letter of May 20, 1905, to Sakai Toshihiko, which is a veritable bibliography.[126] While intellectually the five months proved stimulating, physically it was draining; after being released he stayed with a physician friend to regain his health.[127]

Ōsugi Sakae was imprisoned several times between 1906 and 1910, for violations of the Press and the Public Peace Police laws. During more than three years in Sugamo and Chiba prisons, Ōsugi read Kropotkin, Bakunin, Malatesta, Reclus, and others. Also, he studied Russian, German, Italian, and Esperanto.[128] Reflecting on this period, he wrote in 1919: "Actually when I got out . . . I felt for the first time that I had become a real person. I felt that no matter where I went into the world I could present myself without hesitation as a unique being. And I embraced a kind of religious feeling about my prison life being an ordeal, a blessing imparted by the gods *(kami)*."[129] The dark side of Ōsugi's prison life, however, involved the unavoidable bedbugs, constant hunger, unheated cells in winter, and disease.[130] Like Ōsugi, the Christian socialist Ishikawa Sanshirō, imprisoned in April 1907 for thirteen months for violating the Press Law, read widely, including Kropotkin's work, and emerged from prison an anarchist.[131]

One outstanding labor victory was the 1911–1912 strike against Tokyo streetcar companies. Katayama Sen, who had guided six thousand workers in this strike, was charged on January 15 with incitement to strike under the provisions of the Public Peace Police Law. Besides a three and one-half months' wait in jail, Katayama spent five months in Chiba Prison. While the confinement was difficult, Katayama did begin his autobiography, and he was fortunate enough to be released a few weeks early as part of a general amnesty proclaimed upon the death of Emperor Meiji.[132]

These examples of treatment of political criminals during the last half of Meiji (charges were dismissed in Baba's case) suggest that jail and prison conditions for minor offenders were moderately harsh. Prisoners were allowed limited letter-writing privileges and occasional visits, and books played an important part in their lives. However, obtaining radical books involved subterfuge: Ōsugi received a copy of Kropotkin's *The Conquest of Bread* under the title "How to Bake Bread."[133] Prison did not have to mean total silencing. Ōsugi, for instance, published in two leftist newspapers in August and September 1907 on anarchist tendencies in ancient Chinese thought.[134] Nevertheless, a balanced evaluation of jail and prison conditions also notes that inadequate food and disease appear to have hastened Baba's death, undermined Kōtoku's health, and exposed Ōsugi to pulmonary tuberculosis.[135]

Defending Human Rights

A growing concern for the human rights of prisoners and the procedural rights of criminal suspects developed from mid-Meiji. Concern over the former was indicated in 1887 by the actions of the Osaka Bar Association and the Osaka Municipal Assembly in condemning the "penal rock" punishment. It was the following year that Hara Taneaki led the protest against the sulfur mine at Kushiro Prison. Many farmers were arrested at the turn of the century because they took part in various protest movements to stop the pollution of the Shimotsuke Plain. More than a hundred lawyers took part in these cases, many donating their time, thereby enhancing protection of defendants' procedural rights. "This was the first recorded case in which Japanese lawyers gave their services free to defendants. It must have cost them a considerable amount of time and money, since they were all Tokyo-based, and the hearings were held in the provincial court at Maebashi, in Gunma Prefecture."[136] Even the second Katsura cabinet (1908–1911), remembered for its crackdown on socialists, paid lip service via Home Minister Hirata Tōsuke to the protection of criminal suspects' procedural rights and human rights.[137] The topic of human rights reached the floor of the House of Representatives on February 25, 1912, as Seki Wachi of the Kokumintō excoriated Yamagata Aritomo as "the unique idol of the bureaucratic clique" and "a vestigial survival who epitomizes the feudal oligarchs." Yamagata's ordinances, he stated, were the main cause of unjust taxation, financial disorder, diplomatic stagnation, and "trampling on human rights."[138] In 1914, after a bribery conviction was overturned on appeal, Diet spokesmen charged that procurators abused human rights. From that year, various unsuccessful law bills to protect defendants came before the Diet. Among the provisions in the 1914 law bill, presented by Takagi Masutarō (Kokumintō), and others, were that more than one interrogator had to be present or a suspect could request a lawyer; officials could not lie or threaten; suspects could not be interrogated after indictment.[139]

Outside the Diet, lawyers were involved in the various social problems of the day, defending the poor and workers who struck in defiance of the 1900 peace law. Reginald Smith's *Justice and the Poor* (1915) stimulated the formation of numerous legal aid societies, and the next year Kawakami Hajime's *Binbō monogatari* (Tale of poverty) held the attention of the intellectual world during the three months the Osaka *Asahi Shinbun* published installments. The Japan Bar Association (Nihon Bengoshi Kyōkai) twice in 1918 established committees to investigate possible human rights violations: once during the Rice Riots and again in connection with a bribery scandal involving Kyoto city officials. In the latter case, the bar investigative committee charged that procurators had violated the law and abused human rights.[140] The Rice Riots

began as a peaceful protest in July 1918 in Toyama prefecture over
the spiraling cost of rice, but the movement for cheaper rice grew
rapidly into a nationwide protest, which in some areas turned into
battles between protestors and troops. Vice-Minister of Justice
Suzuki Kisaburō in the August 30 issue of *Hōritsu Shinbun* (Legal
Newspaper) stated that people involved in this terrible affair
would be prosecuted to the fullest extent possible, to act as a warning to others.[141] Lawyers Shioya Kōtarō and Ōi Shizuo went to
Osaka representing the Tokyo Bar Association. At a meeting with
Kobayashi Yoshirō, head procurator, Osaka Appeals Court,
Shioya was curtly told that the investigation of human rights
abuses was ridiculous—the equivalent of a novice procurator
investigating the activities of the procurator-general![142] Thousands of people were arrested and prosecuted, with 1,302 even
convicted of riot under Article 106 of the Penal Code.[143] In the
face of Vice-Minister Suzuki's harsh policy, defense attorney Fuse
Tatsuji argued in the December 18, 1918, *Hōritsu Shinbun* that the
riot law was not applicable and that the lesser penalties of the 1900
peace law should apply. Fuse's view was supported by an editorial
in the same newspaper.[144]

Fuse Tatsuji was experienced at criticizing government officials. Fuse had been a member of the government team in 1904–
1905 as a young procurator in Utsunomiya. However, he was
soured on prosecution by a September 1905 case in which the
defendant, despondent over her husband's debauchery, murdered
her three children and attempted suicide. Before the case was over
Fuse saw the woman as the victim and the husband as the criminal. Writing about the incident thirty years later, he described his
viewpoint as "humanistic." Fuse turned his back on the procuracy
and marched off to help the neglected poor, whom he saw as
nearly defenseless before the courts. During the next few years,
Fuse defended underdogs in various labor dispute cases and supported the rights of local people to use mountainous land in his
home area of Tōhoku. While Fuse doubtless knew about police
brutality and torture before 1915, his defense of murder suspect
Komori Sōsuke resulted in the privately published *Shihō kikan
kaizen ron* (A theory on reforming the machinery of justice) in
1917, the year before Komori was declared not guilty and
released. This case involved a repudiated forced confession. In
this book, Fuse focused on the various illegal interrogation tech-

niques police used to force confession. To break suspects' will to resist, police beat them with *kiseru* (traditional long, narrow pipes), kicked them, gagged them with handcuffs, squeezed their fingers against pencils inserted between the fingers, and forced them to hold chairs over their heads. Long hours of interrogation and various forms of psychological torture were also employed.[145]

A postwar depression firmly gripped Japan by March 1920. Workers responded to widespread dismissals with a wave of disputes and strikes. In particular, the one-month strike at the Kawasaki Dockyards in Kobe, which involved 35,000 workers, was accompanied by much violence, including the killing of one laborer by police. The strike worked itself to a fever pitch, with workers demonstrating in defiance of a ban and the prefectural governor calling in regular army troops. On the evening of July 29, heavily armed police raided the workingmen's headquarters.[146]

On August 10 the Tokyo Bar Association sent to Kobe a fourteen-lawyer investigation committee that included Fuse Tatsuji, Yamazaki Kesaya, Kamimura Susumu, Matsutani Yojirō, and Miwa Jusō. They were aided by labor leaders Suzuki Bunji and Kagawa Toyohiko and by Kobe lawyers. The report issued on August 15 concluded that the so-called riot was police inspired (the workers were attacked by sword-wielding police), for which the governor was mainly to blame. Moreover, police were carrying on improper interrogations of arrested suspects. The committee's conclusions were repudiated by Procurator Koyama Matsukichi's on-the-spot investigation, and his view was published in Tokyo's newspapers. Not deterred, Fuse, Yamazaki, and Kamimura met with Procurator General Hiranuma Kiichirō, urging pressure on the procurators in Kobe to investigate and prosecute the policeman responsible for the laborer's death.[147]

One result of the Kobe strike was the establishment on August 20, 1921, in Tokyo of the Liberal Legal Association (Jiyū Hōsō Dan), promoted mainly by Fuse and Yamazaki together with Katayama Tetsu, Miwa, Kamimura, Matsutani, Miyazaki Ryūsuke, Tani Kenjirō, Makino Mitsuyasu, and Tazaka Sadao. The immediate purpose of the roughly forty lawyers who joined this group was to investigate the administration of justice in connection with the Kobe strike, but a broader purpose was to investigate human rights abuses, aid victims of such abuses, and reform the legal system by removing laws used to suppress laborers and farmers.[148]

Conclusion

A fair evaluation of Meiji laws must conclude that procedural protection was dramatically expanded. The Meiji Constitution, the Penal Code, and the Criminal Procedural Code formed a legal shield for criminal suspects and prisoners, with punishment mandated for officials who committed or permitted illegal acts. Torture was officially abolished in 1879, and forced confessions were declared unacceptable. Deplorable prison conditions were gradually reformed, and the state was generous with amnesties, releasing large numbers of political prisoners in the 1890s. Furthermore, an imperial rescript changed to life imprisonment the death sentences of twelve of those convicted in the High Treason Incident.

Justice Ministry officials were rightfully proud of the legal system and judges of the independence of the judiciary. In both the Ōtsu Incident and the High Treason Incident cases, justice officials resisted outside political pressures and performed their work in the prescribed manner.[149] Moreover, scrupulous attention to the exact meaning of legal provisions is illustrated by the release on a technicality of Baba Tatsui in 1886. In a similar case, three defendants charged with crimes such as violating political meetings regulations and insulting a policeman were freed because "the procurator had not signed the appeal document in person, as the regulations required."[150]

A fair evaluation, however, must also conclude that criminal suspects and prisoners did not always receive the law's full protection and that policemen repeatedly violated laws in the face of orders to stop. This fact is illustrated not only in the Home Ministry's repeated directives on the proper use of the Administrative Enabling Law (1900), but also in orders given by Home Minister Hirata Tōsuke. In an Instruction Address on April 16, 1910, Hirata noted that police had to recognize that the idea of respect for rights and freedom was spreading; without the people's trust, police work suffers. There was, he noted, some criticism of police behavior and even some who said that police violated human rights. To counter this, he concluded, police leaders had to make sure that policemen used laws properly and treated people kindly.

The next year on April 17 Hirata returned to this theme, admitting that there were examples of police misconduct. Severe reprimands, he said, should be given to those who damage the prestige of the police.[151] Despite such commands, police abuse of power to arrest was widespread; torture was used to force confessions, and police brutality was common.

2

Political Crimes: The 1920s

JAPAN IN THE 1920s was a society torn by conflicting ideologies and unsettling events. Against a backdrop of turbulent party politics and postwar depression, the spread of anarchism and communism appalled the directive elite who perceived a disintegration of social harmony. One response to the perceived leftist threat was the *Chian Iji Hō* (Peace Preservation Law), from May 12, 1925 (Law No. 46), which promised up to ten years at hard labor for anyone who organized an association with the object of changing Japan's *kokutai* or private property system (Article 1).[1] Revision of this law in 1928 included a death penalty for advocating a change in the *kokutai*. Police, as the emperor's front-line troops in the ideological war, increasingly became more intolerant of leftist radicalism, turning ever more easily to brutal methods of suppression. Simultaneously, however, an awareness of fundamental human rights took deeper root, with even the police leadership touched by liberal ideas.[2] Lawyers were in the vanguard of the small but increasingly vocal human rights movement, pointing out shortcomings in the enforcement of laws and vigorously defending criminal suspects in political trials. The bench cooperated by insisting that laws be followed and that the trial process be allowed to take its course.

Prosecuting Communists

The Japanese Communist Party was secretly organized in Tokyo on July 15, 1922, by Yamakawa Hitoshi, Sakai Toshihiko, Arahata Kanson, Takase Kiyoshi, and others. This group, with Sakai as chairman, was formally recognized by the Fourth Comintern Congress (Moscow, November 1922) as a branch of the Comintern. While the Japanese reported two hundred fifty members and eight hundred candidates, in fact as late as May 1923 there were only between fifty and sixty members. On March 15, 1923, the new organization prepared a draft party platform, but the drafters split over whether or not to proclaim the radical notion of abolishing the imperial institution. Takase, acting as secretary, shrewdly recorded none of this. Perhaps Takase instinctively felt that such a treasonous statement was too dangerous; perhaps he thought about Kōtoku's fate.[3]

Police, using informants and following up rumors, prepared to crush the party. Lecturer Sano Manabu, Waseda University, provided authorities with an opportunity. Concerned that a dispute between ideologists on the Waseda campus might attract police, Communist Party member Sano moved party documents to a friend's home. Unfortunately for the party, Sano's "friend" was Shibuya Mokutarō, a coal miner turned police informant. About May 24, acting on a tip from Shibuya, police seized the documents. These documents, which proved the illegal party's existence, became the state's most potent weapon in the criminal trial.[4] At dawn on June 5 police raided party offices in Tokyo and several other large cities and in Korea. A special team led by Preliminary Judge Numa Yoshio and Procurator Takikawa Hideo seized materials in the offices of Sano and two others.[5] Thus, authorities, using previously seized party documents, obtained warrants to search for more documents.

After reviewing the preliminary trial record, Judge Numa announced on February 13, 1924, that those arrested would be prosecuted for violation of Articles 14 and 28 of the Public Peace Police Law (prohibited organizing or joining a secret society; violators were liable to imprisonment for six to twelve months). Given statements by defendants, Numa had to order the case to court. Sakai, for instance, told the judge that at the time he had felt it was too early to form a party, "because it would be discovered right away and produce many victims."[6] Sano also admitted that a party had been created, and Hashiura Tokio confessed that Sano, Sakai, Arahata, and Takatsu Seidō had established the party. Sakai and Yoshikawa Gentarō admitted drawing up party rules, and eleven suspects confessed to joining. In addition, three people told about attending a party meeting at Ichikawa Shōichi's home, and two confessed that an executive committee meeting had been held. And so it went, with others confessing that certain people had joined the party and taken part in meetings. Fortunately for Yamakawa Hitoshi, no one mentioned his name. Why did the suspects seem eager to help the government build its case? Their first decision was to deny everything, but they had second thoughts as they realized that a long trial could result in more jail time than the maximum penalty. Thus, they quickened the preliminary trial by replying to the judge's questions, planning to deny everything at the open trial.[7]

The public trial began on April 7, 1925, at the Tokyo District Court. Judge Uno Yōzaburō presided over a three-judge panel; Procurator Ishida Motoi prosecuted. Defense attorneys were Imamura Rikisaburō, Fuse Tatsuji, Yamazaki Kesaya, Matsutani Yojirō, and other court battle veterans: Imamura was one of Kōtoku's lawyers; Fuse had a long history of defending laborers and leftists. At the first session, Sakai denounced as a pack of lies the entire *yoshin chōsho* (preliminary examination record), which was the only document considered legal proof, and accompanying documents: *yoshin ketteisho* (written decision of a preliminary examination) and *yoshin shūketsu* (the conclusion of a preliminary examination).[8] "I cannot," he continued, "understand people who regard communism as dangerous. . . . We want to smoothly avoid a struggle between capitalists and proletarians. If possible, we wish to organize a free and equal political party officially recognized by the government."[9] The defendants continued denying the official record into the second session of the trial (April 9). Closely questioned by Judge Uno, Inomata Tsunao said: "As for me, I do not even know of the existence of the secret organization called the Japanese Communist Party. Of course, I never joined it!" Judge Uno replied that the preliminary examination proved that Inomata was present at the drafting of the party platform, which was equated with membership. Inomata replied: "I attended that meeting at the invitation of Sano, but the purpose of that gathering was to exchange opinions about organizing a proletarian party. Therefore, I do not feel that it had any connection with the Japanese Communist Party, as held in the preliminary report." "The court has been informed," noted the judge, "that at the meeting you all discussed the timing and manner of a revolution."[10] While Arahata did admit to being a Communist, Nosaka Sanzō and Yamakawa denied everything. Tokuda Kyūichi used the public courtroom as a platform from which to give a speech on communism.[11]

Defense lawyers requested permission for expert opinion on the authenticity of the party draft platform document, which was the strongest government proof. They also asked that these people be called to the witness stand to ascertain the source of this document: Tokkō officer Yamada Yoichi, Police Inspector Ōsawa Toyozō, Police Sergeant Nagamori Kaoru, Shibuya Mokutarō, Shibuya Hana (wife), Sakaguchi Kakuji, Sakaguchi Kō (wife), and Sakaguchi Yoshiharu. The first request was approved and the second was denied. Handwriting experts Professors Kuroita Katsumi and Watanabe Yosuke and newspaper reporter Ishii Keizaburō took writing samples from Nakasone Genwa and Takase at the third session (April 18), and at the fourth (June 30) they identified the two defendants as the authors of the document.[12]

Following this, Procurator Ishida demanded one year in prison for nine people and ten months for thirteen. Imamura attacked the penalty as too extreme. Furthermore, he pointed out the terrible social discrimination both Koreans and socialists received in courts, contrary to the idea of equal justice. Another lawyer insisted that the point of this trial was to illustrate the need for harsher control legislation. On July 11 (fifth session), the procurator demanded penalties for three defendants who were absent on June 30 (one year for two and ten months for one). Sano Manabu and two others were added to the procurator's list on August 20 (one year for Sano and ten months for the others). The bench announced its decision for the twenty-nine on August 20, 1925. Twenty-three defendants received either eight or ten months for violating the 1900 peace law. Yamakawa, Ichikawa, and Tashiro Jōji were held not guilty, since there was no proof of their having joined the illegal organization. Kondō Eizō, who was in hiding, and Kawauchi Tadahiko, who was in the military, were not sentenced. Watanabe Mitsuzō had died. Interestingly, the court did mention that the defendants had violated Article 1 of the new Peace Preservation Law, although it could not be used in this case. Furthermore, the days spent in detention were subtracted from the sentences (for ten people this meant 120 days less prison time each). Court expenses were charged to the guilty, and party documents, because they had been used to commit a crime, became government property.[13] The penalties imposed were substantially lighter than demanded by the prosecution, which had asked for one year for thirteen people. One newspaper reported: "When the sentence was pronounced, the suspects looked at each other and their faces beamed with joy, since their sentences were much lighter than anticipated."[14]

The government and some of the defendants appealed; Judge Nagaoka Kumao presided over the first appeal session on April 5, 1926. The verdict (April 28) let stand the decision on Yamakawa (innocent); reversed the decision on Ichikawa (to guilty; eight months); and increased the penalty for two others from eight months to ten months. Again defendants appealed (ten at first, but four withdrew) as did the prosecution (in one case over a dispute on how many days had already been served). The defendants based the appeal on factual mistakes made in the Appeals Court record. On August 4, 1926, the Supreme Court dismissed all appeals.[15]

The government's handling of the investigation, interrogation, and trial of members of the Communist Party was meticulously correct. Documents seized at an informant's home were used to obtain search warrants, which in turn produced additional incriminating documents. It is almost certain that the defendants were not excessively abused by police; had they been, they undoubtedly would have used evidence of brutality as a court weapon, especially since lawyer Imamura raised the issue of court discrimination against socialists and Koreans. Documentary proof and statements made before the preliminary judge determined the outcome; suspects were even linked to specific documents by handwriting experts. Further indication of the state's methodical handling of this case is evidenced by the fact that it lasted three years and two months from the time of arrest (the court time, starting with the open trial and ending with the Supreme Court, was sixteen months). As for the sentences, all parties agreed they were moderate. Moreover, the veteran leftist Yamakawa, whom police and procurators must have known in their bones was at the center of this conspiracy, was released for lack of evidence. Furthermore, many of these defendants were out on bail during the trials and in some cases took short trips abroad. An amnesty granted after the death of the Taisho emperor in 1926 shortened their sentences.[16]

Legal Murder

An earthquake devastated the Tokyo-Yokohama area on September 1, 1923, killing tens of thousands of people and producing mass hysteria. The government responded by issuing a limited form of martial law on September 2, putting the capital under the command of General Fukuda Masatarō, mobilizing army reservists and civilians into vigilante patrol corps, and putting under protective confinement leftist radicals. Unfortunately, rumors about terrible deeds done by Koreans egged on by socialists quickly spread.[17] As a result, thousands of Koreans were butchered by vigilante groups. Leftists, too, lived in fear of sudden death.

The Kameido Incident involved the murder of ten labor activists some of whom were communists. The head of the Kameido Police Station claimed that these men were arrested on September 3 because they sang illegal revolutionary songs from atop the Nankatsu Labor Union building and spread rumors. Unable to keep them quiet in jail, the chief asked on September 4 for help from a nearby military detachment. Police cooperated with the soldiers by removing prisoners from cells. The ten men were killed by Sublieutenant Tamura Harukichi, and the bodies were burned on the bank of the Arakawa Canal three days later. Pictures of these bodies show some with hands tied and others decapitated. Best known among the victims were Hirasawa Keishichi and Kawai Yoshitora.[18]

What occurred at Kameido Police Station is murky, but two eyewitness reports cast some light. One person who was jailed there recalled hearing fearful screams and seeing a young man on the ground and a shiny sword blade among the shadowy figures. More terrible screams followed, but he could not see what was happening.[19] Another account comes from Minami Kiichi, whose younger brother Yoshimura Kōji (name change due to adoption) was one of the ten murdered. Minami was a small factory owner and a respected community leader. An officer he knew from the Kameido Police Station secretly informed him that Yoshimura had been arrested that day and executed by a sublieutenant of the Narashino Eleventh Cavalry. After checking with other police sources, which indicated that these murders were ordered by higher authorities, Minami visited Chief Komori at Kameido

Police Station. The chief's polite attitude changed when he discovered Minami's connection to Yoshimura. A police sergeant seized Minami by the neck, pulling him into the cell area of the station, where Minami slipped on blood on the concrete floor. Certain now that Yoshimura was dead, he broke loose and scaled a concrete wall as policemen yelled and fired two shots, one of which hit his left calf. Minami reported this affair to the martial law headquarters.[20]

News of the murders quickly circulated. One of the first people to get involved was the lawyer and social activist Fuse Tatsuji, who accompanied about twenty others to locate the ten bodies. Fuse dealt with police, who insisted they stop, while others dug out the bodies. Fuse's involvement was just beginning, as he launched a campaign to discover the perpetrators of the crime. Two of his long articles appeared in the *Hōritsu Shinbun*. Suzuki Bunji, a moderate labor leader, joined the verbal assault in the November 1923 issue of *Kaizō* (Reconstruction), pointing out that there was no evidence that the prisoners had caused trouble at the Kameido Police Station. Furthermore, one witness to the police arrest stated that the ten men were simply helping earthquake victims. The police response came from Shōriki Matsutarō, a highly placed official in the Metropolitan Police Board, who stated that he accepted the military's view that their men acted in compliance with military regulations. Shōriki concluded that policemen as well were innocent of any crime. The government blessed this conclusion when Justice Minister Suzuki Kisaburō announced his satisfaction.[21] While authorities could argue that this was a proper protective arrest, these men were stripped of legal protections and illegally executed.

Authorities arrested other leftists, such as Fukuda Kyōji, Kondō Kenji, Ishikawa Sanshirō, Inamura Junzō, Katō Kazuo, and Asanuma Inejirō. There is a record of Asanuma's treatment. After returning to Tokyo on September 1 from a political rally in Gunma, Asanuma was arrested and brought to a cavalry regiment headquarters. Soldiers, threatening death, beat him and sent him off to Ichigaya Prison.[22] A friend, Miyake Shōichi, wrote: "He was so badly beaten we could hardly recognize him."[23] Miyake claims that Ōyama Ikuo was another military target, but perhaps friendship with Lieutenant General Terauchi Hisaichi, which dated back to student days in Berlin, saved him.[24] That some leftists were marked for death before the earthquake is documented in the trial record of Military Police (Kenpei) Captain Amakasu Masahiko, who studied socialism and concluded that it would harm the nation. Anarchism, he believed, was a special evil and, if an opportunity arose, Amakasu planned to kill Ōsugi Sakae, Sakai Toshihiko, and Fukuda Kyōji.[25]

The September Anarchist Cases

Two anarchists caught up in the tragic events of September 1923 left indelible marks in official records and the public mind. Arrested first was Pak Yŏl (Pak Chun-sik), who was charged with plotting to kill the emperor. The second arrested was Ōsugi Sakae, who was murdered by Captain Amakasu.

Pak Yŏl was the central figure among Korean anarchists in Tokyo and on good terms with anarchists Ōsugi and Iwasa Sakutarō. Late in 1921 Pak and other Koreans in Tokyo established the Kekkyo Dan (Bloody Fist Group) to punish Korean collaborators. About that time, Pak also joined Kokutōkai (Black Current Association), whose members were primarily Korean socialists and anarchists. This group, which Iwasa helped start, centered on Kim Yak-su. Kaneko Fumiko, who met Pak the following spring, also became a member. About September 1922, the Black Current Association split into Hokuseikai (North Star Association) and Kokuyūkai (Black Friends Association), with communist members entering the former and Pak and Kaneko and other anarchists joining the latter. About April 1923 Pak was the prime mover behind the formation of Futeisha (Insubordinate Organization), with a membership mainly overlapping Black Friends Association. Thus, by the time Pak was twenty-one, his name acted as a magnet, drawing young Korean political activists; it drew attention as well from the police, who worried about deepening ties between Korean nationalists and Japanese leftist radicals.[26]

By September 3, because some police believed rumors that Koreans were planning to harm Japanese, some Tokyo police stations were arresting Koreans. Many Koreans brought to the Kameido Police Station were, like the ten union men, brutally killed.[27] Using the broad scope of the Administrative Enabling Law (1900), police from the Setagaya Police Station took Pak Yŏl into protective custody on September 3; Kaneko was picked up the following day. The prescient police suggested to Pak's landlord that it would be best to clean up the house and rent it, since Pak's return was doubtful. Shortly thereafter, Pak and Kaneko were charged as homeless vagrants under the provisions of Regulations for the Punishment of Police Offenses (1908). By October 20, after many days of interrogating Pak, police declared Futeisha a secret terrorist organization and therefore in violation of the 1900 peace law. Fourteen others were indicted, of which four were Japanese. Interrogations continued, and on February 15, 1924, Pak, Kaneko, and one other person faced an additional charge of violating the Explosives Control Penal Regulations. Pak's plan, said authorities, was to smuggle explosives in from Shanghai to be used when the time was ripe. At this point authorities dropped the 1900 peace law charge, citing lack of evidence; however, they had evidence of Pak's discussion about explosives in 1921 with merchant seaman Sugimoto Sadakazu and with a Korean nationalist. Nevertheless, Pak had received no explosives.[28]

   The defendants were hostile during the preliminary examination. Procurator Shiono Suehiko, Tokyo District Court, who was involved in this case, said: "It seemed to me that the judge [Tatematsu Natsushi] had various difficulties until Pak Yŏl confessed."[29] The problem, of course, was the leap from a comparatively minor explosives possession charge to a conspiracy to assassinate the emperor. Judge Tatematsu, however, managed to extract a violent statement from Pak: "A Gift from a Disloyal Korean to the Japanese Authoritarian Class," in which Pak said that he would fight the Japanese until "I vomit red blood and fall down." Similarly, Kaneko's feelings were vehemently expressed: she denied all authority and had a goal of "exterminating mankind."[30] On May 2, 1925, Tatematsu photographed the couple in an intimate pose in his private office. This was an unusual and unauthorized act, which, after a copy of the photo reached the press, damaged the Wakatsuki Reijirō cabinet and forced Tatematsu's resignation on August 11. The photo was taken, claimed the judge, as a memento of an exceptional court case, which he planned to use in his memoir. Moreover, the relaxed intimacy of the picture, he said, was unplanned; Kaneko suddenly moved close to Pak as the shutter tripped. Was this photo session part of Tatematsu's campaign to obtain a confession, or does it reflect an inexperienced and romantically inclined young judge being drawn into a symbiotic relationship with the prisoners? Whatever the answer and whatever relationship developed during this intense interchange, the result was a turning of talk about buying explosives into a plan to kill the emperor and his son, a violation of Section 2, Article 73 of the Penal Code.[31]

When the preliminary examination was completed on July 17, 1925, the Supreme Court took jurisdiction, because the case involved high treason. A panel of five judges led by Makino Kikunosuke heard the evidence in open court from February 26, 1926. Koyama Matsukichi, chief procurator for the Supreme Court, was aided by Ohara Naoshi. Pak was defended by lawyers Arai Yōtarō and Tazaka Sadao (court appointed) and Fuse Tatsuji and three associates. Given the prosecution's evidence, the death verdict of March 25, 1926, was expected. Surprising was the reduction in penalty to imprisonment without term as part of the new Shōwa emperor's amnesty, as recommended by the Wakatsuki cabinet. Kaneko killed herself at Tochigi Women's Prison in July, but Pak outlived the Great Empire of Japan.[32]

This case raises questions about violations of procedural rights. While the first protective custody arrest was legal, the holding of Pak and Kaneko under Article 1 of the 1908 law as vagrants (i.e., people without a regular address or an occupation) after police urged the landlord to clean up the house and get a new tenant and after they witnessed the sale of the couple's possessions leaves only one possible conclusion: police officers turned the jailed couple into vagrants in order to hold them as they looked for additional violations. Doubtless, since Pak was under surveillance, police had some information on his activities and perhaps suspected criminal violations. Nevertheless, the police methods were illegal. At the preliminary examination, the suspects became Judge Tatematsu's partners in a cooperative effort to inflate rather petty antiauthority and antigovernment activities into something much grander. Defense lawyer Fuse wrote in the October issue of *Kaizō* that without physical evidence the state's case rested solely on confessions. The process, he said, got twisted, and the suspects ended up as guides for their interrogator.[33]

Postearthquake Tokyo was flooded with wild rumors. Some of them told of the death of Ōsugi Sakae; others said he plotted an evil act against the government. Actually, Ōsugi, watched by detectives, waited at home for the confusion to subside. On September 18 the *Hōchi Shinbun* reported that Ōsugi had been taken

into custody on September 16 in the general Military Police
roundup of leftists. In fact, Ōsugi had been killed on the sixteenth
—together with Itō Noe, his wife, and Tachibana Sōichi, a
nephew—by Kenpei Captain Amakasu Masahiko, a specialist on
leftists with a deep hatred of anarchists, who worried about radicals loose in earthquake-stricken Tokyo. When Amakasu learned
from the Yodobashi Police Station that Ōsugi was free, he single-
mindedly stalked Ōsugi until September 16. Perhaps Amakasu
misinterpreted the willingness with which police gave information
about Ōsugi as tacit agreement to permanently solve the problem
of Ōsugi. At any rate, Amakasu strangled Ōsugi and Itō, leaving
the six-year-old nephew to two soldiers. The naked bodies,
wrapped in straw matting, were dropped into an abandoned well.
The next day dirt and other material were added to camouflage
the brutal murders. An autopsy revealed that the adults had been
severely beaten, but this information was not officially released.[34]

A report meant for limited internal circulation gives the official
police version. Police authorities were not out to get Ōsugi; they
cooperated with the Kenpei because of martial law conditions.
Normally, two men were assigned to Ōsugi, taking turns tailing
him on alternate days; a stakeout near Ōsugi's home reported
anyone who came while the tail was away. Ōsugi was not put into
protective custody for the same reason that Yamakawa Hitoshi
had not been: Yodobashi Police Station was short of personnel,
and a home watch was simply easier. Since police were certain
that anarchists would make no move without seeing Ōsugi, by
watching him they simultaneously watched them all. Around
noon on September 15, Kenpei Sergeant Mori Keijirō, accompanied by a plainclothesman (later identified as Amakasu), came to
Yodobashi Police Station and demanded of Assistant Police
Inspector Matsumoto Denzō and Sergeant Shino Sanshichirō an
explanation as to why Ōsugi was not under arrest. Matsumoto
replied that since Ōsugi was involved in no anarchistic activities,
there was no reason for an arrest. Early that evening the two were
back at Yodobashi Police Station and with Shino's help located
Ōsugi's residence. Mori asked Shino how to lure Ōsugi out. Send
a telegram using the name Fujita Isamu, replied Shino. The next
day about 2:00 P.M. the plainclothesman returned, asking Shino
about Ōsugi. Shino sent Amakasu off toward Ōsugi's house. On
September 17 about 11:00 A.M., Mori returned to Yodobashi

Police Station and told Matsumoto that Ōsugi, his wife, and nephew had been taken by the Kenpei the day before, giving as a reason a desire to discuss the removal of martial law with the anarchist. Matsumoto replied that Ōsugi's tail had reported that a lieutenant from the Kenpei headquarters was scheduled to check on Ōsugi that morning.[35] Mori responded: "The truth is Ōsugi was taken care of last night. Keep this matter absolutely secret. However, if you must say something, then say only that the police took Ōsugi to the Kenpeitai. Say absolutely nothing about anything else."[36] Matsumoto refused Mori's invitation for lunch as well as ten yen to treat the station personnel.[37] This document, which was compiled by the Metropolitan Police Board, may be closer to the truth than the court record.

A detective assigned to Ōsugi reported Ōsugi's seizure to the Metropolitan Police Board. Yuasa Kurahei, head of the board, in turn contacted the Police Bureau, Home Ministry, as well as Martial Law Commander General Fukuda Masatarō. Yuasa also took this matter to Home Minister Gotō Shinpei, who told Prime Minister Yamamoto Gonnohyōe. The next person brought in was Army Minister Tanaka Giichi. At a cabinet meeting on September 19, Gotō criticized the killings as illegal and an abuse of human rights. An investigation was ordered, during which the senior Kenpei officer resigned as did General Fukuda. Amakasu and his colleagues faced a military court. A military procurator told journalists that it appeared that Amakasu killed Ōsugi to remove "poisonous material" before it did additional harm to the nation.[38] Statements in the trial record contradict the confidential police report. For instance, Amakasu stated that Mori had learned from the Yodobashi Police Station that they wanted the Kenpei to exterminate Ōsugi. Also, the defendant said that the police told him they planned to stop tailing Ōsugi. Finally, Amakasu claimed that Shino told him what kind of clothing Ōsugi and his wife were wearing and their destination.[39]

Procurator General Koyama Matsukichi, addressing Kenpei officers on March 9, 1924, ignored the murders of September 1923. Instead, he congratulated the officers: "I see the fact that Kenpei day and night fulfilled their duty of protecting and helping to maintain public peace. They gained the deep trust of the people."[40]

The political murder of Ōsugi Sakae was a private act repu-

diated by higher authority, a repudiation publicly expressed in the
resignation of military officers and the trial of Amakasu and his
men. Home Minister Gotō's outrage was probably heartfelt, since
the incident, as Prime Minister Yamamoto worried, was bound to
cause problems. Actions by police officers at Yodobashi Police Station may have been correct under martial law conditions. Nevertheless, police and government officials must share blame for Ōsugi's death as they must share blame for the Kameido killings,
because by contributing to official panic they encouraged murder.
According to the Metropolitan Police Board's rumor record, one
rumor was that socialists and Koreans were working together to
start fires. Some police stations, it seems, accepted such rumors as
fact. There is no firm evidence that authorities intended to make
socialists and Koreans scapegoats, but there were policemen who
contributed to the spreading of ugly rumors by putting them into
the police and military communications network, thus making the
rumors stronger and removing suspicion about their reliability.[41]
Therefore, to a degree, authorities were involved in Ōsugi's
murder.

   Wada Kyūtarō, a protégé of Ōsugi, fixed blame on former Martial Law Commander General Fukuda Masatarō. Getting help
from Furuta Daijirō and other anarchists, Wada struck on September 1, 1924, as Fukuda spoke at an anniversary ceremony;
Wada's shot, however, merely grazed the general. Police wanted
to know the source of the bomb they found on Wada, but he
refused to tell despite severe interrogations. In the meantime,
Wada's friends tried to blow up a police station, set off a bomb in a
Ginza area train, and delivered a disguised bomb to Fukuda's
home. Police had Wada returned from Ichigaya Prison to a police
station where, under severe torture, Wada gave incriminating
details about the group's membership and hiding place. Judge
Uno Yōzaburō presided over the group trial, which began on May
21, 1925. The state was represented by Kurokawa Wataru and the
defense by Yamazaki Kesaya, Fuse Tatsuji, Matsutani Yojirō, and
two others. Sentence was passed on September 10, 1925: Furuta,
as the group's leader, death; Wada, life; Kurachi Kenji, twelve
years; Aratani Yoichirō, five years (Muraki Genjirō had died in
jail in January 1925 before the preliminary examination). Furuta
was executed on October 15, 1925.[42] While justice officials in this
case appear to have strictly followed the law, police interrogation

methods were illegal.[43] The likelihood that torture was used in this case and others is discussed in Chapter 4.

"The Most Ominous Incident on Record"

On the morning of December 27, 1923, Nanba Daisuke shot at Prince Regent Hirohito, who was on his way to open the new Diet session. Nanba's assassination attempt hit the nation like another terrible earthquake. One newspaper headlined it "The Most Ominous Incident on Record."[44] The Yamamoto Gonnohyōe cabinet, less than four months old, resigned in atonement. Nanba's father, a member of the House of Representatives, resigned, as did the principal of Nanba's grade school and his major teacher; his hometown went into formal mourning. Indeed, Nanba's regicidal attempt left such an indelible mark that Justice Minister Ogawa Heikichi, in a secret session with a House of Representatives' committee (March 3, 1925), said it stood out as the most horrible among various incidents.[45]

Nanba's guilt was plain, but, nonetheless, justice officials made meticulous trial preparations. Preliminary Judge Numa Yoshio met Nanba seven times, beginning the same day as the incident and concluding on January 22, 1924. Numa discovered what the establishment most feared: a young man from an upper-class family radicalized by political lectures, demonstrations, and literature. Increasingly, the conservative policies of the Hara Kei cabinet angered Nanba, and he reconsidered his father's role in the Diet. Violent police actions against the labor movement, coupled with the slaying of Koreans and anarchists after the earthquake, influenced his decision to protest such injustice. Old newspaper accounts about Kōtoku's execution infuriated him, stimulating feelings of revenge. An article by Kyoto University Professor Kawakami Hajime on dedicated terrorists, sacrificing themselves to bring on the Russian Revolution, helped trigger his terrorist act. At the preliminary examination Nanba insisted he was an informal communist. Letters to friends support this claim. Asked whom he most respected, he named Sano Manabu, Yamakawa Hitoshi, and Sakai Toshihiko. Killing the prince, he felt, would profit the communist revolution and avenge the death of Kōtoku. Meanwhile, a professor at Tokyo University Medical School secretly reported that Nanba was rational. Nevertheless, the government chose to follow the line that ill health was one motive for

the crime. Even at the in-camera trial Procurator General Koyama Matsukichi tried to avoid mentioning communism and
stressed that like some of those in the High Treason Case, Nanba
was ill. This was for public consumption, since Justice Minister
Ogawa's view was that Nanba acted because of conversion to,
first, anarchism and then communism.[46]

On February 22, Koyama charged Nanba with violation of
Article 73 of the Penal Code; the trial, presided over by Yokota
Hideo, head of the Supreme Court, began on October 1 and
ended the following day. Court-appointed attorneys were Imamura Rikisaburō, Matsutani Yojirō, and Iwata Chūzō. Yokota
lectured the defendant on the imperial system and communism,
pointing out that the latter was incompatible with the former.
Mostly Nanba remained silent, but he did say that the prosecution's "poor health" argument was insulting. Lawyer Imamura
argued that improper suppression by authorities caused the High
Treason Incident; the present case was a retaliation. Matsutani
joined him in stressing that repressive government policies stimulated the present incident. Iwata, who was from the defendant's
home prefecture, kept a low profile, saying that Nanba's lack of
remorse made it impossible to ask for mercy. The death sentence
was pronounced on November 13, and two days later Nanba was
executed.[47]

This was an open-and-shut case. Unlike the high treason of
Kōtoku and Pak, no legal argument about intent or degree of
involvement was possible. Moreover, unlike the other cases, Nanba's dramatic act evoked little domestic or foreign sympathy.
Indeed, Sakai Toshihiko, one whom Nanba most idolized, wrote
Imamura that he feared a backlash on the social movement.
Despite official shock, the legal machinery functioned correctly
and smoothly, with police, procurators, and judges drawing praise
from newspapers. Justice officials did not neglect the defense;
Imamura's credentials were impeccable: he had experience defending leftists going back to the High Treason Case. And the lawyers put up a spirited defense, bringing the issue of illegal but
unpunished acts by officials in the High Treason Case into the
trial record. Furthermore, they argued that repressive government policies stimulate terrible incidents. Judge Yokota, who lectured Nanba in a fatherly way, urging a display of remorse,
showed some sympathy to the lawyers' argument. Even silent

Nanba softened somewhat by the second afternoon, expressing regret. Six weeks later, however, after hearing the death sentence, Nanba loudly expressed support for the Japanese Communist Party and Soviet Russia.[48]

Applying the New Peace Law

The Peace Preservation Law was first used against the Marxist-oriented Student Federation of Social Science (Gakusei Shakai Kagaku Rengōkai, or Gakuren) in 1926. Normally, police did not interfere with campus activities, but this tolerant attitude changed during the early 1920s in the face of highly vocal national student groups engaged in antigovernment protests. Gakuren upset conservatives by noisily protesting against military education on campuses and for expanded academic freedom. While most Gakuren members concentrated on campus-related concerns, some were involved with communism and other off-campus radical movements.[49] In fact, the organization secretly adopted a platform declaring that "the student movement must hereafter act as one wing *(ichiyoku)* of the proletarian movement with Marxism-Leninism as its guiding principle."[50]

Kyoto's Tokkō head, Kubota Shun, became concerned when Gakuren held a convention in Kyoto in July 1925. Student contacts with a visiting Soviet trade union representative increased Kubota's suspicions. In late November antimilitary posters appeared on the Dōshisha University campus. According to Vice-Home Minister Kawasaki Takukichi, Kubota requested Tokyo's views on Gakuren. The Police Bureau decided to wait, but the Kyoto District Court procurator insisted on arrests. Kubota was then ordered to raid boarding houses, dormitories, and private homes on December 1, arresting thirty-seven Gakuren members whom police suspected of violating the Publication Law (i.e., printing and distributing an antimilitary education handbill). Authorities were embarrassed, however, because the materials seized were inadequate proof. Consequently, most students were released by the next day.[51]

Police and justice authorities began a second series of arrests on January 15, 1926, apprehending a total of thirty-eight current and former students. A special team of "thought procurators" was assembled for this test of the Peace Preservation Law: Ikeda Katsu, Hirata Susumu, and Kurokawa Wataru from Tokyo and

Yoshimura Takeo from the Osaka District Court. At first, investigators looked for Publication Law violations; but as interrogations progressed and the thought procurators read seized documents, the scope of violations was expanded to include the new peace law. By the conclusion of the preliminary examination, investigators felt that the students had made concrete plans to repudiate the private property system. While shocked university officials and parents worried about prison sentences, the defiant and unrepentant students engaged the thought procurators in debate. Completion of the preliminary examination on September 18, 1926, permitted suspects to be released on bail or into someone's custody.[52] The students, having withstood police and prison, must have felt victorious. In fact, except for restriction on movement the ordeal was minor; the students "were treated with respect by police and justice officials and given all the comforts they might desire—including large shipments of the latest communist literature from their comrades outside."[53]

The trial was held at the Kyoto District Court, Judge Arai Misao presiding, between April 4 and May 30, 1927, meeting for thirteen sessions. The government was represented by Procurators Koga Yukitoshi and Nanbu Kaneo, who requested prison sentences for the thirty-eight defendants, up to three years for four of them. All were charged with violations of the peace law: They were members of groups supporting Gakuren's policies; they believed in Marxist-Leninist doctrine and had plotted to overturn capitalism and introduce communism; they had drafted a statement of purpose and discussed ways to carry out this plan. Defense lawyers (Imamura Rikisaburō, Kiyose Ichirō, and six others) emphasized that the students' activities were protected by academic freedom and that the Peace Preservation Law was not designed to retard educational activities. The court's decision reflects a rather tolerant attitude: Four defendants were sentenced to imprisonment for one year and the others to from eight to ten months; of this latter group fifteen had the sentence suspended and were put on probation. Judge Arai closed the case by saying that they were young men with a promising future, and he urged them to obey their parents. Defense lawyers appealed the case.[54]

The case was heard on April 5, 1928, by Judge Maezawa Kōjirō at the Osaka Appeals Court. Only eleven defendants appeared, however, since many were under arrest in connection with the sensational March 15, 1928, arrest (described below). When the judge proceeded, the defendants staged a protest that included singing revolutionary songs; the court was closed. The trial began again in camera on September 24, 1929, with the defendants divided into two groups: A Group included those caught in the March 15 arrest; B Group included those facing only the original charges. Only twenty-one were present. In the A Group (nine people) the longest sentence was seven years of penal servitude and the shortest was three years. In the other group (twelve people) two got the maximum of two years' imprisonment (lighter than penal servitude), seven received one and one-half years' imprisonment, and three were freed. The court in passing sentence was very specific, citing meetings, discussions, and other actions in which the defendants violated the law. In these clearly illegal actions, declared the court, the students had moved outside the protective umbrella of academic freedom. An appeal for review by the Supreme Court was rejected.[55]

Why authorities decided to make this the first test case for the new peace law is not clear. One scholar speculates that Kubota Shun's "inordinate ambition was the deciding factor."[56] Vice-Minister Kawasaki, however, states that within the Home Ministry there was a fatherly feeling and concern for the future of student radicals and a desire to guide and reform them rather than to apply harsh laws. The fact that many student activists came from upper-class families and attended elite universities probably contributed to this attitude. At any rate, Kawasaki shifts the blame to the Kyoto chief procurator, Koga Yukitoshi, who insisted on an arrest. Koga's remark to a journalist after the news blackout on the arrest was lifted in September 1926—that the affair "was a great incident similar to the High Treason Incident" and that left undisturbed it would have become even more serious—reinforces Kawasaki's viewpoint.[57] Whatever the truth of this matter, the law was first used in the academic freedom area which had so concerned some lawmakers.

Educators and the informed public apparently regarded the students as youngsters playacting at social change and no danger to the state. This understanding attitude plus the fatherly feelings of officials no doubt influenced not only the first court decision (May 1927) but police and prison officials as well. After the first trial, the *Tokyo Asahi Shinbun* noted that the sentences were much lighter than requested. Yamada Shozō, head of the Faculty of Law, Kyoto Imperial University, added to this feeling by stating that university authorities planned no additional punishment.[58] Given this general attitude, it is not surprising that this case was handled properly without the slightest whisper of police brutality or legal irregularity.

March 15, 1928

During the spirited first national election (February 1928) under the 1925 Manhood Suffrage Law, the hitherto clandestine Japanese Communist Party emerged in a flurry of propagandizing: the first issue of the illegal *Sekki* (Red Flag) was published, and party handbills were widely distributed. Also, about eleven of the forty candidates of the legal Labor-Farmer Party (Rōdō Nōmintō) were disguised communists. The government, which followed communist movements via informants, responded with a massive round-up of suspected communists.[59]

Authorities gambled on a nationwide sweep to find documentary proof of Peace Preservation Law violations. Procurator Matsuzaka Hiromasa, part of the justice team that spearheaded this arrest, pointed out that information from police spies was not acceptable in court. Consequently, he said, the justice team "had to obtain the evidence by searching their homes. If they had letters or party organization papers in their possession, these could be used as powerful evidence against them. . . . To carry this out, we had to get the evidence in our hands before they discovered the danger and burned the material. Therefore, we had no choice but to carry out a wholesale arrest."[60] Procurators, concerned over paperwork technical flaws, exercised care in obtaining domiciliary search orders and arrest warrants. In Tokyo fifteen suspected communists were named on warrants, but in other districts local officials made the choices. Since little was known about party activities and membership, arrest warrants were deliberately vague. In Tokyo it was planned to have six teams of police led by preliminary court judges and procurators raid suspected union organizations, newspapers, and private homes. Police were to seize party documents, orders, publications, and private written material. This latter kind of evidence would be used to tie individuals to the illegal party.[61] "We arrested them," concluded Matsuzaka, "as stipulated in the text of the Criminal Procedure Code."[62]

At dawn on March 15, 1928, government agents raided more than 120 places nationwide, seizing about sixteen hundred suspects and thousands of valuable documents, including a party name list. In Tokyo, Matsuzaka and his colleagues were under great pressure as they interrogated more than two hundred mainly uncooperative suspects, because to be within legal limits they had only ten days. Eventually, after many sleepless nights, the first suspect confessed to joining the Communist Party.[63] That confession was crucial, according to Matsuzaka: "We had them in our power! From that time we could relax, because we had proof that the party existed."[64]

In the meantime, arrests of communist suspects continued, since key leaders remained at large; more than 3,400 people had been seized by the end of 1928.[65] The crippled party, however, stepped up propaganda activities and even managed to increase its membership from a low of thirty in December 1928 to more than two hundred by April 1929. Increased party activity again brought another nationwide dawn raid on April 16, 1929, in which most of the key leaders and more than seven hundred suspects were taken. By the end of 1929, unremitting police pressure raised the total arrested communist suspects under the provisions of the Peace Preservation Law to 8,368.[66]

Every soldier's war experience is different, and so it was with each of the arrested communist suspects in what became the biggest event in Japan's judicial history. Shiga Yoshio, in the party's agitation-propaganda department, was awakened at dawn on March 15 by someone calling "Telegram!" Police took him to Yodobashi Police Station. No exceptional brutality or torture occurred in his case.[67] Communist Tokuda Kyūichi, an unsuccessful Diet candidate for the Labor-Farmer Party, was not so fortunate. On March 15, Tokuda was already in the hands of police, having been picked up on February 26 in Fukuoka and sent two days later to Tokyo's Takanawa Police Station. After he complained about an illegal arrest, police transferred him to the Metropolitan Police Board, where he stayed for a month. To gain his cooperation, police inserted needles under his nails.[68] Kimura Kyōtarō and his colleague Matsuda Kiichi, both involved in the Zenkoku Suiheisha (National Equality Society) in Osaka, were seized on March 15 and taken to the Ashihara Police Station, where they were interrogated in a second-floor room used for judo and kendo practice.[69] Kimura, who had been arrested before in

National Equality Society protests, immediately sensed a changed atmosphere when the chief detective yelled: "You traitors, be prepared to die!" When the suspects refused to admit to distributing communist posters and handbills, the same detective screamed: "All right then, we will hear from your body!"[70] Kimura's fingers were crushed against a pencil inserted between them. Next his exposed thighs were beaten with an iron rod around which a *furoshiki* had been wrapped. Afterwards, with blackened, swollen thighs, he was dragged off to a cell. The next day his tormentors switched to a kendo sword, breaking an eardrum. Day after day the torture continued, with the suspect passing out from time to time. At one point, the interrogators built a small fire from wood chips in a hibachi and held Kimura's face in the smoke. This treatment continued for about two weeks. Matsuda received similar treatment.[71]

Katayama Nobutada, a labor union official, was taken to the Sugamo Police Station (Tokyo) on March 22. Police suspended him upside down and forced water into his nostrils.[72] In Okayama four days later, Moriya Fumio, who had entered the Faculty of Law, Tokyo Imperial University, in 1926, visited the home of Nagata Misao just as the police were arresting Nagata. Police hit Moriya and took him along to the station. Moriya wrote that although he was released the following day, he was unable to forget the severe interrogations, as he saw law in action and the reality of torture.[73] On May 7, Ishioka Matsugorō, a laborer, was taken to the Shinagawa Police Station. After an interrogation that included severe torture, three Tokkō forced him to apply a thumb print to a prepared statement.[74]

During late 1928 and early 1929, district courts dealt with indicted communists. Okayama District Court Judge Kashima Tsurunosuke heard the first case on October 31, 1928. Among the defense lawyers was Unno Shinkichi from Tokyo, who took the case because eight of the fifteen defendants had attended his old higher school. In reply to the prosecution's request for stiff penalties (e.g., six years for three people and five years for seven), Unno pleaded that these were youngsters whose thought remained unformed. Judge Kashima responded by ordering only one five-year sentence (for Nagata Misao as ringleader); two years for two defendants; one and one-half years for three; one year for two; three years probation for seven. This outcome probably reflects the judge's consideration of the youths' ages and their slight involvement in party activities.[75]

The trial at the Osaka District Court, which began on November 21, was different. First, it was a larger group (ninety-eight), including important party members such as Kasuga Shōjirō, the local chairman for the Kansai area; second, it was disorderly. Judge Shibata Sadaki and two colleagues faced Fuse Tatsuji and twelve other lawyers; the prosecution was led by Kaneko Rikichi. As Kaneko read the indictment, Fuse interrupted, asking the judge to move the trial to Tokyo. He noted that the Japanese Communist Party was a single organization and that its central committee was then undergoing preliminary examination in Tokyo. To maintain fairness in the penalties meted out, he maintained, a unified trial was most proper. Suspects clapped hands in agreement. Judge Shibata urged Fuse to reconsider: a quick trial in Osaka would be fairer to the suspects. Lawyer Koiwai Kiyoshi said that if the judge sorrowed over the suspects' long time in jail he should release them. When defendant Kasuga supported Fuse's argument, Shibata ordered a recess. That afternoon and the next day the bickering between lawyers and the bench continued, with suspects refusing to reply to questions. When Shibata ordered them from the room, they broke into a revolutionary song, whereupon the judge ordered a closed trial. After Shibata's order, Fuse screamed that he was completely opposed. The judge lectured Fuse on the sacred nature of the court and recommended disciplinary punishment for disrespect. Eventually, the trial was concluded. Penalties were heavier than at Okayama: Kasuga was sentenced to eight years imprisonment; two others received seven years; five got six years; thirteen got five years; eighteen received two years; and the balance got one year.[76]

The Tanaka Giichi cabinet, determined to eradicate communism, took harsh measures against suspected support organizations. On April 10, 1928, Home Minister Suzuki Kisaburō, citing violations of Article 8 of the Public Peace Police Law (1900)— which gave the minister wide discretion to disband any organization endangering public peace—ordered dissolved the Labor-Farmer Party, Zen Nihon Musan Seinen Dōmei (All-Japan Proletarian Youth League), and Nihon Rōdō Kumiai Hyōgikai (Council of Japanese Labor Unions). A secret government report noted that leaders of these groups were concurrently members of the Communist Party and that the three organizations followed the lead of the illegal party.[77] Tanaka moved on another front as well, by introducing a bill into the Fifty-fifth Diet to strengthen the 1925 peace law: a sentence of from five years to death for organizers and leaders of any group trying to change the *kokutai* and imprisonment up to five years for anyone, including nonmembers, who "furthered the aims" of an illegal organization. Because of the Diet's dissolution this bill was shelved, but the Tanaka cabinet, after getting the Privy Council's approval, reproduced the law bill as an emergency imperial ordinance (No. 129, June 29, 1928); the Diet certified the law at the next session.[78]

Leaders of the legal leftist parties and others criticized government actions. Outstanding was lawyer Fuse Tatsuji, an unsuccessful Labor-Farmer Party candidate (Niigata, Second Electoral District) in the February 1928 election, who turned into a one-man army, battling the government in both the media and the courts. Writing in the May 1928 issue of *Hōritsu Sensen* (Legal Battle Line), Fuse criticized the government's plan to have local trials for communist suspects before the completion of the preliminary examination in Tokyo: "If we do not have a unified trial of these leaders together with the other suspects' trials, we will not be able to establish the truth about the so-called Communist Party Incident."[79] Unifying the trials, he pointed out, was possible under Article 16, Section 2, Criminal Procedure Code, which allowed the transfer of cases from one court to another. Next he criticized the Tanaka cabinet for censoring truthful accounts of the great arrest and for frightening the general public by issuing distorted information. Furthermore, he wrote, without waiting for the legal disposition of this case, the government precipitately took administrative actions to disband proletarian organizations, saying that this was done not because of general policies or declarations, but because they were somehow touched by the so-called Communist Party Incident. True, wrote Fuse, the home minister was empowered under Article 8 of the 1900 law to disband groups, but this power was circumscribed: there had to be some proof of danger to public peace. Since the facts about the current communist case were not yet established, he concluded, the government's actions were illegal.[80]

Another of Fuse's targets was the revised Peace Preservation Law, which he excoriated in the September 1928 issue of *Rōnō*

(Labor-Farmer), placing the blame for this bad law on Home Minister Suzuki, Justice Minister Hara Yoshimichi, and the groups behind the former justice minister, Hiranuma Kiichirō. This revision was accepted by the Privy Council, he noted, after only seven hours of discussion and in a lightning-fast move announced the same day. In the November issue of *Hōritsu Sensen,* Fuse disputed the government's contention that suspects had to be held without bail to prevent escape or the destruction of evidence. Since authorities had announced that they had enough evidence for trials, he noted, this could not be the real reason. Critical articles about the mass arrest also appeared in *Musansha Shinbun* (Proletarian News) in May and *Kaizō* in October.[81]

In November 1929, the first part of Kobayashi Takiji's *1928-nen 3-gatsu 15-nichi* (March 15, 1928) appeared in *Senki* (Battle Flag) and generated much discussion, with illegally distributed issues passed hand to hand. The second part of this thinly fictionalized account of the March 15 arrest in Otaru, Hokkaido, was out the following month in spite of police censorship. This story, which gave the public a good look at brutality and torture, was based on Kobayashi's own experience and what he was told by others.[82] In one case, police forcing a confession beat the back of a naked man for thirty minutes with a bamboo fencing sword. Later he was choked into unconsciousness, stuck with tatami mat makers' needles while suspended in the air, and then kicked and hit. This treatment took three hours. Another suspect, standing barefoot, was repeatedly kicked in the heels. Next, as his hands rested palms up on a table, they were stabbed with a pencil. Finally, his fingers were pressed against a pencil inserted between them. The next victim was eight times choked into unconsciousness, as a police doctor stood by monitoring his pulse. One suspect was suspended upside down by a rope attached to a pulley in the ceiling and then suddenly dropped to the floor. This torture was followed by forcing his hands into hot water and then beating his naked body with a rope. After the police squeezed out enough information to prepare interrogation reports, suspects were ordered to sign. Shortly before the suspects were transferred to Sapporo, the Tokkō and regular police became almost friendly, ordering food and eating with the suspects.[83] Police said: "There will be no problem if you tell it exactly the way you said it during interrogations. But if the story is different, the result of your insincere attitude will become a problem that will work to your detriment."[84] Not only would a repudiation of a confession reflect badly on police, but it would make the job of the procurator at the Sapporo District Court difficult, because his report to the preliminary judge was heavily dependent upon police documents, including a confession. Faced with a repudiation of a police interrogation report, a procurator might return a suspect to the police. Kobayashi's story indicates that police were not novices at forcing confessions. That ceiling beam pulley, so handy for suspending suspects, had been used before. Also, socialist Masaki Kiyoshi points out that Otaru police carefully prepared for the anticipated extra-heavy interrogation load by quickly constructing a soundproof area within the station.[85]

Two proletarian party members of the House of Representatives interpellated the government about police actions. On January 25, 1929, Asahara Kenzō, Kyushu Minkentō (Kyushu People's Constitutional Party), challenged Home Minister Mochizuki Keisuke (who had replaced Suzuki on May 23, 1928) to explain why thirty people in Sendai had been arrested as they prepared a hall for a lecture by Yamamoto Senji (Labor-Farmer Party). It was reported that a police spokesman told a journalist that Yamamoto, too, would be arrested if he got off the train in Sendai. Continuing, Asahara complained about the dissolution of the Labor-Farmer Party. Next he quizzed the minister about police arresting people for no stated reason and illegally detaining them by circulating them from one station to another or rearresting them as they stepped outside a police station. Actually, said Asahara, under the Tanaka regime police often did not even bother with such legal camouflage, but arrested and detained as they saw fit. In Kagawa prefecture, Asahara noted, one person was kept for seventy days and in another case when a man was not home police arrested his wife. He asked whether such activities were legal.[86] Next Asahara turned to the reports of torture: "Some people might say that such a thing is not happening today, but it is going on under the current cabinet."[87] Among the techniques Asahara exposed were tying up suspects and hanging them by the hands or legs; throwing water on and tickling the nostrils of suspended suspects; inserting pencils between fingers; violently pushing them back and forth; dressing suspects in kendo gear and police beating them with a bamboo sword; depriving suspects of water and sleep; burning them with an incense stick. Home Minister Mochizuki denied these charges. Asahara concluded by exposing three deaths by torture among the several hundred people arrested in preparation for the emperor's coronation: the person in Mie prefecture was simply starved to death; the one at Osaka had a heart attack after a bad beating; the person at Kanazawa was beaten to death. Was it, Asahara asked, the policy of Mochizuki to kill men like this? The home minister denied the charges.[88] Yamamoto Senji interpellated government representatives at a budget committee meeting on February 8. Why, he asked, were police funds being misused to arrest so many people unnecessarily? In 1919, for example, fifteen thousand people were placed under preventative arrest *(yobō kensoku)* as people who endangered public order, but by 1926 the number had jumped to fifty-two thousand. And people arrested on March 15 were held one month—some even two months—without being properly charged, when ten days was the legal maximum. Furthermore, criminal suspects were badly mistreated nationwide. In the Hakodate Police Station, for example, Fukutsu Masao was beaten with a bamboo sword as policemen forced him to crawl on and lick a concrete toilet floor until he passed out. Shizu Hideo (no location given) was beaten into unconsciousness with a bamboo sword. There were, he said, many cases like this. As for the torture tools and techniques, they varied: inserting pencils between fingers; placing stone weights on the thighs of suspects forced to kneel on corrugated sharp-edged boards; hanging upside down; beating the head with a bamboo sword after tying a *zabuton* around it; applying sudden strong pressure on the lower chest. There were many cases like this at Fukuoka, Osaka, and Hokkaido. Government authorities themselves were abusing the law, he pointed out.[89] At various places, police said something like this: "Even if we kill three or four of you, our superior will take care of it. We are really going to do it, since we are Showa's Amakasu."[90]

Comments by government officials on police lawlessness lend credence to leftist charges. For example, on March 7, 1925, at a committee meeting investigating the government's Peace Preservation Law Bill, Representative Yuasa Bonpei (a member of the Kakushin Club, part of the coalition supporting the Katō Kōmei cabinet) said: "We have no choice but to suspect that today's police and judges will use this law in the manner the government wishes. . . . [M]any policemen . . . when they control a move-

ment . . . are misusing the Public Peace Police Law [1900]. As
you know, people who are arrested are not handled as human
beings. . . . They are giving extremely inhuman treatment to our
people, like hungry lions chasing a herd of sheep." Yuasa continued: "Furthermore, they are much worse in their actual control of
the labor movement and the proletarian movement. Truly, they
are committing wanton cruelty. Despite the fact that it is not the
desire of the government to use [the 1900 law] in this manner, the
authorities who are in contact with the people are using it
this way."[91]

Procurator General Koyama Matsukichi, speaking to chief
procurators on June 8, 1927, said: "Recently, the justice police,
who are in charge of investigations, are inclined to punish suspects
by beating or torturing them, if there are disagreements between
the statements of suspects and other people involved in the case. I
very much regret that people pressured by violent force are still
being prosecuted in the above way. Looking at this sort of thing,
you see that it is done by low-level government officials overconscientious about their duties." Koyama continued: "Thus, uncon-
sciously, they reach the point where they abuse their professional
rights and make this kind of mistake. This is caused because they
do not understand the basic meaning of criminal policy. If anyone
under interrogation is forced to give a false statement, that will
cause the procurators to make mistakes and furthermore mistakes
will be made in court." Next, Koyama ordered his audience to
correct this situation, so that the wrong people would not be
imprisoned. "Each one of you strictly use the laws and regulations
for such cases to punish justice police. At the same time, on the
other hand, always educate justice police and make sure that they
do not bring embarrassment upon their occupation." At a meeting with heads of prefectural police on July 11, Koyama repeated
this message, adding: "As everybody knows, the revised Criminal
Procedure Code is based on moral principles and protects human
rights. However, I am very disappointed to look at the record
. . . and still see that some justice police are inclined, during an
investigation of suspects, to yell, to beat, and to torture." The
abuses had to be corrected, he concluded.[92]

During the great March arrest, Procurator General Koyama
addressed Kenpei officers (March 26). The role of justice police,
he said, was to protect public peace and human rights. "There-

fore, during the interrogation of suspects and other involved people, justice police should carefully pay attention to the interrogation itself. Of course, it should not be done illegally or improperly. . . . If an interrogation is carried out in a brutally severe and extremely outrageous manner, then the justice police will completely lose public trust. Luckily, in the case of the Kenpeitai I can share your happiness, not having heard any criticism of this kind."[93]

On June 27, Koyama spoke to prefectural police heads and returned to the subject of proper interrogation techniques: "During interrogations for important criminal cases, it appears that some of the justice police ignore the procedural laws and regulations, because they are overenthusiastic about arresting criminals. . . . However, in the case of officials ignoring laws and regulations that guarantee the people's rights, even if suspects temporarily do not complain, it . . . will become a cause for losing the dignity of laws and regulations." If there are officials such as described above, he continued, "who treat innocent people in this manner, it is an extreme abuse of human rights. . . . No matter what kind of criminals you arrest you must not go even one inch past your official rights, which are regulated by law; carry out your duties in the most proper and fair manner. Make sure that all those under you understand this and that they do not make mistakes."[94]

Koyama's plea for police to obey the procedural laws and regulations was not always obeyed. Nanba Hideo, editor of the *Proletarian Newspaper*, another unsuccessful Labor-Farmer Party Diet candidate, was arrested on March 23, 1929, and taken first to the Sakamoto Police Station (Ueno area) and then sent to the Manseibashi Police Station (Kanda). Interrogators used torture in an attempt to learn the hiding places of Ichikawa Shōichi, Nabeyama Sadachika, and Mitamura Shirō. After authorities apprehended these fugitives in the April 16, 1929, mass arrest, Nanba says that the police grew less zealous in interrogations. Miura Ume was apprehended in the April 16 roundup by the Kanagawa prefectural Tokkō. While she was suspended by arms and legs, the officers burned her waist and pubic hairs with cigarettes. Besides this sort of thing, day after day they manipulated a bamboo spatula in her vagina until she passed out.[95]

Speaking again to heads of prefectural police, on June 28, 1929,

Koyama returned to the subject of interrogations: "As I have instructed many times before, justice police should not interrogate in a severely brutal manner. I am very disappointed, however, to have heard about brutal treatment both inside and outside the courts. . . . Suspects are repudiating their statements in court, charging police brutality. . . . There are cases where in fact beating and torture were employed by justice police to force confessions. Each one of you must prohibit your men from using rough treatment."[96]

Finally, on September 18, 1929, Koyama spoke to Tokkō section chiefs: "I understand that some justice policemen said that it is all right to exceed the law in order to interrogate such bad criminals [i.e., communists] who plan to change the *kokutai*. If people think this is the way to do the interrogating, it will result in not only an abuse of human rights but also in an unsuccessful interrogation, because it will stimulate suspects' resistance. Although extremely rare, there are some cases in which regular [i.e., administrative] policemen eyewitnessed brutal interrogations done by other policemen, which angered them enough to cause them to resign and join the Communist Party!"[97]

Another justice official had harsh words for police actions. Judge Sakamoto Hideo, Nagoya District Court, who was in Tokyo from July 1928 to research *Shisōteki hanzai ni taisuru kenkyū* (Research on thought crimes), discovered one case in which police waited outside a prison for the release of an anarchist. They seized him as he left the gate and immediately placed him in detention. This was a case, Sakamoto wrote, of government officials destroying the state and not the ideologists destroying the state.[98]

Representative of liberal academics were the views of Professor Minobe Tatsukichi, Tokyo Imperial University. Minobe was opposed to both the 1925 peace law and the 1928 revision. It was, he wrote, "a law of rarely equalled iniquity in modern constitutional government."[99] In a 1927 university newspaper article on police detention, Minobe wrote: "I want to take this occasion to discuss the proper limits of police detention . . . so that its legal limits will be made clear, and the people, being familiar with them, may check its abuse."[100] While police detention was legal, he continued, it should never exceed the law's bounds. Unfortunately, abuse was frequent, especially in connection with preventive custody, "which police officials employed without regard for the requirement that such detention was permissible only when it was possible to suppose a person was not merely capable of breaking the public peace but was preparing to do so."[101]

Cases of police lawlessness were discussed in foreign journals as well. In Professor Harry E. Wiles' November 1928 article, for example, entitled "The Japanese Police," Wiles not only mentioned the 1923 killings of leftists, but also exposed third-degree methods. Forced confessions leading to wrongful imprisonment, he noted, had become such a serious problem by July 1926 that Chief Justice Yokota Hideo condemned them. Furthermore, Wiles contended, in July 1926 alone, four deaths were reported due to police torture.[102]

Shisō keisatsu gairon (An introduction to the thought police), published in 1930, provides a police official's reaction to charges of police brutality and torture. Ishihara Masajirō, the book's author, was for nearly three years chief of the Peace Section, Police Bureau, and at another time the vice-director of the Police Training School. It is easy, he wrote, for a public that dislikes police to believe that police are brutal, severe, and cruel. Moreover, the public tends to show sympathy for criminals. It is painful, he continued, for a member of the political police to be bombarded with criticism, sometimes even being referred to as a "dog."[103] When police handle criminals, "it is common to interrogate them until late at night and to give them mental pain, but not to inflict physical pain. People also criticize this as torture or police brutality."[104] A very strange comment, indeed, in light of the overwhelming evidence to the contrary, some of which Ishihara must have known.

As the arrest and police interrogation experiences of suspects varied, so, too, did their treatment in detention places and prisons, where they awaited the completion of preliminary trials. Nosaka Sanzō, a veteran Communist Party member, was caught again on March 15. He not only escaped physical torture, but after being released on bail to enter a hospital managed to escape from Japan.[105] Getting a temporary release for medical treatment or another reason was an involved process, but Nosaka's case was not unique. Yamamoto Kenzō, a central committee member like Nosaka, fled to Russia after being released because of poor health.[106] Satō Satoji, from the Niigata area, was released to attend his father's funeral.[107]

Igarashi Motosaburō, arrested in the March 15 sweep, recalls that after the death penalty was added to the Peace Preservation Law in June 1928, guards at Ichigaya Prison said: "It is all right to kill people like you!" This sort of talk was not too worrisome, but Igarashi was concerned by a procurator's comment after Igarashi called for the abolition of the emperor system: "As long as you hold such an idea you will not be able to leave prison alive."[108] Government-issued food at Ichikawa was terrible, and Igarashi was always hungry, but prisoners were allowed to buy supplemental food from outside. On the first anniversary of the March 15 arrest, prisoners were punished after a demonstration in which they demanded improved living conditions. Guards restrained Igarashi's hands with leather handcuffs, placed a tight, water-soaked hood over his face, and walked on his backbone. After this punishment, his hands remained cuffed behind his back for three days.[109] Kamei Katsuichirō, who became a leading literary critic after renouncing communism, had a very different experience. Arrested on April 20, 1928, while on a trip to Sapporo on party business, he was returned to Tokyo. The detention houses in Sapporo and Tokyo were similar: filthy and bug ridden. But judging from his prison diary, he suffered only at his own hands: guilt, remorse, and fear of punishment.[110]

Conclusion

During this crucial decade, police leaders were at least superficially influenced by liberal thought currents, and the idea of a "people's police" became popular. Police leaders through addresses and publications urged the rank and file to display more politeness and kindness in place of threats backed up by a sword. At the same time, however, policemen were warned against too much intimacy with the people.[111] Actually, while the humanitarian message was now more sharply focused, police had long been given this dual command: maintain firm preventive control and simultaneously be kind to gain the people's goodwill. According to one scholar, the police view of their role changed during the 1930s mainly in response to external developments, and the people's police turned into the "emperor's police."[112] Undoubtedly, the traumatic events of the interwar years influenced police outlook, but beneath these changes certain practices remained basically undisturbed. An outstanding example of continuity was illegal arrest and detention of criminal suspects. A wider public concern over basic human rights and police leaders' talk about reforms notwithstanding, this abuse, like a broad, deep river, flows through police history. Furthermore, police brutality, a strong current in this river, increased its force during the 1920s, the era of the "people's police." Procurator General Koyama Matsukichi's repeated complaints about brutality and torture is a revealing indictment. Obviously, illegal interrogation methods were common even before the era of massive arrests from March 15, 1928: brutality and torture were not simply a product of the arrest of many communist suspects. Indeed, the evidence points in one direction: police officers, both regular police and Tokkō, had long used force to get confessions.

The Peace Preservation Law introduced a new fierceness into the relationship between police and political criminal suspects. Tanno Setsu, the wife of communist leader Watanabe Masanosuke, recalled that the prison sentences under the 1900 peace law were short enough not to be feared: one went off for eight or ten months of study. When her husband was arrested in June 1923, he took a German language book along to improve his German.[113] Tanno collided with this fiercer police attitude on October 4, 5, and 6, 1928, at the Tomisaka Police Station (Tokyo); Tokkō Yamagata Tamezō applied torture to wring from her the location of Watanabe's hiding place.[114] Other political cases add to this picture of the growing ruthlessness of some policemen who employed illegal strong-arm tactics, resulting in numerous injuries and deaths.

Why did police become more ruthless in dealing with leftist political offender suspects? Prime Minister Tanaka Giichi's address to the nation on the March 15 Incident is often cited as a catalyst: "I am horrified by the Communist Party's activities. . . . They have printed and distributed unspeakable assertions regarding the government—diabolical acts beyond description, which neither heaven nor man can permit."[115] Furthermore, Tanaka's address opening the Fifty-fifth Imperial Diet on April 23 that year was entitled "Absolutely No Mercy for the Traitors Who Tried to Change the *Kokutai.*"[116] Other officials and many opinion makers also jumped on the anticommunist bandwagon, demanding harsh punishment for those endangering the *kokutai.*[117] These strong comments undoubtedly encouraged police to forget rules and regulations.

Postarrest official and mass media pronouncements, however,

are an inadequate explanation for brutality and torture, especially since a black curtain covered the mass arrest, and many violations of suspects' procedural rights occurred before the news ban was lifted on April 10. A longer view is needed. In fact, police thinking about "Reds" was influenced by a deluge of books and articles on the "thought problem," "dangerous thought," "bad thought," "extreme alien thought," and on communism pouring out to the public from about 1920. Continuous pronouncements by government officials, from the prime minister down to mayors, reinforced the sense of national danger from radical leftists. At the opening of the Forty-second Diet, December 26, 1919, Prime Minister Hara Kei attacked the "evil ideas" from abroad.[118] As the leftist movement spread, accompanied by strikes, violence, and assassination attempts, government officials used even harsher words. Police were not immune to these messages, which must have produced anxiety. The 1925 peace law enshrined the highly emotional term *kokutai* in the legal code, and policemen, like most people, were solid supporters of the emperor and *kokutai*. Communists, then, were easy to despise and, if a policeman accepted only a portion of what government officials said, the very worst criminal type. Thus, the mind-set of police who interrogated communist suspects was influenced by government propaganda, the 1925 peace law, media fixation on dangerous thought, and traditional police attitudes and habits (i.e., contempt for the people and a history of lawlessness).

3

Janus-Faced Justice

THE SUCCESSFUL CAMPAIGN to imprison the leadership of the Japanese Communist Party did not end the "Red scare," which expanded as the party contracted. Indeed, renewed state efforts to stamp out pernicious communism stimulated an expansion of the police and procurators. By 1932, the thought police had spread to every prefecture, with personnel overseas to watch Japanese and foreign radicals. The Justice Ministry paid special attention to expanding the ranks of thought procurators, whose function was to prosecute illegal actions termed "thought crimes" committed by communists and other "thought criminals." Mainly, these imperial officers in the thought war concentrated upon leftist ideological offenses, but their mandate expanded into many other areas, as events of the 1930s were to demonstrate. By July 1928, the ten main district courts, the appeals courts, and the Supreme Court were staffed with thought procurators. Besides increasing the number of personnel, the state moved on the legal front by submitting to the Diet a harsher version of the 1928 peace law. Party politics and bureaucratic rivalries, however, delayed this law bill until May 15, 1941, when a greatly strengthened Peace Preservation Law went into force.[1]

The 1930s also witnessed a major innovation in the state's handling of thought offenders: *tenkō* (change of direction *or* conversion). What begin in the late 1920s as a modest policy of releasing communists on parole, if they recanted their radical beliefs, became by the mid-1930s a major criminal policy, with police and thought procurators prodding all communist suspects to renounce the faith and accept reintegration into normal community life. The 1936 *Shisōhan Hogo Kansatsu Hō* (Thought Criminals' Protection and Supervision Law), Law No. 29, May 29, provided "protective supervision" for "thought criminals" arrested under the provisions of the 1928 peace law, whether indicted or not. This law aimed not only at keeping watch on leftist ideological offenders but also at formally reintegrating them into society.[2] In spite of the formal acceptance of the "soft" *tenkō* policy (i.e., reeducate and reintegrate rather than imprison or execute), there was opposition by some justice and police officials, as well as by members of the public. The actual working of the system of handling communist offenders, therefore, might accurately be termed a "Janus-faced" approach: *tenkō* was but one face; the opposite side was characterized by a harsh policy of strict punishment for those against the emperor and *kotutai*. This partly explains the illegal brutal treatment of some communist suspects. It was one thing for cabinet officers or thought procurators to promote a *tenkō* policy and to announce that after all even Japanese communists were children of the emperor, but such abstract reasoning was less appealing to policemen who handled communists at police stations.

In the face of expanding police power, an active and vocal human rights movement (i.e., procedural rights for criminal suspects, including communists) developed. Not surprisingly, the main figures were lawyers, some of whom had long fought for procedural rights under the law and who, as police pressure steadily increased after 1928, fought all that much harder. These attorneys were in fact locked in a complex symbiotic relationship with highly placed government officials who led the attack on the Communist Party; both the lawyers and the ranking officials in the Justice and Home ministries used the same argument: the rule-by-law system on which the state was presumably based must be respected. In the case of some defense lawyers, however, "respected" is perhaps the wrong word, since they held "bourgeois" law in contempt; but as it was the only real weapon defense lawyers had, they supported the very laws they despised. Government officials were caught in the same bind: an inbred respect for rules, regulations, and law that was often at war with their intense dislike of communism.

Defense Lawyers

Lawyers who defended clients charged with violations of the Peace Preservation Law fell into two fairly distinct groups. One group, which may be called the Radical Bar, closely identified with the political left and saw itself as a protector against government attacks. The other group may be termed Civil Libertarians; though often conservative in politics and with little sympathy for communism, they took leftist political cases. The prominent examples are Fuse Tatsuji for the Radical Bar and Unno Shinkichi for the Civil Libertarians.

Attorney Fuse, who was intimately involved in trials of communist suspects from the very first one in 1925, shared an ideological outlook with his clients. Fuse was a prominent critic of the legal system and a promoter of legal reforms who loudly proclaimed his views in both the courtroom and the media. While not a Communist Party member, Fuse was eventually caught by the same peace law that imprisoned his clients. Fuse's fall from grace resulted in part from his unorthodox courtroom style, which ran against the grain of procurators and judges. An attorney's traditional role was to humbly point out extenuating circumstances, beg leniency, and promise no future violations.[3] Fuse broke this basic rule. The wheels of justice, however, turned slowly and deliberately: a disciplinary hearing (resulting from the Osaka District Court incident) in April 1929; disbarment confirmed by the Supreme Court in November 1932; indictment for a violation of the Peace Preservation Law in March 1934; conviction in December 1935; appeal to the Supreme Court denied in May 1939; Chiba Prison from June 1939. Fuse was not reinstated as an attorney after release from prison in July 1940.[4]

Unno Shinkichi in contradistinction to Fuse managed to avoid the pitfalls attached to handling peace law cases. While Unno's sense of social justice and concern over abuses of human rights is obvious, he was not politically in sympathy with communist suspects, a fact obvious to authorities. His first defense of communist suspects was in 1928 (the case of students from his old school in Okayama). In 1934 and 1935, he again dealt with peace law violation cases; but a major case from 1939, which helped make Unno's reputation, involved Professor Kawai Eijirō's violation of

Article 27 of the Publication Law. Again in 1940 and 1941 Unno took peace law cases (in the latter year he defended Yamakawa Hitoshi). That defending accused communists was not hurting his career is illustrated by Unno's appointment as president in 1940 of the Second Tokyo Bar Association. And so it went, with more peace law cases until the end of the war.[5] What was the secret of Unno's success? As his biographer notes: "Many of the lawyers who worked on political or thought trials held ideologies [i.e., were communists or were suspected of being communists], but Unno was a professional. This fact had enormous value during the suppression time of the war period."[6] Put another way, Unno accepted the justice system and worked within that system, keeping well clear of the radical left except in the courtroom. And since the state prided itself on the legal system, and since even radical leftist suspects had to have their day in court, lawyers like Unno were needed.

In the midst of the arrests begun on March 15, 1928, Communist Party remnants organized the Kaihō Undō Giseisha Kyūen Kai (Relief Association for the Victims of the Liberation Movement). Sympathetic lawyers such as Fuse, Majima Kan, Makino Mitsuyasu, and Ōyama Ikuo aided in the establishment of this organization on April 7, 1928. As head of the law section of this group, Fuse began, from among the membership of the Liberal Legal Association, to mobilize attorneys needed for the court battles. At first the relief group received support from national figures, like veteran socialists Abe Isoo and Majima Kan. The former became the group's president and the latter the director; lawyers Fuse and Yamazaki Kesaya were among the twenty-three board members. Soon, however, in the face of increased government pressure on communists, Abe and other socialists backed away from the relief association; by August, formal ties were cut. As the number of people arrested swelled into the thousands, Fuse and others created on April 29, 1931, the Kaihō Undō Giseisha Kyūen Bengoshi Dan (Relief Lawyers' Group for the Victims of the Liberation Campaign). While Fuse was often referred to as the head of this group (eighteen lawyers at first), it was actually run by a five-lawyer executive including Fuse. Directly behind the formation of the lawyers' group was the relief association, and deep in the shadows was the Japanese Communist Party, which hoped to win a propaganda battle in the trial process.[7]

None of the eighteen members of the lawyers' group belonged to the Communist Party, but they made no effort to hide support of some party goals and sympathy for those arrested. Fuse successfully urged members of the Liberal Legal Association—including lawyers untainted by known leftist connections—to support the new group. As the details of the great March arrest became clearer, however, about half of them withdrew support; it seems they worried about possible disciplinary proceedings instituted by justice officials. That this danger was foremost in the minds of members of the Liberal Legal Association is understandable, since Fuse was facing disbarment. Finally, on January 29, 1933, the members of the lawyers' group joined forces with eleven other lawyers to form the Rōnō Bengoshi Dan (Labor-Farmer Lawyers' Association). Even after disbarment in 1932 Fuse continued to take part in the activities of both groups.[8]

The Tokyo Trial

A carefully programmed open trial was staged at the Tokyo District Court (118 sessions) from June 25, 1931, to July 2, 1932, for Communist Party suspects, including the leadership of the party. Because of space limitations, the defendants were divided into three groups: the party kingpins were in group one; groups two and three each had spokesmen from the leadership group. The entire process was over on October 29, 1932, the day of sentencing. The government was represented by Thought Procurators Hirata Susumu and Tozawa Shigeo; the chief judge was Miyagi Minoru, borrowed from the Tokyo Appeals Court. Veteran lawyers, among them Fuse Tatsuji, Kamimura Susumu, and Shindō Kanji, represented the defendants.[9]

For the government, the primary reason for this unprecedented open, unified trial was to score an ideological victory: it was hoped that the show trial would dispel the aura of mystery surrounding communism and shake the faith of communists. If the government could cause some party leaders to defect, the victory would have much greater impact in an open trial. The defendants cooperated because they wished to use the courtroom as a propaganda platform.

Since Miyagi's main concern was to conduct the trial smoothly, quickly, and with dignity, he painstakingly prepared: he read about communism, reviewed earlier foreign political trials, and analyzed the disorderly Osaka trial. Every detail was considered, including the order of entering and departing from the courtroom. To overcome his lack of knowledge about communism and lack of reference materials, Miyagi sent his staff to bookstores to buy material, including illegal items. Then, there was the problem of reading this material in Russian, German, French, and English. This was solved by the suspects, who not only translated it but explained the meaning. Besides this, Miyagi also, in an unprecedented action, met with key party leaders to work out a satisfactory trial plan. The defendants' main demand was for an open, unified trial and freedom of speech; Miyagi's main demand was that defendants obey the rules of court. If they did not, he threatened to close the trial.[10]

Opposition in the Home and Justice ministries to Miyagi's trial plan surfaced in the press. On July 4, 1931, for instance, the *Tokyo Nichinichi Shinbun* printed that the Home Ministry was against handling the Communist Party in an open trial. Miyagi tried to win over skeptical police officials in face-to-face meetings in which he promised to stop the trial and eject spectators if anything improper occurred.[11] Another newspaper carried objections from the procuracy: "Mr. Kanayama, chief of the Procurator's Office, has announced his absolute opposition to the policy of the court, and also his intention of refusing Judge Miyagi as president if his protest is not favorably considered. Mr. Kanayama interviewed Mr. Miki, chief of the Procurator's Office of the Court of Appeal, who referred the matter to Mr. Koyama, the Procurator General."[12] In the end, judges rallied around Miyagi, and the independence of the judiciary was maintained. This was not, however, the judge's last skirmish with Justice Ministry colleagues. On July 7, at the second session for the leadership group, Procurator Hirata, concerned that the open trial was disturbing public peace, requested that the proceedings be closed. Miyagi responded that the open trial would continue, but he warned the defendants not to disobey court orders.[13]

At the first session of the trial (June 25), Chairman of the Central Committee Sano Manabu stated that the party was the vanguard of the working class and that the suspects were not ordinary criminals but political criminals. It was the duty of the leadership group, he said, to reveal to the people the true nature of the Communist Party and the Comintern. Besides Sano, the others in the first group who spoke were Nabeyama Sadachika (on organizational problems); Ichikawa Shōichi (history of the party); Sugiura Keiichi (the party and labor unions); Kokuryō Goichirō (the revolutionary union movement); Takahashi Sadaki (policy toward the farmers' movement); Tokuda Kyūichi (the party and the youth movement); Mitamura Shirō (refutation of the peace law). Sano summed up the various comments. All this propaganda proved too much for the procurators, who requested ten times during the first thirty-two sessions to have the trial closed. Miyagi refused, but he did briefly close the proceedings on July 11, 1931, as Sano began a deposition on the proletarian dictatorship, and on April 19, 1932, as Sano started to discuss violent revolution and destruction of the monarchy. Thus, although Miyagi seldom used the trial closure weapon, it was threatened seventy times.[14] This candy and whip strategy was effective.

One scholar feels that Miyagi closely circumscribed lawyers' speech and that the real stage for the defense team was outside the courtroom, where they acted as go-betweens for the defendants and their free comrades. In fact, he says, it was in this manner that the suspects learned about the 1932 Thesis.[15] As for Miyagi's attitude, it is better to say that he doggedly challenged lawyers' objectionable comments after allowing them to become part of the court record. While ever ready to defend the justice system, Miyagi was unwilling to follow the Osaka example and charge lawyers with debasing the dignity of the court, even though the proceedings were sometimes contentious: "Mr. Fuse vehemently denounced the prosecution. He said that the sentences asked for by the Procurator . . . were cruelly heavy. . . . The attitude of the Court was equally improper . . . it was hardly to its credit that all the arguments advanced by the defense to vindicate the innocence of the accused were met by threats to close the hearings." It was, Fuse charged, "a bourgeois trial under bourgeois law by judges whose decisions are dogmatic and feudalistic, being prompted by class sentiment." Miyagi demanded that he explain what he meant. Fuse replied that after hearing the defendants speak for a year the judge should know what he meant. Miyagi felt "that the terms may be interpreted as implying the negation of the provisions of the Constitution." Fuse answered that "there was no question of repudiating the Constitution. The expressions used were merely critical language."[16]

The defense team was kept busy both in the courtroom and out-side. Yomogida Takeshi had the court's permission to make a shorthand record, which he turned over to Tan Tokusaburō. Thus, details about the trial reached left-wing publications. In addition, the lawyers' group also published a newsletter from March 1, 1932; members gave public speeches and wrote newspa-per and magazine articles, and several ran as candidates in elec-tions. The lawyers' contention that suspects were being mistreated by police and prison guards was substantiated when a battered Nabeyama appeared in court on September 26.[17] Nabeyama, recalling this event, wrote that after he heard a guard scream at a comrade in another cell, he loudly protested. Guards responded by taking him into a soundproof room where they beat him into unconsciousness. The next day, when lawyers saw his swollen face, they made a great fuss, but, he said, actually that sort of thing often happened in jail.[18] A newspaper headlined the incident "Thrashed for Half an Hour." Besides giving details about Nabeyama's beating, the report also mentioned the assaults on four Korean communist prisoners in the same prison.[19] Despite the prison director's refusal to cooperate, the Tokyo Bar Associa-tion investigated the incident and confirmed that Nabeyama had been seriously injured.[20] Brutality and torture became part of the trial record on several other occasions. Kokuryō, for instance, gave an eloquent speech on May 3, 1932. During one week, he said, police tortured him almost to the point of death four times, and his was not an unusual case. Kubota, he noted, was worked over in a Yokohama police station for eighty-five days and killed. In Kobe, Hirai Masao was suspended upside down and tortured to death. At the Matsuzaka Police Station in Mie prefecture, Ōsawa was killed. Police in Ōtsuka released Ōnoki after torture, but when his family arrived they could only claim the body. Pre-liminary judges and trial judges ignored this terrible situation, said Kokuryō, even when the indisputable marks of police brutal-ity were clearly visible on the faces and heads of defendants.[21] Sano also commented on police torture: at the first session of the third group on April 19, 1932, and at the trial's final summa-tion.[22] Shiga Yoshio recorded that guards, angry over some confu-sion among prisoners as they returned from the final session of the open trial, beat ten people with a leather whip, reviving them with water as they passed out and beating them again. Sakai Sadakichi was seriously injured.[23]

News of war in Manchuria in September 1931 quickly eclipsed the courtroom drama. Defendants used the courtroom platform to denounce Japanese imperialism, but they misunderstood the rising mood of public patriotism as the war expanded to Shanghai in January 1932. By March 1932, the lawyers' group was, according to a secret police report, "utilizing their lawyers' position to support the extreme leftist movement."[24] Given the national mood and police feelings about the lawyers' group, the arrest of two members was probably expected. Hososeko Kanemitsu was arrested in July, Tanimura Suguo in August for contributing funds to the Japanese Communist Party. Fuse was charged with a postal violation in connection with letters he sent to communist suspects in jail, but this charge was thrown out at the Appeals Court. More damaging was a Press Law violation charge in connection with an article Fuse wrote about the trial for *Hōritsu Sensen*. In March 1933, the Supreme Court upheld the guilty verdict, and Fuse spent three months in Toyotama Prison.[25]

On July 5, 1932, Procurator Hirata demanded heavy punishment, since the defendants' crime of fomenting rebellion was so serious. Their actions, he stressed, were like those of foreign agents and could not be compared in the same breath with regular crimes. For Mitamura Shirō, he asked the death penalty. Extra-heavy penalties were urged for the unrepentant: five years or more for members of the Japanese Communist Party, depending upon each defendant's activities; three-year terms for those who carried out the goals of the party. For those expressing remorse, the state would consider reduction in sentence. Fuse replied that the prosecution's charges were groundless, that the court had sometimes acted improperly, and that during the judicial process the defendants had been terrorized. Since the defendants attacked neither the *kokutai* nor private property, they should be freed. Other lawyers charged the prosecution with playing politics, attacked the peace law, ridiculed the death penalty request for Mitamura, and read a statement from labor unions asking for the defendants' release. Sentence was passed on 181 defendants on October 29, 1932 (twenty were not sentenced for various reasons; for example, eleven had renounced communism): Ichikawa, Nabeyama, Sano, and Mitamura—life confinement; Kokuryō and Takahashi—fifteen years; Sunama Kazuyoshi—twelve years; Tokuda, Sugiura, Shiga, and nine others—ten years; and so on. The lightest sentence was two years for thirty-five people.[26]

The judges gave stiff penalties but refused the prosecution's request for a death sentence. Miyagi received many letters demanding a death penalty, but from the start it was his goal to push the defendants into a public recantation. This *tenkō* approach to sentencing was shared by Associate Judge Ogonuki Sōtarō, who in February 1932 published an article in which he said that the attitude of hardened criminals could be changed by education. This applied to peace law violators as well, once they were shown the error of their ways. If we believe Miyagi, Procurators Hirata and Tozawa were also inclined to reform rather than execute; certainly their later actions strongly illustrate a support of the *tenkō* program.[27] The death request for Mitamura was an exception, because he had shot and permanently disabled a policeman. At any rate, Miyagi's decision was shrewd, since without executions there were no martyrs. All later courts followed this policy.

Years of imprisonment, the lack of public support during the great trial, the fighting in China, plus the life terms pushed Sano and Nabeyama into "conversion." Although this sensational development, which pleased justice officials, stunned the party, it was not the result of a hasty decision. In fact, it was the result of a mental conflict between the demands of internationalism (i.e., Marxism) and nationalism (i.e., love of one's country), which had long plagued Sano and Nabeyama.[28] Communists were faced with an especially painful dilemma, for if they accepted the party's repudiation of the emperor they simultaneously repudiated the entire social structure, in which all families were supposedly related to the central one. Indeed, society without the ageless imperial system seemed unthinkable. The author of a 1930 Tokkō publication neatly summed it up: "Anyone against our system [i.e., the emperor-centered *kokutai*] is not only disloyal, but ceases to be Japanese."[29] Conversely, this particularistic feeling of blood bonds between Japanese permitted the return to the family-state if the strayed individual renounced the evil foreign ideology and reembraced the *kokutai*.

On June 10, 1933, newspapers broke the story of the two famous communists' conversion. Sano and Nabeyama repudiated the party's antiemperor position and endorsed Japan's imperial mission abroad; a domesticated form of communism, in harmony with Japan's unique *kokutai,* must replace the foreign product. Delighted officials circulated this statement to all communist prisoners, and hundreds quickly followed Sano's and Nabeyama's example.[30] Actually, justice officials did not merely wait on the *tenkō* statement by Sano and Nabeyama. They had been working to create a system for reintegrating thought offenders from as early as 1928, and on March 27, 1931, the Justice Ministry had approved this method of handling thought cases.[31] By the early 1930s, therefore, the Peace Preservation Law, which was spreading out its limbs like a rapidly growing tree, received a graft of *tenkō.* Over the following years this graft took hold, resulting in a very singular solution to the "thought problem."

Justice officials used the apostasy of Sano and Nabeyama as a wedge to split the defendants before the Appeals Court trial; it was made clear that conversion could earn reduction in sentence and even probation. Thus, Sano and others lectured from the courtroom pulpit to promote the state's *tenkō* policy. On May 11, 1934, the government kept its bargain: Sano's and Nabeyama's sentences were reduced from life to fifteen years, Takahashi's from fifteen to twelve years, Sugiura's from ten to eight years, and so on. The holdouts were tried separately, their sentences were confirmed, and their appeals to the Supreme Court were rejected. Nishimura Seiki was an exception who converted late; the Supreme Court reduced his five-year penalty to two years.[32]

The activities of the defense lawyer team during and after the first trial brought repression. Kakuta Morihei was arrested in May 1933; other members of the lawyers' group were apprehended in September and November. All were charged with violations of the peace law (i.e., helping the Communist Party) and all wrote *tenkō* statements except Fuse, who was the only one imprisoned. While lawyers usually received better treatment than other suspects, Kakuta and Shibata Sueharu were exceptions. In the case of Kakuta, perhaps the interrogators were overconscientious in order to squeeze out information needed to indict the others.[33] After accusing him of lying, writes Kakuta, "[They] stepped on me, kicked me, and especially they attacked my thighs."[34] The police were careful, as they kicked his thighs, to leave no marks on his face. After two or three days of this treatment, he was forced to crawl from the jail to the upstairs interrogation room.[35] "Even though I was a lawyer," writes Shibata, "the authorities used shameful threats to force me to confess." As Inspector Hisano Shigemasa showed Shibata a pair of red-hot metal chopsticks in the coals of a hibachi, he said: "If you do not obey, we are going to torture you. Even if we kill a man like you, there will be no trouble; we will ask our police doctor to write heart attack on the death certificate. That will do. Be prepared. If you don't want to lose your life, do as we say and quietly let us make your statement."[36] Shibata also notes that at that time police jails were filled with lice, fleas, and cockroaches and that the food was extremely poor.[37]

Fuse Tatsuji, like the others, was indicted for furthering the aims of the Communist Party (this was on March 15, 1934). The Tokyo District Court charged that he agreed with the communist way of thinking, that he participated in the creation of the lawyers' group, and that he carried out various activities to help the communists inside and outside the courtroom. Knowing well the propagandistic purpose of the funeral of Iwata Yoshimichi, Fuse nevertheless took a leading role, the court noted; Fuse did the same at the funeral of Kobayashi Takiji at the Tsukiji Shōgekijō. Moreover, the demand of the lawyers' group for an investigation of so-called torture incidents was part of a propaganda effort to generate hatred of the police among the people. The court's decision, on December 17, 1935, was four years imprisonment.[38] At the Appeals Court, Fuse's sentence was reduced to two years, but the appeal to the Supreme Court was rejected. From June 1939 to July 1940 he was in Chiba Prison (two hundred days of time served in jail was remitted).[39]

Judicial authorities exercised great care in carrying out the open trial. While in the courtroom, the defendants' procedural rights were protected, and sentences were reasonable, especially in light of the harsh penalties of the 1928 version of the peace law. Moreover, sentences were reduced for those who repented. Doubtless, Judge Miyagi, who was awarded a silver medal and an appointment to the Supreme Court, regarded this as a perfect outcome. However, police and prison guard brutality leaves a stain on this record. The arrest of all the attorneys in the lawyers' group, while legal under the expanding terms of the vague provisions of the peace law, looks like an act of vengeance on the part of authorities who, with the *tenkō* process now in place and no more plans for show trials, simply did not need the services of this group. Torture of one of these men of the law and threats to the other were procedural violations. One wonders what Miyagi in his Supreme Court chair would have said.

Procedural Rights for Communist Suspects

Outside the courtroom, authorities increased pressure on communists and their allies. Between 1930 and 1935 more than 50,000 communist suspects were arrested: 6,124 in 1930; 10,422 in 1931; 13,938 in 1932; 14,622 in 1933; 3,994 in 1934; 1,718 in 1935.[40] A dramatic drop in the totals for the last two years is in no way indicative of a slacking in police efforts; rather it indicates a shortage of targets. In this effort to exterminate communism, the enforcement of procedural rights for criminal suspects slipped to a record low, at least in the case of some police units and individuals who disregarded both standing police orders and the legal codes. Therefore, as the judiciary was showing moderation and flexibility by permitting an open, unified trial and simultaneously the Justice Ministry was adopting the softer *tenkō* policy, the police were not only following traditional methods of interrogating suspects, but were even becoming more ruthless.

William J. Sebald, who translated the 1908 Penal Code, wrote in the preface (in 1936): "Many criticisms have been levelled against the [Penal Code]. . . . But the criticisms might better be directed where they are most needed: at the methods only too often adopted by those responsible for carrying out the provisions of the substantive law. These methods still savor of the Tokugawa era in that they are often brutal, unreasonable, short-sighted, and generally senseless." He continued: "[P]rosecution, more often than not, is primarily based upon confessions wrung from the unfortunate accused by means of irresponsible detention and severe grilling often lasting for months or even years. Occasionally, instances of torture are brought to light, but in almost every case strong denials are made by the authorities concerned, thus ending the matter."[41] Sebald, of course, spoke of brutality and torture occurring during interrogations in both regular and political criminal investigations, with regular cases by far outnumbering political ones. With that in mind, it is useful to regard illegal

actions in communist suspect cases as a merely "normal" police
investigative technique, but applied with added relish and vigor to
antiemperor suspects.

Let us look at how some communist suspects fared between
1930 and 1935. Hoshino Yoshiki, a Waseda University student,
was arrested sometime during 1930 in Shizuoka. For ten hours
detectives used a leather belt and bamboo sword to squeeze out
information about a subversive student group. Released into custody of an elder brother, Hoshino joined the Communist Party in
1931. He was arrested again by the Kanagawa police in January
1932. Again, he was beaten.[42] The writer Nakamoto Takako was
arrested on July 14, 1930, as a communist sympathizer (she had
sheltered Tanaka Seigen). Ten days later at the Yanaka Police Station (Tokyo), when she refused to answer, three policemen hit her
face, twisted her hair, kicked her upper back, and hit her head
with a bamboo sword. Next they stripped her, tied her hands and
legs, and threw her on the tatami where, as one man choked her,
another poked a broom handle into her vagina. Finally, they beat
her thighs with an iron rod around which a *furoshiki* was wrapped.
The interrogation was repeated the following day.[43] Katayama
Nobutada was another July 1930 arrest. As a union activist,
Katayama had been caught in the March 1928 roundup and subjected to water torture. Near the end of 1929 he was released for
medical reasons and promptly went underground. After the July
1930 arrest, he was hospitalized for head injuries and never fully
recovered.[44]

The following year Ueda Shigeki was killed in April. Details are
unknown, because he simply disappeared while in custody.[45] That
same month proletarian movie actor Matsumoto Katsuhira was
arrested and taken to the Tsukiji Police Station. He was beaten for
about two hours on the thighs and elsewhere.[46] The most sensational case, however, involved central committee member Iwata
Yoshimichi, who died on November 3, 1932. Officials went to
some lengths to camouflage this death, saying that the cause was a
combination of beriberi, tuberculosis, and heart disease. Lawyer
Fuse Tatsuji pushed for an autopsy, which was done by Dr.
Yasuda Tokutarō at Tokyo Imperial University Hospital. Yasuda
found no evidence of beriberi, tuberculosis, or heart disease, but
there was evidence of massive internal bleeding and a swollen
chest and thighs. According to Iwata's sister, the chest was swollen

and purple, as was the face, with marks on the wrists and below the knees. Representing Iwata's parents, Fuse took the case to the Procurator Bureau, Tokyo District Court, demanding an investigation and naming specific police inspectors and Mōri Motoi, Tokkō Section head at the Metropolitan Police Board. The parents, however, dropped the case under pressure from procurators.[47]

The watershed year of 1933, which witnessed Sano's and Nabeyama's change of course and the destruction of the lawyers' group, was also the year police killed the well-known proletarian writer Kobayashi Takiji, the best remembered victim of police interrogation. Kobayashi, like lawyer Fuse, was an irritating thorn in the government's side. Following the great success of *March 15, 1928,* his fame increased with the publication in March 1929 of *Kani Kōsen* (The Crab Factory Ship) in which he excoriated the brutal treatment of workers on floating crab canneries. While Kobayashi remained outside the Communist Party until October 1931, police arrested him in May 1930 on suspicion of collecting money for the party. Later the charge of lèse majesté was added, because a character in *Kani Kōsen* said he would like to put gravel in the crab meat eaten by the emperor. Torture in a police jail and six months in prison stimulated Kobayashi to more effort, but on February 20, 1933, a police spy lured Kobayashi into an ambush.[48] He was killed the same day. A newspaper account stated: "The death of Mr. Takiji Kobayashi . . . has been cleared up. . . . About 4 p.m. he suddenly complained of feeling unwell, and asked for medical care, which resulted in his being taken to hospital where he died. The suddenness of his death roused suspicion of police torture, but it is now revealed that a heart attack was responsible."[49] Friends demanded an autopsy, but the medical schools at Tokyo Imperial University, Keiō University, and another university refused. Even attendance at the funeral was severely limited by authorities.[50] Dr. Yasuda, however, did view the body and found evidence of internal bleeding, a large bruise on the left temple, narrow cordmarks on the neck and wrists, thighs swollen to double size, testicles swollen, scrape wounds on various parts of the skin, fifteen or sixteen hole marks in the thighs (punched in with a sharp tool), marks all over the back, and a broken right index finger.[51]

Other communist suspects who died in police hands or soon

afterward in 1933 were Kagaya Tomegorō in Tokyo (released on January 12 and died two days later); Itō Tadataka, Suwa Police Station, Nagano prefecture (died on February 5); Nishida Nobuharu, Fukuoka Police Station (date unknown; case suppressed until after 1945). Miyamoto Kenji, arrested on December 26, 1933, and taken to the Kōjimachi Police Station (Tokyo), was more fortunate. His interrogators boasted of their torture skills as they beat Miyamoto's thighs, pouring water over him each time he passed out.[52] One of them said: "Would you like a labor-farmer funeral, like Iwata and Kobayashi?"[53] Writing after the war, Miyamoto identified the leader of this interrogation team as Tokkō Section head Mōri Motoi, who also interrogated Iwata and Kobayashi.[54]

During January 1934, Suzuki Masashi was tortured at the Atago Police Station (Tokyo) with a bamboo fencing sword, a wooden sword, and fire. Besides subjecting him to water torture, police forced him to kneel on an abacus.[55] Five policemen worked on Tanikawa Iwao at the Hisamatsu Police Station in Tokyo (arrested in February 1934) to pry from his mouth the time and place of a meeting with central committee member Hakamada Satomi. Besides crushing fingers against pencils and throwing him around, they put a pole several inches in diameter across his lap and sat on the ends. Then he was given electric shocks and suspended from the ceiling.[56] Noro Eitarō, chairman of the central committee and head of the political bureau, was arrested in November 1933; he died on February 19, 1934, in the Shinagawa Police Station. If he, too, died of "heart disease," it was probably Tokkō induced.[57] Wanibuchi Kiyotora was killed by the Tokkō chief at the Nishijin Police Station (Kyoto) on April 7, 1935, because he denied violating the peace law and refused to cooperate. The officer (name deleted in the confidential Justice Ministry document) was sentenced to two years imprisonment, but this was reduced to a stay of execution.[58]

The experience of the proletarian writer Takumi Jun illustrates the fear torture and brutality generated among potential victims. In February 1933 he was arrested for agitating factory laborers and for having a copy of *Red Flag*. During the interrogation, the police officer boasted of having recently killed Kobayashi. Takumi, who was not a party member, was released after three months. In a postwar story, Takumi, calling himself Tsunomi, described how pencils were inserted between his fingers and how he was kicked mercilessly. This treatment was bad enough, but the real fear was caused by the reputation of this officer notorious for his brutality.[59]

How did high officials in the Home and Justice ministries react to these and other cases of brutality and torture and to police lawlessness in general? What were their instructions to police, procurators, and prison officials during this stressful era? Did high officials publicly admit these serious flaws in the system of administering justice? And, if they did, what did they do to correct the situation?

Home Minister Adachi Kenzō, addressing a conference of prefectural police chiefs in May 1931, said: "It sometimes happens that petty police officials abuse police power in the examination of suspects . . . with the result that charges of infringement of personal rights are laid against the police in general. . . . [C]onstant care must be taken to avoid such public accusation by restraining petty officials from unwarranted restriction of personal freedom."[60] At a meeting the following month for police chiefs specializing in radical thought control, Tsugita Daisaburō, head of the Police Bureau, told the audience that radicalism had to be perfectly (i.e., totally; completely) controlled.[61] Home Minister Nakahashi Tokugorō, at a conference of governors in January 1932, said: "No hesitation should be shown in the exercise of police power where it is necessary to correct irregularities. . . . Care must be taken, however, not to use police power in the wrong way. . . . Regard must always been [*sic*] had for personal rights and for the vindication of justice."[62] Speaking to governors in July 1932, Home Minister Yamamoto Tatsuo stressed the need to maintain public peace but noted that police must also protect "the rights and interests of individuals. They must, therefore, be not only kind but just and fair in their treatment of individuals."[63] A few days later prefectural police chiefs heard a similar message: "The Minister strongly warned his hearers against all acts of unfairness which have sometimes been committed by police officials. . . . To the public . . . [police] must be kind, and care must be taken to compel trust and attachment from it."[64] Addressing Kenpei commandants in April 1933, Yamamoto urged "rigorous control" of communists: "Seeing that the Communist movement is absolutely incompatible with the existence of the State, those connected with it must be sternly dealt with. The duty of the police consists . . . [in] the maintenance of perfect peace and order."[65] The following month prefectural chiefs in conference were told to punish communists sternly. Moreover, the efficiency of Tokkō was ordered increased.[66]

In January 1934, Karasawa Toshiki, head of the Police Bureau, told a conference of chiefs of criminal affairs sections to stop their subordinates from abusing the Administrative Enabling Law (1900) and the Summary Trial Regulations for Police Offenses (1885).[67] A clearer admission that the police were illegally extending their arrest powers would be difficult to find. Home Minister Yamamoto again addressed prefectural police chiefs in May. Unfortunately, he said, police had "committed irregularities or otherwise acted in a manner derogatory to the prestige of the police. . . . They must be fair and upright in their behavior. . . . They must be kind to the people generally, instead of arrogant and harsh. . . . The local police authorities must make special endeavors to eliminate all subversive movements."[68] In May 1935, Prime Minister Okada Keisuke called for the enforcement of strict discipline. Home Minister Gotō Fumio ordered police to take "stern measures" to guard public peace.[69] In August, Home Ministry authorities ordered police to use care and not infringe on personal rights.[70]

Justice Minister Watanabe Chifuyu, at a conference of high justice officials in May 1931, pointed out that "in criminal searches all improper methods, if not actually illegal should be conscientiously avoided."[71] Procurator General Hayashi Raisaburō said to high judicial officials in June 1932: "[I]t is most important for public peace and order that scrupulous regard for the national Constitution and law should be inculcated among the people. Where there is no regard for law there can be no peace and security."[72] Two months later Justice Minister Koyama Matsukichi, speaking to governors, said: "Close attention must be paid to the doings of radicals in order to prevent them from crafty instigation of the local people to disorderly acts. . . . Sternness must be shown in the treatment of elements who deserve stern treatment, while leniency should mark the treatment of those who merit it."[73] When he addressed the conference of prefectural police chiefs in May 1933, Koyama "reminded his hearers of charges often laid against police officials of infringements of personal rights. The speaker believed that some of these charges were not entirely unfounded. If irregularities are committed by the police, it is a very serious matter. It will lead the public to hate the police and tend to engender radical ideas. The speaker hoped that the Police Chiefs will strictly warn subordinates against malpractices." In connection with subversive movements, it was "important for the Police Chiefs to see that their subordinates keep close watch and exercise strict control over these movements."[74] Addressing a meeting of attorneys from the nine provinces in the jurisdiction of the Osaka Appeals Court in November 1933, Justice Minister Koyama asked for cooperation in protecting the authority of law. He condemned those who disregarded the law and used force. "Should such a state of things be left to take its course, the authority of the law would be completely undermined and the foundations of society destroyed. Judicial officials and barristers can serve the State by protecting law for the sake of justice as much as soldiers who fight on the battle fields for the State. It is incumbent on all those present, the Minister declared, to endeavor in harmonious cooperation to ensure the independence of law and to protect judicial power, for which their seniors have done so much in the past."[75]

In May 1935, Justice Minister Ohara Naoshi "warned the police against exceeding their proper limits in criminal searches. . . . In the fulfillment of their duties . . . they ought to be particularly careful not to commit any irregularities. Unfortunately, there have been cases where, in the examination of criminal cases, police officials have used brute force against suspects and unwarrantably detained them."[76] A few days later, at a conference of high judicial officials, Ohara noted that "in spite of the warnings repeatedly given by the judicial authorities in successive Cabinets, the judicial police are not yet entirely free from public complaints that in the discharge of their duties they trample on personal rights. There have been several cases recently where police officials have been indicted on charges of illegal detention of individuals and the use of force against suspects." Ohara asked those present "to give the necessary instructions to police officials under their jurisdiction to refrain from any such illegal action."[77] In August, Ohara repeated the message, this time for procurators,

that procedural rights must be protected and that "their enthusiasm should not carry them beyond the proper limits in the examination of accused."[78]

These pronouncements soundly condemned the use of illegal
investigative methods, as officials from both ministries admitted
abuse. Police, who were the major offenders, were repeatedly
ordered not only to formally obey the law but to go a step beyond
and show kindness and courtesy; personal rights were to be
respected. Justice officials exalted the bedrock of law and deplored
its abuse. Simultaneously, intertwined with this "obey the law"
theme was one that called for stern, rigorous, perfect control of
communists and other radicals. In light of the expanding "Red
scare," the latter message must have been more in harmony with
the national mood and must have held more appeal for police.
Moreover, these two messages were contradictory, since "perfect"
control was impossible for police operating within legal limits.

Police textbooks provide one method of investigating what went
on inside policemen's heads and offer hints at the motivation
behind actions. A textbook published in 1930 stressed police guidance to keep people from straying into the swamp of dangerous
thought. "Police should use humanistic consideration in carrying
out their duties."[79] This same author, however, after noting that
Japan's *kokutai* was uniquely superior, stated that those opposed to
this view ceased being Japanese.[80] Another publication catego-
rized "thought criminals" (i.e., communists) as the national
enemy: "Unlike a murderer, who kills only one or perhaps several
people, and there it ends, thought criminals endanger the life of
the entire nation."[81] In the past, said the author, this kind of criminal had been killed; more recently, leniency had been favored;
however, the future trend appeared to be stricter punishment. A
special goal of Tokkō, he noted, was the prevention of crimes;
when that goal was missed, strict punishment should be given to
offenders. As for law, all Tokkō must study pertinent regulations
to learn how far they were permitted to go.[82] The Police Research
Institute in a 1932 textbook for regular policemen stressed that it
was often necessary for regular policemen to perform the work of
Tokkō.[83] "To deny that Japan is the ideal nation, is like denying
the power of the sun." Therefore, concluded the authors, "[a]ny-
one who tries to reform our *kokutai* is no longer one of our people."[84] When interrogating thought criminal suspects a policeman

must, wrote the authors, follow the articles of the Criminal Procedure Code and other regulations. Moreover, while police should
display kindness and warmth, they should not become the people's servant.[85] A 1933 Tokkō textbook boasted about the tremen-
dous expansion of the thought police and concluded: "The Tokkō
Age is almost here!"[86] Since prevention of thought crimes was the
Tokkō's most important duty, the author urged that the seventy
thousand regular policemen be fully mobilized as an auxiliary.
While police had to prevent thought crimes, they were not to
abuse arrested suspects. However, the provisions of the peace law,
wrote the author, were to be interpreted as widely as possible; just
to suggest an illegal action would be a violation.[87] About Sano and
Nabeyama, the author said: "We do not know their real feelings,
but at least the people who are only tinged with pink can be
saved."[88] A former Tokkō officer wrote in 1935 that police must
have a military-like spirit firmly based on an understanding of
Japan's unique *kokutai*.[89] A textbook published two years later
stressed the oft repeated themes of strict control and prevention of
thought-related incidents. Indeed, communists were so dangerous
that they should not be permitted to exist for even a day.[90]

These textbooks reflect the numerous demands placed on the
elite Tokkō, who were expected to discover thought crimes before
they occurred and, if they failed, capture all violators of the peace
law, guiding and reforming those who renounced communism.
Another common theme was the vagueness clinging to the concept
of a thought crime, but all authors repeatedly stressed the need for
prevention. In fact, Tokkō were to perfect a special sense, one
which would allow them to "hear what has no sound and see what
has no shape."[91] Strict orders to protect the unique *kokutai* at all
costs were mixed with commands to be humane in order to garner
the people's support. Obey the law, they were instructed; but in
the same breath communism's terrible nature was underscored.
Suspects were not to be abused, but, on the other hand, communists were no longer Japanese. It is impossible to know how each
policeman interpreted such contradictory orders, but many must
have decoded this message: protect the *kokutai* at all costs and
smash the no-longer-Japanese communists. Just in case the point
was missed, in 1935 the Home Ministry stated that the highest
mission of the Tokkō was the protection of the *kokutai*.[92] What
Tokkō officer Nakagawa Shigeo supposedly told communist sus-

pects represents the extreme form of this attitude: "The Communist Party is a traitor, which denies the imperial system. Therefore, it is all right to beat you to death."[93]

Prison

The government was extremely proud of the modern prison system. Not only did the Justice Ministry take control of prisons in 1903, but a program was begun to construct new facilities, including juvenile reformatories and separate prisons for women. By the 1920s, some penologists were trying to change the old regulations (e.g., prisoners to work in silence with no recreation facilities) into more humane ones. Scientific ideas about prison management were flowing in from Germany, stimulating reformers to move toward the progressive stage system for treatment of inmates. This system, which was designed to encourage prisoners to reform, was divided into four stages; as a prisoner met certain criteria he was given more privileges.[94]

After the appointment of Shiono Suehiko to head the Prison Bureau (September 1930), the reform movement gathered speed. In 1932 Shiono decided that from the viewpoint of the new penology, underground labor was undesirable, so prison labor at the Miike Coal Mines was abolished. The *Gyokei Ruishin Shogūrei* (Progressive Treatment in Prison Affairs Ordinance) went into effect on January 1, 1934.[95] That leftist political criminals, the so-called thought offenders, were included in the Justice Ministry's progressive treatment plan was made clear by Justice Minister Koyama Matsukichi: "Regarding the treatment of 'thought' convicts . . . some people are under the impression that true amendment and conversion on the part of such convicts is impossible. . . . Such a view is negatived by actual experiences. It is by no means impossible to convince them of their mistaken course of conduct."[96] About five years later, a Justice Ministry article on the progressive system stated: "The penal system . . . must have as its main object the rousing of convicts to the consciousness that they are Japanese subjects. The system must aim at the cultivation of the Japanese spirit and always have in view the return of the prisoners to society."[97]

Speaking to the directors of prisons in June 1931, Justice Minister Watanabe Chifuyu "emphasized the need of strictly correct behavior on the part of prison officials. . . . In all spheres of activity the behavior of those placed high has an immediate effect on subordinates, but the influence of prison officials on convicts under their care is particularly marked. . . . They should also see that their subordinates behave equally correctly, so as to set a good example for convicts to follow."[98] While it is obvious that orders from on high were not always obeyed, violators were sometimes apprehended. For instance, in December 1939, when two guards were accused of beating two inmates to death at Fuchū Prison, the local procurators investigated by questioning some three hundred officials and prisoners. The whistle blower in this case was the prison physician, who on one body found wounds caused by a heavy weapon.[99] Besides ordering strictly legal treatment of inmates, the Justice Ministry also expressed concern for their health: "Food is so prepared as to be as nutritious as possible. . . . Furthermore, the inmates are called out of doors once in the morning and once again in the afternoon during recesses to take part in walking . . . and physical exercises with a view to exposing them to fresh air. Thus every effort is made to preserve and promote the health of the inmates and to improve their physique as well as their morale."[100]

Jails and prisons served different purposes and were in some respects quite different. The jails and detention houses were under the supervision of various police stations and used to house suspects under interrogation. Justice officials had inspection rights. Some prisons were used for housing suspects who were being tried (e.g., Ichigaya Prison). Convicts went into the regular prison system (e.g., Kosuge Prison was for long-term prisoners).

Jails and detention houses were often dirty places filled with biting bugs; cheap, inadequate food was served. That the vermin bites Ōsugi Sakae complained of were still plaguing prisoners is attested to by a member of the lawyers' group. Another prisoner said in court that he put up all-night fights for a month in his insect-ridden cell.[101] Kamei Katsuichirō also recalled that he spent many sleepless nights fighting lice.[102] As for the jail fare, one female communist wrote in a book published in 1930 (and immediately censored): "[T]hey brought us rice which appeared to be rotting. The miso soup and the pickles seemed fit only for pigs. . . . They call a jail a pigsty, a befitting name."[103] Igarashi Motosaburō, arrested during the March 15 Incident, found the government ration at Ichigaya Prison poor in quality and barely enough to sustain life. However, prisoners could buy supplementary food from outside. Another common complaint focused on the filthy conditions of police cells. Sano Hidehiko, who was imprisoned in Toyotama during the 1930–1932 period, contracted such a bad case of itch in jail that later in prison he took medicated baths to cure it. There were others like him, he said, and some prisoners died of skin disease.[104] Even those favored by authorities complained about jail conditions. The writer Akita Ujaku, for example, who was detained in a police station between August 21 and September 14, 1933, while undergoing a mild form of interrogation and writing a life-history statement, found the food poor (although adequate). Most bothersome was the hard bed, which caused him restless nights for a week, and the terrible smell of the toilet. Ordinarily, he wrote, one comes to accept such a smell in an hour or so, but in this case it grew worse each day.[105]

Most, if not all, police jails had no bathing facilities. This fact was noted in a discussion among justice officials about the need to upgrade jail facilities under the 1941 peace law regulations, which allowed procurators to detain suspects legally for periods of up to one year. Not mentioned is that police had been illegally holding suspects for months or even more than a year. The socialist Suzuki Mosaburō, for example, was arrested on December 15, 1937, and kept at the Suginami Police Station for one year and nine months. He was not charged with a specific law violation during this period.[106] No wonder suspects contracted skin diseases or other illnesses; little else could be expected under prolonged confinement in such dirty conditions. At any rate, the thought procurators wanted baths added to jails not primarily out of humanitarian considerations, but for the practical reason of avoiding the bad publicity connected with a mass outbreak of illness. Food costs also came up at this meeting, with Akiyama Kaname, head of the Criminal Affairs Bureau, admitting that the twenty sen per day per prisoner was inadequate. Kanazawa Jirō, head of the Prison Bureau, noted that it had been eighteen sen for many years until 1940.[107] The fundamental problem, of course, was not a shortage of food money, but an illegal misuse of police jails, which were not designed for long-term incarceration.

Prison, while hardly a hotel, was a great improvement over a police detention facility. Kishi Seiji, in Toyotama from May 20, 1932, to December 22, 1933, said that prison was called *bessō* (villa) and that in comparison with a police jail, it was one. The food was tasty, and money could be earned to buy soap, tissue, and other items. Igarashi Motosaburō, in Toyotama during 1931–1932, remembered the great improvement in the food after he left Ichigaya; and when he moved on to Kosuge, he gained weight.[108] Tokuda Kyūichi, who refused to *tenkō*, got an extensive tour of prisons: Abashiri (1934–1940), Chiba (1940–1941), Toyotama (1941–1945), Fuchū (1945). He wrote that many prisoners died from malnutrition during the final four years of his sentence and that things got so grim that officials stole the prisoners' rations. His friend Shiga, who also refused to convert, spent seven years in Hakodate Prison before being assigned to Chiba in 1940. When he first saw Tokuda and Ichikawa (who also had been in Abashiri), he was shocked by their emaciated look. Unfortunately, however, they found Chiba one level worse than the Hokkaido prisons. After Shiga was moved to Kosuge, he felt an improvement in living conditions even though the nation was falling more and more under wartime conditions.[109] Nabeyama, who had donned Kosuge's red prison outfit in December 1934, quickly gained weight. Over the years he made paper brooms, worked as a cleaning man, grew vegetables, and ran the prison kitchen.[110]

Books played an important role in the lives of political prisoners. The rule, according to Tokuda, was four per month and an extra one by special request. Shiga adds that authorities carefully regulated books and encouraged prisoners to read about the imperial system. No newspapers were allowed. Nabeyama, like anyone else, was rationed to five books a month, but thanks to a kind guard newspapers were sometimes available, and after long negotiations prison authorities allowed him to have a set of Marx and Engels in German.[111] Kamei Katsuichirō (three years in prison) spent much of the time reading: "I devoured all kinds of classical works of literature and kept reading them. It was a joy, a great joy. . . . The prison cell was a paradise for me. . . . I wrapped my legs with warm *futon* . . . nibbled cookies and indulged myself with Tolstoy and Goethe."[112] The distinguished economist Kawakami Hajime, who spent three years during the mid-1930s in Kosuge, worked in the prison library. Books were available, as was a censored newspaper. If his diary is an accurate reflection of desire, however, food was more often on his mind than literature.[113] The proletarian writer Hayashi Fusao, who was impris-

oned from 1930 to 1932, enjoyed reading good literature in a manner reminiscent of Kamei. Also, not only did he like the food, but
he found nice things to say about the guards. Japanese prisons
were, for the most part, he concluded, humane and enlightened
institutions.[114]

Other reports expose a darker side of prison life. When one
prisoner attempted to pass some sugar to another, a guard spotted
this infraction of the rules. Punishment was a beating with fists
and feet. Another prisoner was badly beaten for tapping messages
on a wall. Guards made sure others heard his screams, so as to set
an example. Both incidents occurred at Toyotama Prison between
1933 and 1935.[115]

Those who write on the imprisoned communists usually stress
the "difficult conditions of prison life" and the fact that some prisoners, like Kokuryō and Ichikawa, did not survive the war's
end.[116] Another theme is that the "jails and prisons in the pre-war
era were damp, cold, unfriendly and unhealthy. Many prisoners
became ill."[117] These views, however, need further elaboration
and refinement, because facilities to hold prisoners varied as did
the reactions of prisoners. From our review of conditions in jails
and detention houses, as compared to prisons, it is obvious that
most prisoners were most miserable in police jails, given the inadequate facilities and poor food. Also, because they were in these
jails during the interrogation stage, the prisoners' distress was
intensified. Prisons, too, were not all the same, with Kosuge in
Tokyo, which was under the prying eyes of big-city newspapers,
seemingly one of the best. Prisons like Ichigaya, used for holding
suspects until after trial, would have ranked low, had inmates
voted on this issue. Geographical location was another important
factor, with places like Abashiri in cold, remote Hokkaido disliked
by those from the main islands. Shiga, who was in Hakodate for
seven years, felt that those held in Hokkaido's prisons were
unfairly treated. As an example of the better conditions at
Kosuge, he pointed out that in Hokkaido winter clothing was
issued in late December, but in Kosuge, which was in a warmer
area, such clothing, and of a better quality, was issued earlier.[118]
Indeed, government policy may have been to send diehards like
Tokuda, Ichikawa, and Shiga to Hokkaido as part of a softening-
up process to induce them to convert. If so, then the state was
punishing those who had symbolically cut the umbilical cord to the

kokutai by sending them to an area traditionally regarded as out-side the pale.

People reacted differently to conditions in jails and prisons. Someone like Nabeyama, with a laboring background, was able to adjust quickly, making friends among guards and eventually tak-ing over the prison kitchen. Intellectuals must have suffered more, but such suffering also depended upon the person and the situa-tion. Tokuda, for instance, used his lawyer background to provide legal advice for guards who in return did him favors.[119] The writer Akita Ujaku's physical suffering was mild, but his internment in a neighborhood police station jail was eased by a friendly police chief. Undoubtedly, those who played the government game were handled more gently than those who required sustained pressure to force conversion. Even here, however, there were exceptions. The proletarian writer Shimaki Kensaku, who was arrested on March 15, 1928, surrendered because of illness and the loneliness of solitary confinement. At his trial in late 1929, he promised to reform, but the court replied with prison for three more years. Not surprisingly, prison life, as depicted in Shimaki's fiction, is miser-able.[120]

The amount and the quality of food was of prime interest to prisoners. In most accounts, prison meals were better than jail food, but here, too, the time must be considered, since the food situation became grim during the Pacific War. While mass starva-tion did not sweep Japan in 1944–1945, there were numerous cases of malnutrition, and in many areas life without black-market food was impossible.[121] As Kawakami Hajime noted in January 1943, people were "thinking from morning to night only of food."[122] This grim situation is captured in Tokuda's comment that prison officials were reduced to stealing rations from the pris-oners' mouths. It is against this desperate situation that the death of long-term prisoners like Kokuryō and Ichikawa should be viewed, because prisoners were experiencing, albeit more intense-ly, the same problem as the general population: people weakened by malnutrition succumbing to disease.

In observance of the fiftieth anniversary of the Meiji Constitu-tion, the government in 1938 extended an amnesty to prisoners, including those sentenced under the provisions of the peace law.[123] Another amnesty was granted in 1940 during the grand celebra-tion for the nation's 2,600th year. Among those who benefited

from this humanitarian policy were converts Sano and Nabeyama, whose sentences had already been reduced from life to fifteen years. They left Kosuge on October 2, 1943. Nabeyama had
served fourteen years and three months, so amnesty reduction
earned him nine months.[124]

Overall, Justice Ministry penal policies appear enlightened.
Tokuda and Shiga, for example, lived to write about their experiences. The reduction in sentence and then an amnesty-shortened
term for Sano and Nabeyama similarly reflects a humane policy.
Policies set in the minister's office could be modified, however, to
fit the needs of tyrannical guards, as we have seen. Without doubt
brutality by guards was underreported, but the fact that the ministry took action in some cases indicates a desire to follow regulations. The deaths in prison of Kokuryō and Ichikawa do raise difficult questions about harsh treatment. For example, if a prisoner
died of stomach problems or tuberculosis, was the death attribut-
able to maltreatment? A review of fifty-eight biographical sketches
of communists identifies six who died in prison (three in the early
1930s and three near the war's end). Ten who survived long-term
sentences are listed as well, which suggests that there was no Justice Ministry policy to kill imprisoned communists.[125] In fact,
responsibility rests with the Home Ministry, which had primary
jurisdiction over the police stations, where most violations of prisoners' procedural rights took place. Police were flagrantly abusing
the law, and everyone was aware of this situation, from the prime
minister down to day laborers. Most of the brutality and torture
occurred at this initial level in the justice system, and it was in the
police station exercise rooms that murders were committed.

Expanding the Peace Law Net

Two significant developments during 1936 played major roles in
expansion of the Peace Preservation Law System: passage of the
Thought Criminals' Protection and Supervision Law and an
administrative reinterpretation of Article 1 of the peace law. The
1936 law was a logical outcome of the state's war on ideological
crime and the establishment of the *tenkō* solution. Besides firmly
establishing the category of thought crime *(shisō hanzai)*, the law
was designed to keep thousands of released thought criminals
under indirect surveillance and to reintegrate them into society. A
broadening of Article 1 of the peace law was a reaction, by justice

anus-Faced Justice97

officials, to the new popular front line pushed by the Comintern, which ordered the remnants of the Japanese Communist Party to take on the protective coloration of legal labor unions and political parties and to take united action with such groups. After the China War began in July 1937, justice officials, accelerating a process already in motion, further expanded the law.

Speaking at a conference in early November 1936, Justice Minister Hayashi Raisaburō urged justice officials not to be overly optimistic over the decrease in leftist violations of the peace law, in light of the recent decision of the Comintern. On the surface, he noted, communists avoided illegal activities, but underneath the camouflage they were busy. The new infiltration policy made control of communists doubly difficult.[126] Unable to expand the peace law's scope by enactment of a revised law in the Diet, justice officials administratively solved the problem of controlling camouflaged communists and their supporters; the scope of Article 1 was simply expanded to catch those who had formerly enjoyed borderline legal status.[127]

A month after Justice Minister Hayashi spoke, about thirteen hundred communist suspects were rounded up in thirty-five prefectures; several hundred were subsequently indicted. In December 1937, spurred on by the outbreak of war with China, authorities moved against the formerly legal left as well as communists, removing the distinction between ideological Marxists and communists. Among the targeted organizations was the National Council of Japanese Labor Unions (Nihon Rōdō Kumiai Hyōgikai), the Labor-Farmer Proletarian Conference (Rōnō Musan Kyōgikai), and the Labor-Farmer Faction (Rōnōha). Among the leading socialists arrested were Katō Kanjū, a Diet member, and Suzuki Mosaburō, a member of the Tokyo Municipal Assembly.[128]

Suzuki Mosaburō was not tortured at the Suginami Police Station, but some of his colleagues were terribly abused. Moreover, Suzuki saw and heard Koreans and Taiwanese tortured: compared to that, he writes, his pain was simply to spend two years and eight months in jail without knowing, for the first year and nine months, what law he had violated. Though the law did not permit this illegal detention, he writes, each month the police filled out the renewal forms and went through the technical motions of rearresting him. Suzuki also blames the preliminary

judge for allowing his case to hang in limbo. After one year and
nine months in jail, he was sent to the Tokyo Prison Hospital for
treatment of beriberi; there he was interrogated daily.[129] The waiting and wondering, while not as hurtful as holding heavy stones or
hanging suspended from the ceiling, did take a psychological toll.
The agony might have been shortened, of course, had Suzuki
been willing to confess and sign a statement prepared by police.

Justice officials were well aware of improper and illegal actions
by Tokkō justice police, and they often discussed this problem.
Finally, in August 1936 an educational program was established to
train the Tokkō in the correct handling of thought criminal suspects and specifically in the proper methods of collecting evidence
for trials. Special attention was paid to the matter of confessions,
since forced confessions were causing problems in court.[130] Justice
Minister Hayashi emphasized at a conference in November 1936
that justice police had to "correct their fault of relying too much
upon confession. . . . They must correct the fault of not collecting
enough material proof."[131] At the June 1937 meeting of officials
dealing with thought criminal cases, Procurator Kuriya Shirō,
Tokyo District Court, stressed the importance of correct interrogation methods: "Police must not give unlawful suppression."[132]
Unfortunately for victims of improper police practices, the Justice
Ministry was unable to wean justice police away from near total
reliance on the queen of evidence.

On February 1, 1938, more than thirty persons in the "Professors' Group" were arrested.[133] According to Procurator Hasegawa Akira, Tokyo District Court, procurators, while interrogating those arrested on December 15, 1937, discovered a "front"
group (i.e., those arrested on February 1). Among those arrested
were such distinguished scholars as Ōuchi Hyōe and Minobe
Ryōkichi. To indict these noncommunists, Hasegawa focused on
the origins of this group in November 1928, when a few scholars
had begun meeting to study international economics; among the
reports they used were those by the Comintern. They published
books and magazine articles, and in January 1931 they opened a
seminar room in Kanda, where they kept research materials.
Other Marxists joined the group research, said Hasegawa, and
they gradually became a front group for the Labor-Farmer faction. Hasegawa concluded that the scholars had confessed to carrying on group research and publishing the results. As for the

Labor-Farmer faction (a group of Marxists centered on the former communist Yamakawa Hitoshi), Hasegawa described this group as—under the provisions of the peace law—an "organization" that advocated the overturn of the *kokutai* and repudiated private property. Proof that the group's ultimate goal was a communist society, said Hasegawa, was found in seized documents and published material plus confessions.[134] Stretching the scope of Article 1 of the peace law helped push the total of arrests to more than sixty-three thousand by the end of 1938.[135]

Alert to patriotic war sentiments, justice officials increasingly favored the stricter punishment side of the Janus-faced policy. At the June 1938 conference of procurators and judges concerned with thought criminal cases, while two judges continued to recommend a more lenient approach to sentencing, others called for increased penalties. Judge Watanabe Hikoshi, Hiroshima Appeals Court, called for stricter punishment in light of the war. Those who committed a serious crime or falsely converted, opined Judge Yamazaki Katsuyoshi, Nagasaki Appeals Court, should be shown no mercy. Procurator Katsuyama Takumi, Osaka Appeals Court, worried over light penalties, noting that justice officials had to keep one eye on social circumstances. In the past, said Judge Watanabe Hikoshi, a more lenient approach had been acceptable, but times had changed: with the Imperial Army battling communists on the mainland, the judiciary could not appear disloyal. Stricter punishment, at least for those who do not convert, was in order, he concluded. Justice Minister Shiono Suehiko agreed that officials must fully support the war effort.[136]

Even as the range of legal dissent narrowed, justice officials made public pronouncements on the sanctity of the law and urged reform of police abuses. In March 1936, Justice Minister Hayashi Raisaburō said: "In view of prevailing conditions, it is particularly important to uphold the sanctity of the Constitution and the law, and to this end the independence of the judiciary must be safeguarded above all things. . . . In any case, however, infringements of the law must be sternly punished. Both Rightist and Leftist offenses require stern punishment. No matter what the motives, recourse to illegal means is wrong, and such offenses must be dealt with vigorously, irrespective of the motives."[137] The following June, Hayashi called for reform of the detention system: "[T]here have been cases where the accused have been detained too long. This calls for reform. . . . It is up to the officials in charge to use every care and circumspection and endeavor to remove evils."[138] Addressing the gubernatorial conference a few days later, Hayashi stressed reform of police practices: "One regrettable thing is that there are still many Government and public officials who abuse their official positions. A speedy end must be put to this deplorable state of things, and discipline enforced in all quarters. Offenders must be brought to justice without fail. . . . At the same time . . . the methods and procedure taken by the police must be not only legal but moderate and proper. Special care must be taken to avoid infringement of personal rights and interests."[139] At a judicial conference in June 1937, Justice Minister Shiono Suehiko remarked on the special efforts made from August 1936 to teach justice police correct methods of investigation and interrogation. One reason for this program, he noted, was to "clean up criticism of their so-called infringement upon people's rights."[140] The following February, Shiono again discussed violations of procedural rights: "[I]n some cases these accusations have been substantiated. This, coupled with the fact that many of the accused in sensational cases have been acquitted as the result of trials, has led to public uneasiness about the method of prosecution. . . . It is urgently necessary . . . that every effort should be made to remedy the situation."[141] In October 1938, Matsuzaka Hiromasa, head of the Criminal Affairs Bureau, recalled the March 15 and April 16 incidents. Throughout this lecture he stressed the importance of following procedure and obeying the law: "Too much ignoring of their human rights must not occur, even though they are Communist Party members. There is a limit to it."[142] Hardly a ringing endorsement, but, doubtless, a frank comment, since this was a closed meeting.

Also in 1938, Procurator General Motoji Shinkuma issued to procurators *Kensatsuken Unyō no Shishin* (A Policy for Enforcement of Prosecution Rights). They must, he said, maintain the dignity of and trust in prosecution rights by "adhering to the spirit of the law and respecting human rights; avoid making severe judgments and take a moderate course." Next, he reminded readers that while a similar message had been delivered at a prior conference, public criticism about prosecution methods remained. "Recently, however, it is a regretful phenomenon that there are cases which resulted from improper application of investigation and arrest.

We should strictly prohibit such a grievous phenomenon."[143] Although current laws needed revision to strengthen prosecution rights, he said, "it [was] always the duty of the prosecution to be loyal to the current laws and to do its best to skillfully utilize them."[144] On examining badly handled cases, he noted, one could easily recognize that the problem stemmed from the improper investigative methods of justice police. Moreover, procurators then compounded these errors by not correcting mistakes. To correct this problem, procurators must educate justice police.[145] "Do your best," urged Motoji, "to transplant to justice police officials the fact that when they carry out an investigation they must always have a sincere respect for human rights. Also, you must do your best to see that the methods used by justice police officials are moderate and impartial. Simultaneously, procurators must look at the changing times and try not to stick unthinkingly to customary conduct. Rather they must try to reform the management of affairs in order to fulfill the employment of prosecution rights." Procurators, he concluded, must pay special attention to self-confessions. "I regret that recently there are more than a few actual cases which do not follow this point [i.e., proper procedure]."[146]

The Justice Ministry's public message was little changed from earlier years: respect the law, sternly punish violators, protect legal rights of suspects, and correct police abuses. Basically, this same message circulated within the ministry as well except for one modification: in-house, the illegal interrogation techniques of justice police were identified as a problem urgently needing correction. These public and private messages about respecting laws, even as the China War expanded, reinforce the notion that many justice officials did truly respect them.

The Home Ministry's public message to the police was similar to that of the Justice Ministry. At the conference for prefectural police chiefs in June 1936, Home Minister Ushio Keinosuke stressed that the bad behavior of even one policeman eroded public trust. Therefore, it was "very important that all in the police force should be careful in the exercise of their power and in the treatment of individuals."[147] Speaking before the same conference two years later, Home Minister Admiral Suetsugu Nobumasa ordered the chiefs to "maintain peace and order perfectly"; simultaneously, police were "to gain and retain the confidence of the public."[148] In October 1939, Home Minister Ohara Naoshi noted that while maintaining public order was important, government officials "must be kind in their attitude toward the people with whom they come in contact. . . . The charge of unkindness and lack of civility has often been imputed to . . . police officials . . . who come in daily contact with the public."[149]

Behind the scenes, the Home Ministry reacted sharply to the war, with an order going out from the Police Bureau's Public Peace Section on July 17, 1938, to each prefectural police chief to "promote absolute national unity" and "strictly control" all radicals.[150] On July 30, chiefs were ordered not to allow anyone or anything to interfere with Japan's "Holy War." Each police officer, said the message, had to be willing to devote himself solely to doing his duty for the emperor (i.e., to die, if necessary).[151] Chiefs were ordered to lead the public "to the belief that the common good of the Emperor and his subjects comes before their private good."[152]

The Home Ministry messages to the public from 1936 were basically a repeat of earlier pronouncements: police should maintain public order and obey the law. Home Minister Ohara's willingness to confess that police were sometimes less than civil might be attributed to his earlier career as justice minister. At the same time, a new urgency and an added note of harshness appeared in the secret instructions from the Peace Section to Tokkō: all individual rights were subsumed by the larger national need. In view of the Tokkō record prior to 1938, this order for all-out support of the "Holy War" was an invitation to gross abuse of procedural rights. Of course, invitation to abuse the law was not new to police leadership ranks. For example, Hida Takuji (Seiyūkai) interpellated Home Minister Suetsugu in February 1938 about the appointment of Tomita Kenji as head of the Police Bureau the previous December. While chief of police in Osaka, Hida pointed out, Tomita had distributed a pamphlet among subordinates in which there was "a passage to the effect that police officials must observe the law but that 'on occasion they must be ready to break it.' This is a very dangerous teaching . . . and may have very bad effects on young and reckless policemen." Suetsugu replied that he had not read the pamphlet, but he thought the passage was "presumably intended not to encourage police officials to break the law, but to emphasize that the law is not almighty."[153] Superficially, this remark seems out of character from a home minister, since for decades ministers had at least carefully paid lip service to the supremacy of law. Admiral Suetsugu, however, was much admired by prominent rightists and was himself recognized as a leading member of the *kakushin uyoku* (reform right wing), which wished to move Japan closer to the fascist model of the national defense state. Moreover, Suetsugu saw "Reds" behind every door and was a bitter critic of political parties. Under Suetsugu's leadership, police were sometimes encouraged to act illegally.[154] It would be unfair, though, to place all blame on the admiral, since police had a long tradition of acting illegally; furthermore, wartime pressures must be considered.

Protecting and Supervising

A general feeling among Japanese that all were brothers under the emperor contributed to the notion that no thought criminal was beyond salvation. This feeling was reinforced by a deeply rooted tradition of confession and rehabilitation, which was imbedded in Article 6 of the 1925 peace law: amnesty or reduction of punishment was promised to those who voluntarily surrendered. Not everyone subscribed to this soft approach, but justice officials were drawn mainly to a rehabilitative solution. Indeed, Procurator Shiono Suehiko, who headed the Tokyo bureau during the March 15, 1928, arrest, decided to recognize conversion by party members.[155] The following month, at a meeting of procurators in Okayama, the problem of converting and protecting thought offenders was debated; in June it was discussed at Sapporo and in April 1929 at Hiroshima. Nagoya took up the matter in September 1929. A key question was how to prevent thought criminals who had served their sentences from backsliding.[156]

Developments within the Japanese Communist Party as well encouraged justice officials to move from a primary reliance upon harsh punishment to a Janus-faced approach, with conversion as a strongly sought goal. By the summer of 1929, Kawai Etsuzō (head of local committees in Niigata and Nagano prefectures) and Mizuno Shigeo (chief of the party secretariat) were undergoing a self-generated conversion and leading others out of the party. While in an Osaka jail Kawai started this movement by writing material critical of the party's frontal attack on the imperial system. Instead, he felt, the party should have focused on cleaning up corruption around the throne while retaining the unique imperial symbol. This argument was presented at the Osaka Appeals Court in June. Stimulated by Kawai, Mizuno concluded that the party should shift tactics to conform with Japan's special conditions (i.e., fit the party movement into the framework of the imperial system). Under Mizuno's influence a number of party members announced their defection in a written statement that renounced the Comintern and called for a legal Communist Party.[157]

Procurators and judges, faced with numerous thought offenders and increasingly certain that the negative policy of arrest and prison was insufficient, moved toward a supplementary policy of recantation and reintegration. Finally, on March 27, 1931, conversion for peace law cases was formally approved by the Justice Ministry.[158] In November of that year, justice officials discussed this and other problems at a meeting in Tokyo. While confused on many aspects of handling thought offenders, officials generally agreed on the need to promote conversion and to extend aid to converts. Procurator Inoue Nagamasa, Urawa District Court, suggested that if an individual appeared repentant, suspension of indictment should be used. If a jailed person looked reformed, he recommended parole. Procurators should go so far, in fact, as to help such people find employment. Procurator Kinoshita Yuhei, from a lower court in Nagoya, agreed that for those who had a change of heart, a stay of execution was best. Other procurators and judges agreed on this policy. Procurator Miyazato Tomehachi, Shimonoseki Ward Court, supported this dual policy of strict punishment for unrepentant ones and forgiveness for those who repented, pointing out these figures: out of 85 given suspension of indictment, 55 appeared reformed (65 percent success); out of 10 given a penalty, 5 reformed (50 percent); out of 25 given stay of execution, 14 repented (56 percent); out of 3 who completed a sentence, no success. The "softer" policy appeared to work.[159]

In September 1932 the Justice Ministry reacted to pressure from Tokyo's procurators by issuing "Official Regulations for the Procedure of Charges withheld for Thought Offenders." The "charges withheld" technique allowed procurators to keep suspects in a sort of limbo between prosecution and release. While this indeterminate state must have upset suspects, it allowed the procurator, who held the suspects under his thumb, to urge conversion. In many cases, suspects went back to a job, but with guarantors, submitting monthly reports on their mental attitudes and general living conditions while police kept a discreet watch. Tokyo considered this administrative technique far superior to the old one under which suspects sometimes felt that their thought crime was not only forgiven but acceptable. The charm of this approach was that it forced suspects to prove themselves, and it kept suspects out of overcrowded jails and prisons. Between January and October, procurators at the Tokyo District Court had more than 1,100 cases, with most handled under the new administrative technique (about 370 were prosecuted).[160]

By the end of 1933, more than 53,000 suspected peace law violators had been apprehended, with only a fraction indicted and imprisoned. Justice officials were deeply concerned about released people and discouraged over the lack of an official organization to supervise their thought, to help them find employment, and to keep them out of trouble. Procurator Moriyama Takeichirō noted at a May 1934 conference that the Keihin area was especially troublesome, since many laborers lived there and it attracted converted people. Procurator Inohara Takakatsu, Kanazawa District Court, reported that private groups helped converts, but, unfortunately, most of them did not fully understand such work. Former thought offenders, said Procurator Kubota Tokujirō, Nagoya District Court, needed jobs and understanding people with whom they could talk. Hirata, from Tokyo, mentioned the Teikoku Kōshin Kai (Imperial Rehabilitation Club), but said it was limited to about a hundred former thought offenders, since the club's main activities were directed to regular criminals. Kobayashi Morito, a former communist who converted for religious reasons, was in charge of this section of the club. The success rate was 100 percent—mainly, Hirata said, because Kobayashi was careful in enrolling people. Kimura Naotatsu, head of the Criminal Affairs Bureau, urged the establishment of protection and inspection groups in each district, but this had to be done with help from volunteers and donated funds, because the Justice Ministry was unable to support such a system until the Diet approved one.[161] Speaking at a conference for thought officials in June 1935, Justice Minister Ohara Naoshi pointed out that the communist movement was in rapid decline and that the number of people prosecuted and in prison for peace law violations was dropping in direct proportion to this decline. However, he stressed that it was impor-

tant to make sure that the converted communists remained converted, and for that purpose it was necessary for the creation of a
Justice Ministry–directed protection and supervision organization. Those in attendance enthusiastically supported this idea. A
special concern was, as usual, exprisoners who had not converted
and converts who for various reasons were backsliding, since such
people could become a grave social problem.[162]

Justice Minister Hayashi Raisaburō appeared before the House
of Representatives (May 16, 1936) and House of Peers (May 22)
to urge the passage of the Thought Criminals' Protection and
Supervision Law Bill. Numerous former thought offenders, some
of whom were unconverted, were circulating in society, he noted.
Besides that, others would soon complete prison terms. Passage of
this law bill, he said, would allow the government to isolate
thought crime repeaters and help others in their economic and
mental struggles.[163] The fourteen-article law passed in May and
was implemented by Imperial Ordinance No. 401 on November
13, 1936. Article 1 of the ordinance delegated authority to decide
which violators of the Peace Preservation Law fell under the law's
scope to Protection and Supervision Examination Commissions.
Article 2 explained that "protect" meant that a person would be
protected from the danger of again violating the peace law;
"supervision" meant that the thoughts and activities of each person would be watched. The protecting and supervising, said Article 3, would be overseen by the personnel of the Protection and
Supervision centers. Article 4 restricted movement, association,
communication, and so on. The term for people was set at two
years, with the possibility of renewal (Article 5). Twenty-two centers were established throughout the nation to deal with people
placed under the law.[164] Enactment of this law was a logical outcome of the government's public policy. Since normal criminal
procedures were inadequate for removing the ideology behind
thought crimes, it was necessary to devise a method formally to
reintegrate thought offenders.

In November 1936, Justice Minister Hayashi addressed a conference of thought administrators. The secret of preventing
thought crimes, he said, was, on the one hand, to firmly arrest
suspects, and, on the other hand, to guide them with the new law.
Repetition of thought crimes could be prevented, he emphasized,
by stimulating the Japanese spirit within each offender and by

helping each to earn a reasonable living.[165] Several months later, Protection Division head Moriyama Takeichirō wrote that the "father-and-mother-type policy to control thought crimes has been established."[166] The stern fatherly part, of course, was the peace law and penal servitude. The mixture of strictness and tenderness would vary with each offender, depending upon the nature of the crime and the criminal's mental attitude. Basically, Moriyama saw the law's purpose as twofold: change wrong thinking and keep it changed. For nonconverted and semiconverted people, the law would be used to stimulate their Japanese spirit and make them truly understand what it meant to be Japanese; for converted people, the object would be to move their thought further along the proper path. The spirit of the new law, said Moriyama, drew upon the historical fact that Japan was one great family.[167]

A few months later Moriyama wrote: "Instead of forcing a new outlook upon the violators, the law is designed to lead them to a realization and voluntary acknowledgement of their offense. Simultaneously it prepares them for a return to active and grateful service to society. . . . Through guidance and help it is expected that the offenders will also be brought to realize the worth of the family system and to experience the privilege of being welcomed back to membership in the great family that is the Japanese nation."[168] He continued: "The fact that a rigidly suppressive and intimidatory law has developed within a few years' time into a protective and benevolent statute may be regarded as an expression of the cultural development of the human race at large, and particularly of the Japanese people. . . . Their [i.e., thought offenders'] sense of being Japanese is strong. . . . [O]nce they have given up their radical convictions they are easily awakened to a strong consciousness of being members of the Japanese nation and loyal subjects of the Emperor."[169]

At a conference of thought officials in November 1936, Moriyama said that up to the passage of the new law the Justice Ministry standard for conversion was unconverted, semiconverted, or perfectly converted. Thought offenders in categories one and two —and in some cases people in category three—fell under the law's scope. The standard for a perfect conversion, he felt, would be raised under the new law: perfect conversion presupposed a person who had totally discarded revolutionary thought and whose nationalistic feelings were fully awakened.[170] Protracted warfare in China together with serious international problems did stimulate higher standards for conversion. Judge Ishii Kiyoshi, Takamatsu District Court, for example, said at a September 1940 meeting: "The standard for full conversion should be whether they worship the Emperor as a personal god."[171]

How effective were the Protective and Supervision centers? At a conference in October 1938, Protection Division Chief Moriyama announced that among thought offenders in protection groups, the percentage of repeaters was only one percent. In September 1940, Hiroshige Keizaburō, head of the center in Fukuoka, said they had no repeaters, and the Tokyo center reported the same. However, in Tokyo among people not in the center, there were more than a hundred repeaters.[172] These figures indicate that the system was probably working better than planned.

Official Efforts to Limit Procedural Abuses

Japan faced one crisis after another during the 1930s: the Manchurian problem, the collapse of the world's economic system, the failure of political parties to maintain control of cabinets, the collapse of a liberal interpretation of the Meiji Constitution, and protracted war with China. One state response was to narrow the range of legal dissent. Another response, however, was a liberalization of the state's handling of criminal suspects: the *Keiji Hoshō Hō* (Criminal Compensation Law), Law No. 60, April 1, 1931 (effective January 1, 1932).[173] While the enactment of a government law bill to open an avenue of appeal for victims of false arrest and imprisonment may appear contradictory, since the state was simultaneously narrowing the range of legal dissent, it illustrates widespread and continuing concern over enforcement of procedural rights by bar associations, legal scholars, politicians, and bureaucrats and that humane laws can be enacted during a time of national crisis. Furthermore, this seemingly contradictory law is best viewed as one of the many contradictions inherent in the era of so-called Taisho Democracy. For example, 1925 witnessed the passage of the Peace Preservation Law and the Universal Manhood Suffrage Law; and the same year as the *Baishin Hō* (Jury Law), Law No. 50 of 1923, which provided an opportunity for citizens to participate in the administration of justice, went into effect (October 1, 1928),[174] the Tanaka Giichi cabinet crushed the legal Labor-Farmer Party and revised the Peace Preservation Law to include a death penalty. In part these apparent contradictions reflect the confusion about social values within the political and intellectual worlds during the interwar era.

The humanitarian impulse that led to prison reforms at the turn of the century also stimulated a movement to compensate victims of false imprisonment. In 1900, three years before the Justice Ministry took charge of prisons, Dr. Okada Asatarō published "National Compensation System for Falsely Charged People" in a scholarly journal.[175] Over the following years, bar associations, legal scholars, the mass media community, and politicians increasingly criticized government authorities for permitting police violence and neglecting human rights. As protests of victims increased, an embarrassed government at last recognized that deficiencies in the system of justice required the enactment of a compensation law. During 1923–1924, the Justice Ministry produced two draft law bills, and in 1929 and 1930, politicians introduced two other law bills. While none of these bills became law, it is interesting to note that trying to get them passed was a bipartisan effort: Miyako Keizaburō (Seiyūkai), a lawyer, in 1929 and Ichimatsu Sadakichi (Minseitō), a former judge, in 1930, brought them before the Diet. Finally, a law bill was passed in 1931 by the Hamaguchi Osachi cabinet (Minseitō).[176]

The provisions of the Criminal Compensation Law applied to suspects acquitted after a trial, prisoners who had a guilty verdict reversed by a higher court, and people detained but never tried (Article 1). Excluded from applying for compensation (Article 4) were those acquitted or released based on Articles 39–41 of the Penal Code: persons of unsound mind, deaf mutes, and persons under age fourteen (Part 1, Section 1); those who were prosecuted for offenses against public order or morals (Part 1, Section 2); those whose actions, whether deliberate or in error, caused the prosecution (Part 2); those who committed a serious error, intentionally or unintentionally (Part 3); those involved in multiple criminal cases (i.e., acquitted in one case but judged guilty in another) (Part 4). Applicants were to apply within sixty days of acquittal at the court issuing the decree (Articles 6 and 9); the trial judge made the decision after confering with the procurator (Article 10). A maximum award was five yen compensation per day of detention and imprisonment (dated from the issuance of an arrest warrant). If a falsely charged convict was executed, an additional sum was added (Article 5). No appeal right was granted for the amount awarded, but an applicant could reapply if refused relief (Article 11). Articles 2 and 3 listed eligible family members and explained that if a criminal suspect died, the family could apply. The court making the decision was to publish the judgment in the *Official Gazette* (Article 19).[177]

During the Diet discussion over the law bill, Article 4 (Parts 2 and 3) emerged as the most controversial item. Legislators hotly debated the exact meaning of the phrase *jūdai naru kashitsu ni yoru kōi* (an action based on a serious error), with Seiyūkai members (e.g., Makino Ryōzō), urging the removal of this peculiar phrase. It was the duty of the prosecution, not of the defendants, to discover serious errors, he argued. Moreover, the issue of *kyōsei gōmon* (forced torture) became a part of the debate, as concern was expressed that criminal suspects forced to confess would become ineligible for compensation. Komata Seiichi (Minseitō) stated, for example, that like Ichimatsu he knew of numerous cases of police beating suspects to force confessions. This sort of brutality continued, he pointed out, even though the government insisted that such practices were rare.[178] Representative Makino also expressed dissatisfaction with the maximum compensation of five yen per day. This amount, he noted, could "hardly recompense the wronged person for the mental and physical suffering to which he or she ha[d] been subjected during detention." Moreover, all falsely charged persons, "including those detained in police stations, must be compensated."[179] Ōyama Ikuo (Rōnōtō), who insisted that the law only pretended to protect personal rights, stated: "A careful study of the Bill reveals the fact that it is contrived as to make the State immune from compensation to wronged labourers, farmers, and proletarian citizens. . . . It is easy to suppose . . . that the judicial authorities will go on infringing the personal rights of proletarians under cover of this clause [i.e., Article 4, Part 1, Section 2: Offenses against Public Order or Morals]."[180] Other legislators attacked the government's position that compensation was a special favor extended by the grace of the emperor (i.e., an extension into law of the traditional *mimaikin* [a sympathy gift of money]). Zeroing in on *hoshō o kyūyo su* (to grant compensation) in Article 1, they demanded that *kyūyo* be dropped because it means "to do a favor for a person" (i.e., benevolence from above). Yokoyama Kintarō (Minseitō) noted that a falsely charged person endured dishonor and pain; therefore, authorities should not mask reality by talking about benevolent government. Finally, *hoshō o nasu* (to give compensation) was substituted for the offensive *kyūyo*.[181] Justice Minister Watanabe Chifuyu, replying to interpellators, clearly exposed the law's character by pointing out that even though the state had no obligation to give compensation, it wished the law enacted to illustrate that the government rested on a foundation of benevolence. Giving compensation, he emphasized, would not mean that the state had any obligation to compensate people because of the state's illegal act;[182] instead, compensation was to be viewed not as an inherent right of the erroneously prosecuted, but rather as a special favor extended by a paternalistic state.

Table 1 gives an overview of this law's application. No figures are available for 1944 or 1945, because the records were burned; the amount of compensation for 1940 is missing because of a printing error.[183]

Table 1. Redress under the Criminal Compensation Law of 1931

Year	Suspects acquitted	Compensation applied for	Compensation received	Application rejected	Application undecided moved to next year	Average amount paid per person per day (yen)
1932	340	82	37	45	14	2.04
1933	210	93	33	60	3	2.08
1934	375	56	26	30	12	1.90
1935	419	105	32	73	9	1.97
1936	552	78	31	47	13	2.51
1937	444	78	28	50	103	2.34
1938	458	192	137	55	78	2.83
1939	232	67	23	44	74	2.84
1940	299	198	166	32	7	
1941	277	37	8	29	6	2.05
1942	263	16	3	13	2	2.41
1943	256	33	13	20	10	2.46

Applicants for compensation were faced, as legislators pre-
dicted, with a narrowly written law that excluded many victims of
false arrest and police brutality. Indeed, so restrictive were court
decisions during the first six months of 1932 that the Justice Ministry urged judges to adopt a more liberal interpretation (only
twenty applications for redress were received, and not one from
Tokyo or Osaka).[184] Nevertheless, over the following years applicants for compensation faced courts less than eager to grant relief
and seldom willing to give the maximum amount of money.

Not unexpectedly, the vaguely worded Article 4 proved a difficult hurdle for many applicants, and most cases rejected by the
Supreme Court were in connection with the public peace and
morals and the error parts of this article (see table 2).[185]

In the following case, the appeals court rejected the applicant's
plea for relief by citing Article 4, Part 2: "No person will be compensated whose actions, deliberately or in error, are the cause for
prosecution, detention, and trial." The criminal suspect in this
case was tried for robbery but was acquitted at the District and
Appeals courts. The Appeals Court, however, rejected his applica-

Table 2. Reasons for Denying Redress under the Criminal
Compensation Law of 1931

Year	Part 1, Section 1 (based on articles 39–41)	Part 1, Section 2 (public peace and morals)	Part 2 (error)	Part 3 (error)	Part 4 (multiple crimes)
1932	2	12	24	0	1
1933	0	13	30	2	1
1934	0	8	18	0	0
1935	0	9	58	1	1
1936	0	13	29	0	0
1937	0	10	34	3	0
1938	4	21	23	0	0
1939	3	1	28	0	0
1940	0	4	21	0	0
1941	0	2	21	1	0
1942	0	5	7	0	1
1943	0	2	11	1	0

tion for compensation, noting that he had confessed, and that confession had caused procurators to prosecute. The "error," then, was his. The Supreme Court, too, refused to recognize a possible mistake by procurators and the preliminary trial judge, and the application was rejected on August 8, 1940.[186]

A majority of the applications for which compensation was awarded involved *miketsu kōryū* (unconvicted detention).[187] Even in such cases, though, court interpretation was narrow. The following case was decided by the Supreme Court on December 14, 1934. A suspected arsonist was held without warrant by police for thirty-four days (April 10–May 14, 1932). At both District and Appeals courts he was found not guilty. An application for compensation, however, was rejected (based on Article 5: payment granted only after issuance of a warrant). Time in detention after the thirty-four days was also discounted because of the defendant's confession, which had misled police and procurators. The court cited Article 4 (defendant's error).[188]

As has been illustrated, police were inclined to squeeze confessions out of criminal suspects, and courts—even though policemen were sometimes indicted for brutality—were inclined to regard all confessions as legally obtained. In fact, judges were so imbued with this idea that it was nearly impossible for an acquitted victim of a forced confession to receive compensation. In such a case, a judge was likely to say that the suspect caused the "error" by confession and, hence, led the procurator and preliminary judge astray. Suspects, then, unless their bodies carried obvious marks of torture, found little sympathy. Judges thought it was up to applicants to prove charges of brutality or torture, but since interrogations went on behind closed doors, with only interrogators present, such charges were virtually impossible to prove.[189] A Supreme Court decision of August 8, 1932, set the tone for court attitudes on confessions: if a suspect made a voluntary confession, it was correct to interpret this as the suspect's error even if the suspect was later acquitted. The judges felt that as long as no illegal acts were involved (e.g., leading questions or torture) then it was a willing confession. In theory this was acceptable, but in fact it was nearly impossible for a victim of brutality to prove that an illegal act occurred.[190]

On the one hand, it is easy to criticize this law's shortcomings: applicants faced a narrowly drafted and narrowly interpreted law,

with compensation at an average of 2.00–2.50 yen (the maximum
was 5.00 yen)—a niggardly amount for the 537 people who
received payment (1932–1943). On the other hand, this progressive legislation was a step in the right direction, since it did open
an appeal channel between victims and the state. While it is
impossible to discern the law's impact on police practices, it may
have deterred some illegal actions.

Procurators, frustrated by procedural mistakes and incidents of
brutality and torture, were acutely aware of the need for better
educated and more obedient justice police. This pressing need was
one subject of discussion at conferences from 1933 onward, when
Thought Procurator Tozawa Shigeo urged officials to better educate justice police.[191] At a June 1935 conference, the need for better trained and more obedient justice police was again discussed.[192] Justice Minister Hayashi Raisaburō, at a November
1936 conference, condemned unskilled justice policemen for not
collecting enough material proof and instead relying upon confessions. Procurators must, he stressed, teach them the proper procedure. At a conference in June 1937, Procurator Kuriya Shirō,
Tokyo District Court, urged the improvement of justice police
practices to stop public criticism about infringement of people's
rights.[193] As the China War expanded, the actions of military policemen caused concern. One procurator pointed out, at a July
1938 conference, military policemen's deficient legal knowledge,
which sometimes resulted in criminal cases and in civil disputes.
Another frustrated procurator agreed, saying that military police
acted like country boys. Procurator Masaki Katsumi, Supreme
Court, who was teaching criminal law at a military police school,
said that one reason for the deplorable situation was the inadequate one to six months of study time, which included instruction
in subjects other than criminal law.[194] Complaints about methods
police used to get confessions and other procedural problems surfaced again at conferences in June 1939 and May 1940.[195] Procurator Shibata Noboru, at a September 1940 conference, noted that
Tokkō "had a tendency to create antipathy [during an investiga-
tion]. . . . They must not cause antipathy, but must instead give
the people with whom they come in contact a good feeling."[196] At
a conference in April 1941, Procurator Nakamura Yoshirō,
Nagoya District Court, pointed out that police held suspects too

long, trying to force conversion. Police tactics came under fire by Judge Suzuki Taijirō, Kanagawa District Court, who asked how much trust should be placed in confessions and other documents produced by police, since it appeared that in thought cases many statements were forced.[197] Judge Kawakami Kan (confidential report of February 1938) argued that human rights abuses by police stemmed from a lack of education, improper training (i.e., a lack of knowledge about laws and scientific investigative techniques), and an arrogant attitude of superiority over the common people. Police, reflecting these deficiencies, illegally held criminal suspects and forced confessions. Indeed, wrote Kawakami, immature investigative techniques and forced confessions were inseparable and together were the primary cause for human rights abuses. It was unfair to blame only police, he concluded, because courts, by overemphasizing the importance of confessions, contributed to this problem.[198] While these comments were made in closed meetings and a confidential publication, the matter of police shortcomings surfaced in the press. For example, in late May 1935, Justice Minister Ohara Naoshi noted that "in spite of the warnings repeatedly given by judicial authorities in successive Cabinets, the judicial police are not yet entirely free from public complaints that . . . they trample on personal rights." Four days earlier Procurator General Mitsuyuki Jirō, addressing prefectural police chiefs, "warned those . . . in charge of judicial police business against the use of brutal force against suspects."[199]

A more concrete action to stop police illegality was the *Shihō Keisatsu Kanri Kunren Kitei* (Justice Police Officials' Training Rules) of July 22, 1936. Under these regulations, procurators were to teach policemen proper investigative techniques in order to stop illegal procedures. One of the more novel innovations, however, was the order for procurators to inspect police stations periodically. Justice Minister Shiono Suehiko, at a June 1937 conference, judged that the one-year-old training program for policemen was working well.[200]

How much police brutality and torture decreased is an open question, but it is clear that procurators were unable to bridle police. In fact, as Judge Kawakami Kan noted, procurators who harped on human rights abuses not only demoralized police but also stimulated resentment against the prosecution.[201] Given the police tradition of ignoring the Criminal Procedure Code and the pressing investigative needs of procurators, the 1936 rules were doomed to have only a limited impact on police practices.

Nevertheless, police were prosecuted for violations of Articles 194 and 195 of the Penal Code (the former article provided imprisonment not exceeding seven years for abuse of arrest power; the latter ordered imprisonment not exceeding three years for cruelty or violence; see Chapter 1 for the full text). Between 1926 and 1940 (statistics are not available after 1940, when the Justice Ministry combined prosecutions for violations of Articles 194 and 195 with those for taking or giving bribes) seven were convicted under Article 194, fifty under 195. Thirteen of those convicted under Article 194 and twenty-four of those convicted under Article 195 had their sentences suspended. It is unclear why the number of police whose sentences were suspended is almost double the number convicted for violating Article 194, but the disparity may result from the time lag in appeal procedures.[202] Most of those convicted received sentences of one year or less, but the six officers convicted in 1935 were sentenced to two years or more.[203] On balance, though, it is obvious that authorities were not eager to imprison policemen: out of fifty-seven convicted, thirty-seven were put on probation. The less-than-zealous prosecution of police lawlessness is also reflected in statistics collected by Judge Kawakami Kan for the years 1932–1936 (see Chapter 4).

4

Brutality and Torture

DURING THE 1930s, the state's *tenkō* policy was successfully applied to thousands of thought offenders. While both physical and psychological coercion were used, police and justice authorities relied more on the latter method than on the former. Nevertheless, as the last chapter illustrates, brutality and torture were used by police not only to pressure recalcitrant communist suspects into signing conversion statements, but also to wring out information about comrades, or to force a confession, or simply as punishment for those repudiating the *kokutai*. Up to now we have primarily focused on the elite Tokkō, which had the mission to capture thought criminals, but it is important to remember that the thought police were merely an offshoot of the regular police force. As Miyashita Hiroshi, a member of the Tokkō from 1929 to 1945, stressed in a postwar interview, the Tokkō were similar to the regular police, since they received orders from procurators and especially since they, like regular policemen, were subject to the Criminal Procedure Code. Moreover, he said, they were not a secret police.[1] Therefore, this chapter looks at regular police brutality and torture in nonideological cases as a standard against which to measure Tokkō actions.

Brutality and *torture* are different. Of course, brutality for one person may be torture for another, but in most cases which label to apply is obvious. For example, a slap on the face or a kick in the side by a policeman frustrated by a suspect's lack of cooperation is not torture. But if the policeman keeps on slapping and kicking, brutality turns into a form of torture. Suspension upside down, suffocation, sexual aggression, beating thighs, and so on are forms of torture. In the following cases, most readers will have no difficulty distinguishing one from the other. It is understood, of course, that torture can be psychological as well as physical and that the two are intimately interrelated.

Newspaper Accounts

Early in 1931 the *Kokumin Shinbun* (Tokyo) carried a story about a Korean interrogated by police because he had loaned money to two other Koreans arrested for the murder of a policeman. "The torture he underwent was beyond description."[2] A few weeks later a missing person story from the summer of 1930 turned into a case of alleged torture. Ōmori police (Tokyo) were accused of holding an arson suspect until he died. Details were unearthed after a Diet member helped the family.[3] "The Third Degree Again" read a headline on December 31, 1931. Fortunately for this arson suspect, the real criminal was apprehended, but not before the suspect had been forced to sign a false confession.[4] The *Japan Weekly Chronicle* commented: "These third degree revelations are becoming increasingly common. Last month a youth who had served a year's imprisonment as part of a life sentence for murder, was released after strong comments by the Appeal Court as to the methods used by the police in extorting a confession."[5] In mid-January 1932, the *Kobe Shinbun* printed rumors of a death by torture in the Sannomiya Police Station (Kobe); the story was hotly denied by the chief of police. Subsequently, however, it was admitted that a policeman, angry over the slow pace of interrogation, killed the suspect by throwing him to the floor.[6] In the next case detectives mistook a young man, who was a student, for a bogus student. The young man recalled: "They finally took me to the police station. Immediately they pushed me into the detective room they began beating and kicking me, paying no attention whatever to my explanation."[7] In September 1932, newspapers in Tokyo prominently featured alleged police torture (February 1931) in Yamagata prefecture. Police torture was not the sensational aspect of this case, but rather that sixty policemen resigned to protest the indictment of several colleagues.[8] In June 1933, Kobe detectives were alleged to have tortured three impolite men. At the Amagasaki Police Station, the three "were struck on the head and neck with a bamboo foil until the stick broke. Their legs were also beaten, their faces slapped with geta and slippers, and refuse was flung at them. . . . [They] were detained for several days."[9] The sequel to this incident appeared a few days later: "The three Kobe policemen . . . have now been sent to the Tachibana prison, where they are to await trial. Preliminary examination revealed a *prima facie* case against the men, and the procurators are stated to be determined to push the charges."[10] An Osaka police station, in April 1934, arrested and held for two weeks a man who reported a stolen watch. Police, who suspected that the man was lying, hit him on the head with a geta until he confessed that he had not lost a watch. Fortunately, the real thief was apprehended.[11]

In January 1935, a Tokyo newspaper reported that policemen were being questioned in connection with a death at the Iiyama Police Station. It was alleged that the suspect had been beaten to death.[12] The *Kokumin Shinbun* reported that a man held by the Nakano Police Station (Tokyo) was, after being detained several days, returned to his family. He died without speaking. Police denied any responsibility.[13] "With stories of police brutality coming to light almost daily, a case is reported from Kumamoto which puts most of them completely in the shade. According to the *Mainichi* a Kumamoto girl of twenty, detained for no offense whatever . . . was violated night and day by officials of the Minami station. She was eventually driven mad." Prefectural police authorities were to hold an inquiry, the report said.[14] In Nagano prefecture, a police chief, badgered by journalists in connection with a torture charge against one of his detectives, chased them out of his office at knife point.[15] The following month a Kanagawa prefectural official left a suicide note: "I am entirely innocent, but due to torture I received in prison, I have confessed what I have not done."[16] In September, the Ōtsu police charged Okamoto Heijirō, a candidate for the prefectural assembly, with violating election regulations. "The examination lasted six hours and a half, it is complained, and as it was conducted in a very severe manner Mr. Okamoto got frightened, so much so that he has made up his mind to abandon his candidature."[17] Shortly after this incident, three detectives and a policeman of the Kikuyabashi Police Station (Tokyo) were alleged to have handcuffed and struck one suspect with a club and to have stripped a female suspect.[18] The *Yomiuri Shinbun* reported in July 1936: "The Tokyo Procurators' Office is investigating a case in which a policeman of the Mikawashima police station is suspected of having beaten a prisoner to death early the morning on [sic] May 6th. They face considerable difficulty, however, because the victim, Fukuji Nakazawa (24), was cremated after the cause of his death was diagnosed as heart failure."[19] In September four policemen at the Takanawa Police Station (Tokyo) were accused of stripping four girls, bus ticket takers, involved in a demonstration. One girl was hospitalized with shock.[20] The following month cases of torture and forced confessions were reported in Tokushima prefecture by Minseitō political leaders: "In order to investigate whether illegal house-to-house visits to solicit votes were made, it is alleged, 350 voters out of a total of 380 in that village were summoned to the local police station and detained for periods ranging from three to twelve days. 'Confessions' were extracted from some of them by torture, as a result of which one committed suicide, another went mad and hanged himself, and a third attempted suicide."[21] The *Hōchi Shinbun,* reporting on the Uraga police torture trial, noted that the former chief of Uraga Police Station, Miyakawa Seima, "admitted in the trial that one of his superiors suggested that he dispose of a club 'which was liable to be suspected of having been used in the grilling of persons held for alleged Election Law violations.' "[22] Several days later Procurator Takegami Hanjirō (Yokohama) resigned to take responsibility for a "notorious police torture incident in Kanagawa prefecture."[23] Mrs. Tanaka Shin was arrested in Kyoto on January 9 on suspicion of illegal betting activities. When her answers to questions proved unsatisfactory, police "removed the lower part of the woman's *kimono* and making her sit on a *soroban* (abacus) beat her with a wooden fencing sword. Other detectives subjected her to the same torture on January 18th and 19th, after which further violence is said to have been done to her because her replies to questions were not satisfactory."[24] To "sit" in this case means sitting with the knees pressed against the sharp wheels of the abacus. At the Osaka Appeals Court, a superior of the detective who ordered Tanaka interrogated stated "that though it is possible that policemen examine prisoners in a manner open to question . . . [I am] firmly convinced that the allegations that the prisoners were caused to 'sit astride an abacus or suspended from the ceiling,' are untrue."[25] This second article makes clear that two women were involved.

On February 7, 1938, the long Kanagawa Engineering Scandal trial was completed, with 119 of the 134 accused acquitted. "At the public hearings which totaled over 240 . . . many of the accused bitterly criticized the prosecution, charging them with resorting to torture. Some of them sued the policemen for the use of third degree methods."[26] Near the end of 1938 an arson suspect denied in open court his earlier confession: "I made a false confession because I was tortured. . . . From the very beginning the police suspected me of starting the fire and I had to satisfy them, against my wishes."[27]

Common denominators in these cases of alleged police misconduct are ignoring the legal time limits for holding a criminal suspect and using brutality or torture to extract confessions. These cases also suggest that police attitudes had not changed significantly from those held in late Meiji (i.e., feelings of superiority over and contempt for the common people). Clearly, a signed confession, advances in investigative techniques notwithstanding, remained the queen of evidence in the 1930s. As for the instruments employed to force confession, police used anything handy: fists, feet, bamboo and wooden swords, geta, slippers, excrement, clubs, and an abacus. Women were subjected to stripping, rape, and suspension from the ceiling.

The Teijin Affair

Perhaps more than any event during the turbulent 1930s the so-called Teijin affair focused public attention on violations of suspects' procedural rights. Teikoku Jinzō Kenshi Kabushiki Kaisha (Imperial Rayon Company), or Teijin, was a subsidiary of the old Suzuki trading company, which had declared bankruptcy in 1927. The Bank of Taiwan held 220,000 shares of Teijin as collateral against a loan to Suzuki. These shares, however, were deposited with the Bank of Japan in return for a loan to the Bank of Taiwan. Since the government guaranteed the loan to the Bank of Taiwan, the shares held by the Bank of Japan could only be negotiated with the permission of the Finance Ministry. Over time the value of the stocks rose, and many speculators tried unsuccessfully to purchase them. Finally, in June 1933 a group of financiers purchased 100,000 shares. Rumors of bribes paid to gain access to the stocks and illegal manipulation of the market to increase their value were picked up by the media and in turn by political foes of the Saitō

Makoto cabinet. By the spring of 1934 highly placed government and business leaders were caught in the expanding pool of corruption. Rumors spread that Justice Ministry personnel were exploiting the political situation to promote a new cabinet headed by former Justice Minister Hiranuma Kiichirō. After a lengthy investigation, sixteen people were indicted for corruption, including the former railway minister Mitsuchi Chūzō and Commerce Minister Nakajima Kumakichi. A dramatic public trial went through 265 sessions (June 22, 1935, to October 5, 1937); all defendants were acquitted on December 16.[28]

This trial surprised procurators, because it turned into a severe attack upon the administration of justice. Charges of infringement of personal rights (i.e., procedural rights) and torture were made in both the courtroom and the Imperial Diet, and the procuracy emerged from this affair with a tarnished image. Indeed, for a procuracy already dogged by charges of *kensatsu fassho* (fascism by the procuracy), this trial only exacerbated matters.

An indication of what was coming appeared in early January 1935 in the *Tokyo Jiji Shinbun:* "In connection with the examination of the accused, rumor was set afoot the other day that some accused were subjected to virtual torture and that they were forced to make groundless 'confessions' under physical pain. This charge was taken up in both Houses at the recent extraordinary session of the Diet. . . . It is said that the accused have filed a petition traversing [repudiating] the 'confessions' they have made in the preliminary court."[29] On January 22, Justice Minister Ohara Naoshi, speaking in the House of Representatives, denied that the procurators involved in the Teijin case were guilty of violating the suspects' personal rights.[30] The next day, in his maiden House of Peers speech, Minobe Tatsukichi said that justice had to be dispensed according to the law and all suspects treated with a scrupulous regard for the law. While he had for years heard rumors about procurators moving beyond the law, he had discounted them, but this time there were facts showing violations of procedural rights. Suspects, said Minobe, had been illegally detained in dirty cells, terribly tormented by bugs, and unnecessarily handcuffed.[31] One newspaper report was based on the interrogation experience of defendant Nagano Mamori, the auditor of Teijin. The moment Nagano denied the charge of accepting shares as a bribe the two procurators "thundered out, 'Don't talk nonsense!'

They rushed at him, ordered him to stand up, and then gripping both arms, forced his face up with their fists. He was pushed to the wall behind, and his forehead and jaw were then pushed so that the back of his head was knocked against the wall. . . . The one procurator said: 'A fellow like you had better die. But then, perhaps you have not sufficient pluck to take your own life. If you don't know how to kill yourself, I will tell you.' " The report continued: "It was soon after he was detained . . . that he was handcuffed [with leather manacles]. . . . [H]e could not make his bedding. Nor could he keep off the mosquitoes or fleas. He could scarcely sleep at night. . . . As he kept refusing to confess his guilt . . . he was transferred . . . to another cell. . . . Once inside he was attacked by a swarm of vermin and their bites were terrible. . . . The procurator at one time declared that if he remained obdurate, he would be put into a worse cell."[32]

The *Japan Weekly Chronicle* editorialized that while some of the alleged bad treatment of suspects might be exaggerated, there was a growing suspicion that procurators had "third degreed the defendants. The charges are quite plain, and in certain important respects are not disputed. Defendants have been kept manacled for as long as 48 hours at a time; others have been confined in verminous cells, and all . . . have been subject to little refinements of treatment that—designedly or not—were calculated to break down their resistance and produce the much needed confession."[33] And so this scandal-ridden trial dragged on, finally overshadowed from July 1937 by the expanding war in China. After the acquittal of all defendants, the *Japan Weekly Chronicle* commented: "For the real importance of the trial, it seems to us, is not that a distinguished group of defendants . . . happened to be in the dock . . . but that the Court believed the oral testimony of the defendants as against their signed confessions. . . . In announcing the Teijin acquittals the presiding judge did not, it is true, refer even indirectly to the defendants' charges of harsh treatment during detention."[34]

Although the court was mute on the issue of brutality to force confession, the *Osaka Asahi Shinbun* was not: "[T]he impression is fairly wide that some judicial officials approached the case with the idea—not a proper one—of eradicating, by the application of the law, certain deplorable tendencies in society. It was due to this belief that the judiciary was at one time charged with Fascism.

124   JANUS-FACED JUSTICE

. . . The Teijin case was rendered the more notorious by the
charges of the infringement of personal rights freely brought by
the accused against the judiciary." The paper concluded: "This
gives rise to the thought that there must have been many other
accused in the past who . . . were not cleared of charges wrongfully brought against them, in spite of the possibility that their personal rights had been abused more glaringly than in the case of the
accused in the Teijin case."³⁵

The Teijin affair was a political bombshell, with foes of the government and the Justice Ministry itching to use sensational courtroom charges. Some comments on the abuse of procedural rights
of criminal suspects, of course, were probably not only sincerely
expressed but also accurate in fact. In the House of Peers, on February 6, 1935, Iwata Chūzō interpellated Justice Minister Ohara
by reading from the memoirs of several defendants. Procurators
often remarked, he noted, that "businessmen are responsible for
the corruption of politicians. . . . We hold you, accused, of no
account. It is the bigger ones, lurking in the background, we want
to bring to justice. Our object is to carry out a bloodless *coup d'etat*
in order to purify society." Iwata commented: "When procurators
abuse their power, even an entirely groundless charge can be presented with some degree of plausibility."³⁶ Four days earlier Kuya-
ma Tomoyuki (Seiyūkai), in the House of Representatives, had
quoted from the press recent examples of police lawlessness. One
report alleged that a policeman in Nagano beat to death a bur-
glary suspect; another described the illegal arrest of a religious
group in Kanagawa prefecture. While detained for forty days in
the Hayama Police Station, these people were tortured. To cover
up this case, which included the abuse of two young women,
police authorities circulated distorted accounts to the press.³⁷ On
February 20, in the House of Peers Budget Committee, Uzawa
Sōmei quizzed Home Minister Gotō Fumio about the Teijin affair
and then pointed out cases of police torture in Aomori and Toyama prefectures. Great care would be taken, replied Gotō, to stop
such abuses.³⁸ On May 8, 1936, in the House of Representatives,
Iwasaki Kojirō (Seiyūkai) charged procurators and police with
violations of procedural rights. He pointed out that at least fifteen thousand people had been arrested after the recent general
election and that torture had been used in some interrogations.
Home Minister Ushio Keinosuke pledged punishment for guilty
policemen.³⁹

In February 1937, Kokubo Ki'ichi, House of Peers, recalled being imprisoned three times for political offenses between 1884 and 1887, but he was never tortured. In connection with the 1935 prefectural elections and the 1936 general election, however, he noted that "many cases of the use of torture by the police were reported. Such cases occurred in Kanagawa, Kagoshima, Yamaguchi, Iwate, and Okayama prefectures, and the forms of torture resorted to by the Kanagawa police were most shocking. . . . This is a serious blot on Japanese constitutional government."[40] On February 24, 1937, at a House of Representatives Budget Committee meeting, Tachikawa Taira (Seiyūkai) detailed torture cases from many prefectures, producing numerous photographs of victims. Justice Minister Shiono Suehiko replied that many of the cases were being probed, but, in a majority, incriminating evidence was not found.[41] Several days later the Seiyūkai and Minseitō jointly sponsored a resolution to reform the justice system in order to promote constitutional government. Shiono, promising to enforce the spirit of the resolution, urged the parties to withdraw it, since the Diet criticism had undermined the public's confidence in the police and the judiciary.[42] Nevertheless, the joint resolution was passed on March 31; it said in part: "[T]here have been cases of late where . . . the judicial police illegally placed innocent people under arrest and detention and attempted to extort 'confessions' from them. When the evidence given by these poor people was not such as they wished to obtain, the police often subjected them to shocking acts of violence and indignities, sometimes with fatal results. Nothing can be more shameful for a law-governed country."[43] Diet criticism continued into February and March 1938, focusing on false confessions and lack of regard for personal rights.[44]

Embarrassed police and justice officials, as newspapers and lawmakers exposed one case after another of official lawlessness, sometimes denied the abuses and other times promised reforms. In January 1937, they tried to placate critics with a promise to publicize in the Diet details of police torture cases. The *Osaka Mainichi* noted, however, that police torture cases were verified by the Home Ministry in only Aomori, Kanagawa, and Okinawa prefectures; the political parties, on the other hand, insisted that the practice was widespread. Ranking police officers, said the journal, thought a change in the law would solve the problem: if police were permitted to keep suspects longer, they would not be under such great pressure to solve a case quickly. Under the current system, noted the paper, suspects could be legally held until sunset on the day following arrest unless a procurator's writ extended detention up to ten days. "Under the circumstances, police officials are inclined to become impatient in dealing with suspects who refuse to 'confess,' and to resort to torture occasionally."[45]

What the lawmakers described was a system of justice in which illegal arrest, illegal detention, brutality, torture, and forced confession were commonplace. This is the same pattern of official lawlessness reflected in the newspaper accounts. It should be noted, however, that lawmakers did not discover lawlessness among police and procurators as a result of the Teijin affair. At the Fifty-ninth Session of the Imperial Diet (February 21, 1931), for instance, Nishio Suehiro, Social Democratic Party, demanded an explanation for police violence against labor demonstrators, including a former Diet member who was injured as he tried to enter the Diet building. Asahara Kenzō, Japan Masses' Party, read "extracts from many Tokyo papers describing the outrages committed by the police." Finally, Ōyama Ikuo, New Labor-Farmer Party, declared that "the government ought to put an effectual stop to the practice of extorting 'confessions' by inducement as well as by torture."[46] The following summer a political committee of the Minseitō stated: "An effectual end should be put to cases of infringement of personal rights. It is an undeniable fact that in their criminal searches and in the examination of suspects, procurators are often guilty of infringing personal rights. The authorities concerned must keep a strict supervision so as to eradicate such evil practices."[47]

Infringement of Human Rights

The above evidence illustrates that "normal" police handling of nonideological criminal suspects included illegal arrest, illegal detention, brutality, torture, forced confessions, and other lawless acts. Yet a nagging doubt remains, since newspapers usually qualified such charges with "alleged," and officials often denied such violations. Even indictment of policemen and denunciations of police lawlessness by Diet members do not dispel doubt about the nature and extent of official abuses. Indeed, determining the truth about this elusive subject requires a view over the fence into the government camp, but authorities kept this unpleasant subject secret. Fortunately, however, Judge Kawakami Kan produced *Iwayuru jinken jūrin mondai ni tsuite* (About the so-called infringement of human rights), which removes the veil of secrecy. This document, marked "confidential," was issued for in-house use in February 1938. Kawakami discusses nonideological cases from 1932 to 1936 inclusive, based on confidential information obtained from various procurator bureaus. Since not all bureaus responded, the nationwide total of police abuses is understated. Nonetheless, this report is unique and comes from unimpeachable official sources.

Kawakami was aware of criticism leveled at the criminal investigative organs, including the accuracy of some charges that human rights were violated.[48] According to Kawakami, Justice Minister Shiono Suehiko said: "Well, a recent tendency you can often see is among justice police, of course, but also even the procurators are forcing confessions from suspects and defendants."[49] Therefore, Kawakami researched police violations of Articles 194 and 195 of the Penal Code. The former mandated punishment not exceeding seven years for officials who abused the arrest power; the later decreed imprisonment not exceeding three years for officials who used violence or cruelty against criminal suspects (see Chapter 1 for the full text). Besides this legal protection, Kawakami also looked at Article 254, Criminal Procedure Code, which forbade coercion during interrogation, and Article 127, which permitted police to hold no suspect longer than forty-eight hours (unless they applied to a procurator for additional time).[50]

Kawakami's first example of illegality involved an arrest for suspected payoffs during the February 20, 1936, Diet election. Miyakawa Shizuma, a justice policeman for the Kanagawa Prefectural Police and also chief of the Uraga Police Station, was the senior man indicted for procedural violations. The other justice police defendants (Kanagawa Prefectural Police) were Suberikawa Eizō, Shimada Atsunari, and Koori Yutaka. They had arrested Hishinuma Shunkichi on February 21, and on February 22 they interrogated him in the second-floor exercise room. After the suspect denied offering money, the interrogation team laid five round sticks about one inch in diameter and four feet long parallel on the floor; the rods were secured with judo belts to keep them properly spaced (the author terms this *sunokozeme*, "portable slotted floor piece torture"; sometimes this was used with an additional rod inserted behind the knees). As Hishinuma knelt on the rods, he was forced to hold a chair overhead on which police piled fencing equipment to add weight (Kawakami calls this *isuzeme,* "chair torture"). The treatment was given again the next morning and on March 5; on March 6 the time was extended to six hours.[51]

Thirteen other suspects were involved in this case. On February 23, Takahashi Taichi was given the same treatment as Hishinuma, but in addition police beat him with a piece of bamboo (Kawakami categorizes this as *nagurizeme*). After a noon break, the interrogators returned. Around 6:00 P.M. they forced Takahashi onto the tatami and employed *kusugurizeme* ("violent knuckle-rub of sides" torture). Takahashi confessed, but he later repudiated the statement. Infuriated, Shimada repeatedly kicked Takahashi in the head. Hasegawa Tomekichi (arrested on February 20) was interrogated in a similar manner. In his case, however, Suberikawa, after taking a break for supper, also used a bamboo sword. This pattern was repeated the next day until around midnight. The interrogation of Kakui Homare began on February 24 and was similar. Finally, on the afternoon of February 25, water was forced into Kakui's nose (Kawakami does not name this torture, but the interrogators called it the "Korean Criminal Code, Article No. 2"). Later a new technique was applied—*tenbinzeme* ("shoulder-carrying pole torture"). For this torture, which was usually used in conjunction with *sunokozeme,* a pole about two inches in diameter was inserted in the hollow of the knees. The remaining interrogations were a variation on the same theme; in addition, Takagi Kōjirō was kicked and viciously beaten, and Nagashima Seizō was thrown several times onto the wooden floor. The chief of police not only condoned these actions, but in many instances took part. Koori Yutaka investigated two other suspects in a related case at the Misaki Police Station. Urashima Ukizō was hit with a piece of wood and forced to inhale smoke from a smoldering piece of wood. In the case of Niigura Yoshizō, a bamboo pipe was inserted between his fingers and pressure was applied. He was also kicked, beaten, and forced to inhale smoke. While not continuous, this treatment went on for four days.[52]

At the Amagasaki Police Station (Hyōgo prefecture), on April 25, 1933, officers Nakaike and Okutani forced five men to kneel

on a concrete floor. They beat them with a walking stick, hit them
with a piece of bamboo, threatened them with a gun, and sprayed
them with urine. Police at the Iiyama Police Station (Nagano prefecture), after arresting Ideno Miyoshi as a robbery suspect on
January 17, 1935, trampled him, beat him with a bamboo fencing
sword, and beat him with other things. Ideno died. Police in
Tokushima prefecture arrested Kimura Kanpei on suspicion of
gambling on February 16, 1934. Kicking and hitting resulted in
injury. The interrogation of Sakanaka Juntarō took place on February 11, 1935, at the Iwakuni Police Station (Yamaguchi prefecture). After being thrown to the floor ten times, the suspect died.
Hamamura Rikizō came to the Ainoura Police Station (Nagasaki
prefecture), to report a theft. Policeman Akatsuka Morishige,
however, decided that he was lying and beat him. On April 2,
1933, Officer Minamizato Kōzō took suspect Yamamura Mohei
outside the station and threw him on the ground, killing him
(Fukue Police Station, Nagasaki prefecture). At the Iizuka Police
Station (Fukuoka prefecture), a woman complained when a
policeman hit a suspect; he beat her to death. An auto accident
brought Sudō Masaki to the Hachinohe Police Station (Aomori
prefecture). Policeman "X," dissatisfied with Sudō's attitude,
slapped him until his nose bled. Then he pulled his hair, shook his
head, beat him with a short measuring stick, and banged his head
against a shelf. Policeman Ichinose Seiji, Sasebo Police Station
(Nagasaki prefecture), was on December 1, 1936, on his way
home from an end-of-the-year party when he spotted Egami
Saburō, who earlier had given Ichinose the slip. Ichinose killed
him with a saber. Kawakami notes that the victim's only sin had
been to dodge a routine questioning. This policeman, Kawakami
wrote, was known as a rough and short-tempered sort.[53] "Besides
these examples there are numerous cases in which authorities got
angry for minor reasons over worthless matters and acted illegally." Moreover, he noted, "looking at current conditions, unfortunately, I must agree that many justice police officials do lack
humane feelings."[54]

The next incident in Kawakami's account occurred at the
Kamakura Police Station. Officer "X," who discovered Masubuchi Shōtarō lying drunk in the street, poured several buckets of
water over Masubuchi and then slapped and kicked him. Two ribs
were broken. In Kyoto in 1933 (no location given), a policeman

interrogated two barmaids on suspicion of prostitution, forcing them to show their private parts. Kawakami pointed out that this was not an unusual episode. Police also used threats and violence to influence elections. Officer Nakamura Eiji arrested Uramoto Shūichi, an influential member of the Minseitō, on February 18, 1932 (an election was scheduled for February 20). The victim was slapped twice. Hirashita Mizuho, another influential Minseitō member, was arrested in Kumamoto prefecture by Officer Ikeda Toshirō, who threatened, slapped, and choked him. Another incident occurred in Kumamoto prefecture one day earlier, when two policemen beat businessman Aoyama Katsunojō, who had Minseitō ties. First Aoyama was paraded in front of a business place owned by the head of the Seiyūkai branch office and then beaten on the way to the Misumi Police Station. Kawakami notes that ten days were needed to heal the injuries caused by this illegal arrest.[55] "This kind of act," said Kawakami, "goes against humanity and it debases the dignity of the law."[56]

The following figures are based on Kawakami's research (not all procurator bureaus responded). The first number in the parentheses following the year represents total complaints; the second number, people involved; the third, number of cases in which police were prosecuted: 1932 (84/169/8); 1933 (91/161/2); 1934 (77/142/3); 1935 (83/168/6); 1936 (63/130/4). Kawakami also divides these cases according to the result of illegal police actions. The first number represents injury, the second, death: 1932 (48/1); 1933 (55/2); 1934 (52/2); 1935 (33/5); 1936 (34/4). Of 398 cases taken to procurators, only 23 were followed up with a prosecution (roughly 6 percent)—a remarkably low percentage. In all years except 1935, well over half the cases involved injuries; the number of deaths climbed yearly, dropping by one the last year (14 people were killed during the period).[57]

Kawakami believed that police and procurator obsession with written confessions was in the background of most cases involving human rights abuses. The case of accused arsonist Fujiwara Kiichi, who asked the Miyagi Appeals Court on December 26, 1934, to reverse his conviction, provides one example. The suspect had fourteen interrogations, starting on October 1, 1933, and ending on December 24. Fujiwara alternately denied, confessed, denied, confessed, and denied. Looking at the record, Kawakami noticed that the procurator was present at the police station during two interrogations (unusual) and that even the preliminary judge attended one session (very unusual). Why did the police not simply follow procedure and send the suspect along to the procurator's office? Clearly, concluded Kawakami, this case involved the use of torture to force a confession—which the suspect then denied at the preliminary examination. The Supreme Court agreed with Kawakami in 1935 (Case No. 140) and released Fujiwara. Police alone, concluded Kawakami, were not to blame, since the courts as well placed too much value on confessions.[58] "For a procurator to not absolutely censure this kind of crime [i.e., abuse of human rights] caused by police officials," wrote Kawakami, "and to protect his men for petty selfish reasons, is not to defend the Constitution, which is a procurator's life."[59]

One reason prosecution for human rights abuses was a slim 6 percent of Kawakami's sample is simply that officials destroyed evidence and denied wrongdoing. As Justice Minister Shiono said to Tachikawa Taira (Seiyūkai) on February 24, 1937: "In the majority of cases, however, incriminatory evidence has not been discovered." Tachikawa replied that it was "usually difficult to secure evidence in connection with charges of torture against police officials."[60] A situation existed, then, in which both the top law officer and a conservative Diet member were faced by police officials who closed ranks against outsiders, refusing to admit to lawless acts. While each ministry jealously guarded its turf, including in-house documents, some highly placed police officers must have read Kawakami's report. Neither their reaction nor that of justice officials, however, appears in other documents (e.g., the shorthand record of conferences). Therefore, it seems that this highly illuminating document was carefully shelved and forgotten.

An editorial in the *Japan Weekly Chronicle* pointed out that in the February 24, 1937, session of the House of Representatives, police and procuratorial methods were discussed again, "but it is doubtful whether the interpellations in the Diet will have any lasting effect." The main interpellator, said the paper, was Makino Ryōzō (Seiyūkai), who "did not confine his accusations to the police but went on to attack the general method of handling criminal cases. The procuratorial authorities, he pointed out, are not only in the habit of detaining suspects for an unduly long period, but are occasionally known to re-examine the prisoner after he has gone before the preliminary judge. This, of course, is against all the rules of procedure. . . . [O]nce the original examination is closed the procurator has no more to say on the case until the prisoner comes into court for his first trial." That both the procurators and the police abuse their powers, commented the paper, was a matter of common knowledge. Moreover, Home Minister Kawarada Kakichi "admitted the truth of charges of police torture in certain specific cases, and Mr. Shiono . . . could only agree that the examination of suspects takes much too long a time." The commonest abuse of all, said the editorial in agreement with Makino, was holding suspects past the legal time limit. The law "sets very definite limits to these examinations, and also limits the period of detention during which the questioning may take place. The ignoring of these limits was the first breach in the safeguarding of an accused man; the torture now complained of followed when police and procurators were not at once pulled up for exceeding their authority." Police were permitted, said the paper, to hold suspects until sunset the day after an arrest; an easily obtainable procurator's writ could extend that period for ten days; if special circumstances warranted, a suspect could be held longer on a writ by a preliminary judge. "What happens in practice, however, is that the police go through the motions of releasing a prisoner each night, re-arresting him on the spot, and possibly there are not many police stations where it is deemed necessary to play even this little bit of farce."[61]

Bar associations also were concerned about violations of procedural rights and until the outbreak of the Pacific War published reports about such violations. In January 1935, for example, the Imperial Bar Association at a special general meeting selected a committee to investigate the growing number of human rights abuse cases. Information in this shocking report, which was completed by April, was carried in issues of *Seigi* (Justice). One case exposed in the May 1935 *Seigi* involved members of a Nichiren Buddhist group arrested on the grounds of Tsuruoka Hachimangu (Kamakura). The police, who suspected that this group was a terrorist organization, interrogated members at the Hayama Police Station, Kanagawa prefecture. Two young women received especially rough treatment, being stripped, beaten, kicked, and burned (including the removal of pubic hair). This treatment was not unusual, however, since many similar cases were cited in reports done during the 1930s. Moreover, lawyers pointed a finger not only at guilty police and jail guards, but at procurators as well. But from 1937, the China War muted criticism of illegal police actions; and as the wartime crisis deepened, critics became silent.[62] One scholar, while noting that the Imperial Bar Association and the Japan Bar Association issued reports on procedural violations, points out that neither group was willing to sharply criticize the illegal acts of the Tokkō in thought criminal cases. These conservative associations, he feels, were more likely to denounce official abuses when the police targets were important people like those involved in the Teijin affair.[63]

Unequal Justice

Bias in the police profession reflected general attitudes about social ranking and the sacred nature of the emperor system. While high social rank did not ensure proper treatment, upper-class criminal suspects, or those with close ties to the directive elite, were insulated from police brutality. This double standard, which offered more protection to the elite than to the common people and which irritated policemen with proletarian backgrounds, is confirmed by former Tokkō Miyashita Hiroshi. Procurators, for instance, asked for more lenient sentences for university students; and when it came to arresting suspects like Ozaki Hotsumi (the Richard Sorge spy case; see Chapter 6), who had ties with Prime Minister Konoe Fumimaro, Miyashita points out that the surveillance and arrest were done with great circumspection and that no physical violence occurred during interrogations.[64] Miyashita's view is confirmed by the order Home Minister Adachi Kenzō (Hamaguchi cabinet) issued in August 1929 for more merciful treatment for "children of good families."[65] Police and procurators who forgot that the legal system favored the upper classes were forcefully reminded during the Teijin affair trial. "The Minister of Justice recently agreed [Ohara Naoshi in February 1935] with the Diet that confinement and manacling should not be resorted to when men of obvious substance are concerned."[66] An editorial in the *Japan Weekly Chronicle* (January 8, 1931) bluntly noted that normally the application of justice was unequal: "There have not, it is true, been wanting cases where men of some distinction complained bitterly of their treatment at the hands of police and procurators; but as a rule, men of high position find that the wind is tempered to them." The criminal suspects "who suffer severely . . . are mostly fellows who are not regarded as being of any particular importance."[67] Thus, police treatment of lower-class criminal suspects, in both regular and political cases, was less generous; and, for those opposing the *kokutai*, brutality and torture were not unusual, with the procedural rights of unpopular defendants and their lawyers easily disregarded by police during the "Red scare" hysteria.

Politicians in both major parties were more often than not willing to ignore police abuses unless a special nerve was touched (i.e., their own party or person) and not above sacrificing leftists whether moderate or radical.[68] When Representative Matsutani Kōjirō (Nihon Taishūtō) claimed in February 1933 that police atrocities pushed people into the communist ranks and demanded reform of police practices, he was angrily denounced; his remarks were deleted from the stenographic record.[69] Such shortsightedness on the part of the mainstream politicians must have encouraged illegal police actions. The following year, police, in a secret warning to newspapers, forbade the reporting of injuries due to police brutality.[70]

Lumping all rightists into a unified, undifferentiated mass is a serious error, as is lumping all police together, but it is safe to state that generally police were less brutal in confronting rightists than leftists. Matsumoto Manabu, head of the Police Bureau, frankly explained to Diet members in 1933: "We do recognize the importance of controlling the rightwing . . . and we do try to prevent incidents." He went on to explain, however, that rightist thought was unlike communist ideology, "which extremely disturbs the national public peace and brings danger to the nation. . . . The Communist Party is attempting to change the *kokutai*. . . . The rightwing is different in that it supports the *kokutai*." Therefore, he said, rightists did not fall into the category of thought criminals and "as long as they do not use violence to carry out their ideas, I think we cannot say that this is dangerous thought on the same level as that prohibited by the Peace Preservation Law. . . . As I mentioned before, they [rightists] want to reform politics, economics, and society, but basically these ideas are not a danger to the nation, like an attempt to change the *kokutai*. . . . We have been controlling rightwing groups only when they commit a violent action and not because they are rightwing."[71] While police probably manhandled rightist thugs who robbed through intimidation, or brutalized rightists who injured policemen, the sympathetic picture of police treatment in Mishima Yukio's *Runaway Horses* blends truth with fiction. A police inspector interrogating Iinuma Isao, a nineteen-year-old ultranationalist who had planned political assassinations, said: "With patriots like you and your friends, I don't need to worry about the future of Japan. You shouldn't have violated the law, of course, but that shining sincerity of yours is something that even we can understand." Shortly thereafter, the inspector and the protagonist hear the sounds of kendo swords striking upon flesh followed by the groans of the person being tortured. "Yes," says the inspector, "It's a Red. Stubborn ones bring this kind of thing on themselves." Iinuma asks: "Is it because the Reds won't accept our national structure [*kokutai*]?" "That's it. In comparison to them, Iinuma, you and your friends are patriots."[72]

Liberals, who should have staunchly supported the enforcement of the Criminal Procedure Code, were too often insensitive to violations of the procedural rights of leftist political criminal suspects. Professor Minobe Tatsukichi, for example, who for years criticized illegal police actions, was "shaken and somewhat chastened by the evidence of Communist Party activities disclosed by the police campaigns of 1928–1929, and especially by the revelation of the close relationship between the Japanese communists and the Communist International. . . . He conceded that the scope of the conspiracy was alarming."[73] On January 23, 1935, Minobe delivered a maiden House of Peers speech, in which he interpellated Justice Minister Ohara Naoshi about alleged violations of procedural rights (in the Teijin affair). Minobe said: "The speaker has often heard rumours that procuratorial authorities have overstepped the proper limits in arresting persons . . . but he has hitherto been inclined to discount them."[74] What was it about the Teijin affair that prompted Minobe to make the issue of procedural abuses the centerpiece of this speech? One issue, according to Minobe, was that in this case there were facts illustrating violations; an unspoken reason was the high rank of the defendants. Even though Minobe was well known as a harsh critic of the Peace Preservation Law,[75] he had a blind spot when it came to extending full legal protection to the lower classes and communists. Another prominent legal scholar, Makino Eiichi, wrote in a book published in mid-1941: "In the past, when people commented on cases in

violation of the Peace Preservation Law, they said any method
was permitted in order to carry the investigation and prosecution.
Since they were such cases [i.e., special cases] there would be no
criticism for human rights abuses. I do not know how much of this
comment is based on fact; however, I think this sort of thing [i.e.,
lawlessness on the part of the police and procurators] went on up
to a certain level."[76] If Makino, a professor at Tokyo Imperial
University from 1913 to 1938, heard about mistreatment of leftist
criminal suspects, then we can be certain that his colleague
Minobe also knew; his certain knowledge makes one wonder why
the liberal legalists did not press harder on the issue of procedural
rights for communists. One reason is that Minobe and Makino
shared their colleagues' loathing of communism. Indeed, writes
one scholar, "[h]ardly anyone in the university system was prepared to make a full-scale defense of avowed Marxists as such."[77]
Another reason, of course, was the general erosion of the liberal
position after 1931, in both the political and academic worlds,
with most people moving along with the trend of the times. There
is, however, another factor to consider: most politicians and academics instinctively rallied around the emotional slogans supporting the emperor system. Thus, academics like Minobe and
Makino and members of the bar associations, whatever the legal
part of their brains might tell them, instinctively were not much
concerned about procedural rights for those who repudiated the
kokutai.

Conclusion

It is indisputable that police violated time limits for holding suspects and sometimes used illegal methods, including torture, to
force confessions. These violations were not new in the 1930s but
were a continuation of lawless practices rooted in the Meiji period.
Furthermore, these illegal practices were common knowledge,
with highly placed Home and Justice Ministry officials time and
again ordering them stopped. Thus, a picture emerges of a police
force operating by its own set of very special rules and even disre-
garding direct orders from its leadership. This is the milieu with
which Tokkō Miyashita Hiroshi identified. To this customary
method of handling criminal suspects, the Tokkō, as the elect force
designated to save Japan from the "Reds," added its own set of
"laws" for handling ideological suspects (as we saw in Chapters 2

and 3). Moreover, in light of the police environment in which the Tokkō operated and its feeling that only its shield protected Japan from the "Red tide," the logical outcome was a mistreatment of ideological criminal suspects.

Former Tokkō Miyashita Hiroshi, who served for many years on the Metropolitan Police Board, was by 1943 head of the Tokkō headquarters in Toyama prefecture. In a postwar interview, he said that police had a long tradition of hitting difficult suspects during interrogation. It was, in fact, a police "custom." Indeed, the so-called detectives' room was synonymous with violence. He remarked that soon after he joined the elite force (1929), he inquired of a old-timer if it was all right to treat ideological suspects so violently. The reply suggested that such a question was foolish. Asked if Tokkō violence was not more intense than the traditional police brutality of the detectives' room, Miyashita replied that after all they were facing communists who were engaged in an illegal movement. For such people there were no second thoughts about illegal detention and physical violence.[78] As for torture, Miyashita said: "I will not deny that some people used torture."[79] Itō Takashi, who interviewed Miyashita, concluded that "in not a few cases torture occurred. . . . There was quite a bit of difference, however, based on the individual Tokkō, the geographical location, and the period."[80]

Since policemen viewed the *kokutai* as the essence of morality, they felt free to act in the emperor's name unbound by any other moral code. Therefore, what most determined police action "was neither an abstract consciousness of legality nor an internal sense of right and wrong, nor again a concept of serving the public; it was a feeling of being close to the concrete entity known as the Emperor. . . . [Police came] to identify their own interests with those of the Emperor and . . . automatically . . . [saw] their enemies as violators of the Emperor's powers." Given this attitude, policemen violated the Criminal Procedure Code because they saw law "simply as a concrete weapon of control operating in the hierarchy of authority of which the Emperor was head." Moreover, the equating of morality with power resulted in what Maruyama Masao calls "the transfer of oppression." Using the bad treatment of Allied prisoners of war as an example, he writes that camp guards felt they were helping prisoners, but "at the very same time they were beating and kicking them. Acts of benevolence could coexist with atrocities."[81] Kobayashi Takiji's account of the March 15, 1928, arrest reflects this police mind-set. After hours of brutality and torture, police extended the hand of benevolence, ordering food and eating with the suspects. While the educated elite understood that the emperor system was based on myths perpetuated by the post-1868 state, most policemen were not part of that elite: through 1928 about three-quarters of police recruits had only a primary school education; in 1933 this figure was one-half (most Tokkō officers, however, had graduated from middle school).[82] Therefore, police attitudes reflected the state's ideological propaganda, which stressed the image of an absolute emperor who represented an ancient, unbroken imperial line; policemen who served the Tenshisama (Son of Heaven) regarded their duty to protect the kokutai as a form of religious devotion. Seen in this light, brutal treatment of regular criminal suspects, if they refused to cooperate by confessing, or torture of those who repudiated the kokutai was of little consequence.

To the ideological motivations for illegal police actions, add the Tokugawa legacy of suppression, which was reenforced by the paternalistic authoritarianism of those who built the modern police force (see Chapter 1). Judge Kawakami Kan attributed numerous cases of illegal police actions not only to a lack of education and training, but also to an attitude of arrogance and contempt that was a "remnant of feudalism."[83] This view that the police mentalité was little changed is supported by Railway Minister Egi Tasuku (Hamaguchi cabinet), a former justice minister: "Taken individually, policemen are all good men. But directly they join the force, they recede back [sic] not thirty years but sixty years and develop the characteristics of police detectives in those backward days."[84] Police fixation on confession, which Judge Kawakami detected in a majority of human rights abuse cases, was another feudal remnant. Police and procurators expected suspects to confess and to ask for mercy, and the courts encouraged them by placing undue emphasis on the suspects' acknowledgment of guilt. Kawakami believed that the police tradition of forcing confessions could be broken if police were trained in modern, scientific investigatory methods and if each prefecture had a special indentification department. Unfortunately, the justice system had neither the funds nor the personnel for such training and such sections.[85] Thus, the police tradition of brutality and torture was not broken; in fact, the application of the conversion solution for thought criminal cases encouraged police to labor harder to force confessions.

Finally, it should be noted that a 1930 Communist Party decision to switch to armed action, which resulted in the death of policemen, probably contributed to provoking more police violence against communist suspects. Up to December 1934, there were thirty-three incidents (three officers killed and thirty injured) involving the use of pistols, daggers, and other weapons. Most of the incidents occurred in 1930 and 1931 (twenty-five in the former year and three in the latter), and most were in Tokyo and Osaka (fifteen in the former city and five in the latter). In 1930, pistols were involved in six incidents and daggers in ten; in 1931 it was two pistols and one dagger. There were only two incidents in 1932, but pistols figure in both. Furthermore, between March 1928 and May 1933, police seized one hundred handguns from communist suspects.[86] Perhaps a police perception of communists armed with pistols against police usually without sidearms contributed to the "especially brutal" handling of suspects in 1932–1933.[87] While any killing of a policeman was shocking, death by shooting doubtless angered officers dealing with the radical left.

5

Tightening the Vise

PROLONGED FIGHTING in China, coupled with a steady drift toward the Pacific War, was the background against which suspected violators of the peace law were judged. A hardening attitude of justice officials reflects the heightened concern over national defense. At the May 1940 meeting of the Criminal Affairs Bureau, for example, Akiyama Kaname, conference chairman and head of the bureau, noted that a revised peace law was sorely needed to cope with the unconverted communists due for release in 1941.[1] Procurator Yoshioka Noboru, Sendai District Court, argued: "Because of the need to keep certain people in prison for a long period, we should stop completely all discussion of their human rights."[2] Procurator Masaki Ryō, Hiroshima Appeals Court, urged the establishment of a political police directly under the control of procurators along the lines of the GPU (USSR secret police) or the Gestapo.[3] The government's tougher stance was also reflected in the expanding role of Military Police, who considered anything that might endanger the war effort within their jurisdiction. By 1940 civilians feared not only Tokkō, but Military Police as well, because the latter had established a special section to act as an anticommunist watchdog. Prime Minister Tōjō Hideki, who had a special relationship with the Military Police, appointed friends to key positions and used that organization as a secret police. Civil police, too, redoubled efforts to uncover any remaining communist cells and to unify national thought along approved lines.[4] Communists, said a textbook published in 1941 for Tokkō and other police, were like "evil weeds," which officers had a duty to "kill." Furthermore, the book stressed that the first obligation of the people was to support the throne; "individual rights and freedom cannot be considered."[5] The government, pressured by the expanding war, took extraordinary steps to destroy communists and stop the spread of dangerous thoughts. In February 1941, for example, authorities suppressed the liberal haiku movement, arresting people like Kuribayashi Nobuo and Shimada Seihō. Poets who wrote of chrysanthemums dared not mention death, because authorities equated this flower with the imperial family. Red flowers were also taboo.[6]

The New Peace Preservation Law

Justice officials repeatedly sought to revise the peace law during the 1930s, but it was not until protracted warfare in China silenced Diet critics that the law bill was accepted. Actually, revision does not describe this sixty-five-article law (No. 54), which went into force on May 15, 1941. Indeed, the 1925 version, when compared, looks like a first draft. Part 1 of the law enlarged the definition of illegal activities, aiming at preventing communists from finding cover in legal organizations. The expanded definition included political activities by religious groups. Part 2 widely enlarged procurators' powers to arrest and detain criminal suspects. Procurators were authorized to issue warrants of detention good for two months; this period could be extended to one year with the permission of the head procurator of the court in question. Trials for thought offenders were shortened (the appeals courts were omitted), and lawyers, limited to two, were to be drawn from a pool created by the justice minister. Part 3 concerned preventive detention *(yobō kōkin)* for unconverted thought offenders. This was aimed at people who could not be handled by the protection and supervision system and at die-hards such as convicts Tokuda and Shiga.[7]

Justice officials hoped that preventive detention properly managed would substantially reduce the number of recalcitrant thought offenders. At a May 1940 conference, Procurator Masaki Ryō, who had researched this subject, pointed out that foreign thought criminals had iron wills which made reform nearly impossible; in contrast, Japanese, who were descended from the same ancient blood line, were all amenable to reform. Evil foreign ideologies, he emphasized, could not totally pollute a blood line more than three thousand years old![8] Motivated by such optimism the Justice Ministry began renovating part of Toyotama Prison (Tokyo) in 1941, planning a maximum capacity of two hundred inmates.[9] Internees in the facility would receive a special education program designed to bring out their latent Japaneseness.

The Justice Ministry, on May 14, 1941, issued *Yobō Kōkin Tetsuzuki Rei* (Procedural Ordinance for Preventive Detention), No. 49. Article 1 of this ordinance ordered procurators to interrogate anyone they considered a good candidate for detention or to request another procurator or justice policeman to do so. Article 2 instructed prison wardens and heads of protection and supervision centers to inform procurators about people needing such attention.[10] Procurators requested that the appropriate district court decide each case in which preventive detention was requested. The court would hear the defendant (no lawyers were allowed) and also confer with a seven-person Preventive Detention Committee. Sentences were for two-year terms, which could be renewed. Release depended upon the degree of progress made toward conversion, as assessed by the head of the detention center. Early release was also provided.[11] At a Thought Investigation and Prosecution Conference held at the Nagasaki Appeals Court in late November 1941, Chief Procurator Tokunaga Eiichi stressed the need to find communists hidden in rightist groups or other legal organizations. The new preventive detention system, he pointed out, was not only for unconverted people, but also was for converts who faltered in supporting the *kokutai*. In doubtful cases, he said, it would be better to overuse rather than to underuse the preventive detention system.[12]

Sixty-five inmates were in the Tokyo Preventive Detention Center during the program's lifetime. Fifty-three of these were labeled communists; six were Korean labor activists or fighters for independence; four were connected with the Tenri religion; one was a proletarian labor leader; and one was a female member of the Jehovah's Witnesses. The sixty-five inmates came from prisons or protection and supervision centers (twenty-one who had served their full sentences from the former and forty-four from the latter). Of the sixty-five, only three left early: the communist Fukumoto Kazuo (after four months); the communist Nagae Jinsei (after eight months); and the woman, who was transferred to Tochigi Women's Prison. Some inmates met the high standards for conversion and "graduated" after serving the two-year term; they were then absorbed into various local protection and supervision centers. At the end of June 1945, in an attempt to escape bombing raids, the center was transferred to Fuchū Prison outside Tokyo.[13]

Tsuchiya Shukurō, who arrived at the center in late December 1941 and remained until after Japan's defeat, was a veteran of jails and prisons from 1933, including Kushiro in Hokkaido. Tsuchiya was favorably impressed by the new center: a solid red brick building with white walls and ceilings inside and two rooms per prisoner (one floored with wood and the other with tatami). This facility, writes Tsuchiya, had none of the darkness of a regular prison, since each cell unit had two windows. Most of the time all doors remained unlocked. Moreover, although each door had a peephole, prisoners could see the face looking in, which relieved Tsuchiya, since at Kushiro the peephole was one-way from the outside, and he continually felt spied upon. The view from his second-floor windows took in the prisoners' exercise yard, a wall about twelve feet high, and several trees. Another pleasant surprise was the bedding, which, for a change, was neither too thin nor too short. Furthermore, prisoners wore a choke-collar style uniform instead of the standard red one. At other prisons similar uniforms were worn only by trustees or prisoners who went outside the walls to work. Winter- and summer-weight kimono were supplied as well plus a *haori* (kimono jacket) and a *hakama* (a divided skirt for men's formal wear).[14]

Matsumoto Kazumi, another inmate, writes that the education program centered on *Kokutai no hongi* (Fundamentals of our *kokutai*) and other approved books. Speakers included philosophers, Buddhist priests, heads of protection and supervision centers, thought procurators, and other justice officials. Among the lectures Matsumoto heard, none mentioned communism and none was especially forceful in promoting the imperial system. One vividly recalled was by a thought procurator recently returned from Germany, where he visited a forced labor camp for thousands of communists. The procurator noted that brutal terror was used to enforce orders. The audience needed no explanation to understand this message. According to Matsumoto, the third director of the center was Yamada Noboru, a former thought procurator, who took over sometime in 1944. Yamada, whose attitude was totally different from the attitudes of the two former directors, agreed to many of the prisoners' requests. For example, additional fire-fighting equipment was purchased, and the number of air raid shelters was expanded. Also, when the move was made from Toyotama to Fuchū, Matsumoto spotted books by Marx, Engles, Lenin, and Stalin among the director's possessions; the director gave him about twenty volumes, after pledging him to secrecy. Matsumoto suspected that the war must be going badly. Another approved request was for the release of Tokuda and Shiga from nearly three years of solitary confinement. Prisoners did worry about the Military Police, who came to guard the prison area during each bombing raid. Yamada sought to allay their fears, instructing them to stick close to him in an orderly fashion and promising to lead them to safety. At the war's end, there were sixteen prisoners: one Korean nationalist, one inmate who belonged to a religious group, and fourteen communists.[15]

Pulling "Evil Weeds"

Haunted by the ghost of the Communist Party but frustrated by a shortage of communists, the Tokkō, with the aid of procurators, was not above inventing communists. The best remembered criminal case of this kind was the Yokohama Incident (which began in 1942), during which forty-nine people were arrested; six died from torture and prison conditions. This case began during routine police interrogation of Japanese internees repatriated from the United States. One of these people told of a Kawada who had returned. Kawada Hiroshi and his wife Sadako were already on a police list, because in January 1941 customs officials discovered socialist materials in their possession. Thus, police concluded that Kawada, who had studied labor problems in America, was planning to rebuild the Communist Party. The couple were arrested on September 11, 1942. Three days later Hosokawa Karoku was arrested on suspicion that *Sekai shi no dōkō to Nihon* (The trend of world history and Japan), which was published in the August and September issues of *Kaizō,* propagandized communism. The two cases came together after authorities discovered a photograph taken in July 1942 of Hosokawa and several journalists from *Kaizō* and *Chūō Kōron* at a gathering to celebrate a large royalty check Hosokawa had received. Unfortunately for those involved, several people in the photograph had had contact with Kawada Hiroshi. Perhaps an old hand in the police recalled the famous Goshiki Hot

Spring meeting in December 1926, at which the defunct Communist Party made plans to reorganize, and decided that the group in the photo planned to do the same. At any rate, one interrogation led to another, as Kanagawa prefecture Tokkō tried to build a case. Torture was freely applied. The Kawadas were interrogated with a fire poker, a sharp pointed umbrella, a rope, bamboo swords, and a five-foot cudgel, with which the wife was sexually abused. Other suspects were beaten on the thighs with bamboo staves, hit, kicked, burned, stepped on, tossed around, and so on. All except Hosokawa Karoku signed confessions.[16] The interrogators yelled such epithets as "It is all right to kill you people! Look at Kobayashi Takiji!"[17] Even material witnesses were badly abused. President Shimanaka Yūsaku, *Chūō Kōron,* was hit and spat upon, as Tokkō insisted that he admit that all the editorial staff were communists.[18] Aikawa Hiroshi, a journalist drawn into this affair on May 26, 1943, and interrogated until September 15 in the Tsurumi Police Station, said that many parts of the memoir *(shuki)* he signed were written by the interrogators. As Tokkō Matsushita Eitarō, Morikawa Seizō, and Hirahata tortured him, they wrote out parts of what became the final statement and forced Aikawa to sign.[19] Statements signed by other suspects were undoubtedly extracted in a similar fashion.

Miyashita Hiroshi, chief of the Toyama prefecture Tokkō, heard about the so-called Yokohama Incident from a former colleague at the Metropolitan Police Board. When asked about it by another officer, Miyashita replied that he simply could not imagine the people on the list of suspects rebuilding the Communist Party. All in all, he felt that the Metropolitan Police Board viewed negatively the proof produced by the Kanagawa prefecture Tokkō.[20]

There were, of course, less spectacular episodes of police brutality and torture during the war years. On March 31, 1942, Hayase Masayuki was arrested in Nagoya and held in three different police stations until September. Although Hayase was not a communist, police felt he was not supporting the war effort. Besides being suspended by a rope, he was burned, hit, and given a water treatment. The following October, Professor Kawamura Taku, who worked for the Hokkaido Agricultural Research Center, was arrested for suggesting that one way to solve the labor shortage would be to form farm cooperatives. Local officials thought this sounded communistic. Police beat his thighs to force a confession. The sentence was four years in prison.[21] One bizarre torture case was exposed by the persistent efforts of lawyer Masaki Hiroshi. Masaki, well known as a nonconformist unafraid of offending officials, was asked by a coal mine owner to locate a missing employee. Masaki learned in January 1944 that the man had been arrested and tortured to death by police in Ibaraki prefecture. He located the grave, cut off the corpse's head, and carried it back to Tokyo, where Professor Furuhata Tanemoto, an expert on forensic medicine, confirmed that the man had died of head wounds. Masaki brought suit against the policeman in charge of the interrogation, but at the trial the officer was acquitted.[22] Miki Kiyoshi, the eminent Marxist philosopher, was arrested for a peace law violation on March 28, 1945, and died in Toyotama Prison on September 26. This sad case began with a jail escape on March 6 by Takakura Teru, who turned to Miki and Yamazaki Ken for clothes and a place to stay. When police seized the fugitive communist they discovered Miki's name sewn into his suit. Miki succumbed to malnutrition, nephritis, and scabies.[23] Nakaishi Mitsuhiro, who was in Toyotama Prison where Miki died, wrote that scabies was widespread at that time (i.e., in both jails and prisons).[24]

Perhaps Miki welcomed death, since scabies, which is caused by a parasitic mite burrowing under the skin to deposit eggs, causes intense itching. This terrible skin condition appears to have been widespread among criminal suspects, who lived in filthy jail conditions and who commonly went for eight or ten months without a bath. Wakatsuki Shigeru, arrested on January 29, 1944, spent eight months in the Tobe Police Station in Yokohama without taking a bath. Eventually, scabies covered his entire body. Interrogators, worried about catching this loathsome disease, were careful to wear gloves![25] That scabies was not a product of extreme conditions during the war years is illustrated by the comments of Sano Hidehiko (imprisoned 1930–1932). The disease, he said, was picked up in jail. Together with other sufferers he took medicated baths once he reached Toyotama Prison, but some prisoners died (see "Prison," Chapter 3).

Wartime Justice

Despite the highly nationalistic atmosphere created by prolonged war in China and the Pacific War, the integrity of the legal system was maintained. Overzealous police and procurators ignored the law, but the court system continued to function, even for suspected peace law violators. This fact does not imply, however, that supercharged patriotism had no impact on legal thinkers and practitioners. Indeed, most of them moved along with the current of the times. Professor Miyazawa Toshiyoshi, who replaced Minobe Tatsukichi at Tokyo Imperial University, provides a good example. By 1944 Miyazawa's legal thought accepted the notion that all law was based on the *kokutai* and that it was permissible for the state to break the law. In short, he supported the extraordinary wartime measures.[26] Another example of a change in thinking brought on by wartime pressures is that of the distinguished legal scholar Makino Eiichi. In 1936 Makino criticized the government's plans for the preventive detention system, saying that it was wrong to place people under this system after they had completed a prison sentence. By 1941 he had turned 180 degrees, citing the emergency brought on by war.[27] As for practitioners, conferences of justice officials in charge of thought often discussed the need to read new social conditions into old law. Nonetheless, the wheels of justice continued to turn throughout the wartime period.

The arrest and trial of Yamakawa Hitoshi is a good example of the judicial process at work. Yamakawa was arrested late in 1937 as part of the crackdown on the Popular Front Movement. With the preliminary examination completed on December 28, 1939, the district court trial began on December 18, 1940. It appears that no effort was made to speed up the judicial process, because the case was still in the appeals stage in late 1944 and not decided by the Supreme Court until November 1945. Yamakawa, then, had his full day in court, where he was represented by the experienced attorney Unno Shinkichi. According to Unno's biographer, this case was the springboard for Unno to become the outstanding lawyer for "thought" trials. Moreover, since Unno was well known as a highly skilled professional without an ideological axe to grind, he inspired confidence in both the defendants and the courts. "This is a peculiar thing," writes his biographer, "but during the wartime under that kind of suppression this trust was of the highest value."[28] Unno, therefore, from the viewpoint of authorities was useful for two reasons: he could be counted upon to observe court regulations and the law, and his presence would render verdicts more acceptable to the general public. Unno, no doubt, viewed the situation differently, seeing in each trial a situation in which a strong effort must be made to save the defendant. Among legalists Unno's painstaking preparation and attention to detail were well known.[29]

The Justice Ministry reinterpreted Article 1 of the peace law to use it against defendants like Yamakawa Hitoshi and others in the Labor-Farmer faction. By stretching the law's meaning, procurators tried to prove that Yamakawa and his colleagues were part of an "organization" dedicated to overturning the *kokutai* and repudiating private property. The preliminary examination judge rubber-stamped this argument. Unno countered by pointing to the history of the Labor-Farmer faction. Yamakawaism, he noted, was in direct conflict with Fukumotoism, which advocated changing the *kokutai* and repudiating private property. Yamakawaism, therefore, merely aimed at reforming abuse in the capitalistic system. Moreover, Marxism was not illegal, and Yamakawa's ideas had been in print for many years. Furthermore, the Labor-Farmer faction was simply a loose collection of intellectuals and not an organization as defined by the peace law. Finally, Unno asked why, if the group was illegal and the publications of Yamakawa were illegal, the government had not indicted him many years earlier. Obviously, he concluded, Yamakawa and the others were not guilty.[30]

Unno had a persuasive argument. By the mid-1920s Yamakawa had repudiated Comintern tactics, since there was simply no place in Japan for an illegal Communist Party. What was needed, he felt, was the development of labor unions, farmer unions, and student associations that together would form the basis for a legal proletarian party. Fukumotoism, which emphasized theory over practical means, repudiated Yamakawaism, viewing it as a compromise between unionism and socialism. In fact, much of Fukumoto Kazuo's energy was spent on attacking Yamakawa.[31]

The prosecution asked for a seven-year sentence on July 11, 1941. The verdict, given on September 21, was five years imprisonment (one hundred days of jail time to be subtracted). At the Appeals Court, Unno requested that chief Judge Miyamoto Masuzō obtain expert opinion on the difference between Fukumotoism and Yamakawaism. Former Kyoto Imperial University Professor Kawakami Hajime was chosen, but since he was ill the judges, procurators, and Unno went to Kyoto. Fukumotoism, opined Kawakami, supported the position of the Japanese Communist Party. The verdict, given on September 25, 1944, was three years' imprisonment (minus one hundred days). On November 7, 1945, the Supreme Court announced that it would not review the sentence.[32]

As was noted in the mass trial of communists in the early 1930s, it was not unusual for trial judges to impose lesser sentences than requested by procurators, so in that sense this case was "normal"; however, this trial's progress through the courts during the Pacific War must have strained the fair-mindedness of the most impartial judges. Also, Judge Miyamoto's acceptance of Unno's request for expert opinion, while not unusual in itself, moved beyond the normal when Kawakami was chosen and the court traveled to Kyoto, since Kawakami had been imprisoned as a communist during the mid-1930s. And last, the two-year decrease in sentence suggests a court not fully convinced by the prosecution argument. This trial is in many respects typical of wartime "thought" cases.

The trial of the "Professors' Group" is enlightening in regard to police practices and illustrates again that judges during the war years were not controlled by procurators and the Justice Ministry. In the face of the Comintern's call for communists to make common cause with legal organizations, the Justice Ministry, which was anxious to extend the scope of the peace law anyway, decided to indict selected Marxists (see "Expanding the Peace Law Net," Chapter 3).

One of the thirty-eight professors arrested on February 1, 1938, Minobe Ryōkichi, writes that both he and Professor Ōuchi Hyōe were asked politely by police to come along voluntarily for questioning. Arresting officers did not have warrants (not having warrants seems to have been a police custom except when procurators or judges were leading a police team). Ōuchi refused to cooperate in this illegal procedure, but after an hour's debate with officers and the arrival of more policemen equipped with a net, Ōuchi went along. While Minobe gave in sooner, he did protest this lawless act. Neither professor experienced physical torture, but their psychological stress was extreme. Procurators, for instance, if not satisfied with Minobe's answers, would simply return him to jail for five to seven days and then resume their questioning. Undoubtedly, this tactic of playing on the growing fear of suspects, coupled with unpleasant jail conditions, did produce confessions in many cases. Professor Minami Kinji, Hōsei University, survived the harsh jail conditions, but died soon after being released on bail. The authorities treated Minami badly in other ways, too: no bath was allowed for more than ten months, and requests for a doctor went unanswered. With the completion of the preliminary examination in July 1939, Minobe was released on bail, after one and one-half years in jail. The first trial began in May 1942; the verdict was given on September 28: all defendants not guilty except Arisawa Hiromi (two years imprisonment and three years on probation) and Abe Isamu (the same term). Both the prosecution and the defense took the case to the Appeals Court. At the second trial, which began in June 1943, all defendants were found not guilty.[33] Justice Ministry officials must have been extremely unhappy, since so much effort and publicity had gone into this case.

The prosecution of followers of the Ōmoto religion provides another example of the continuing integrity of the legal system during wartime. However, it also provides examples of police brutality and torture. This popular religious group was crushed in the government's drive to smash so-called evil cults. The prosecution in this case used unsuccessfully the 1928 peace law, which was designed for use against leftist groups.

Arrests of Ōmoto leaders and members began on December 8, 1935, and continued throughout the following year, by the end of which three thousand people had been interrogated. At least one person under torture died, and several were hospitalized. Patriarch Deguchi Onisaburō signed a confession, as did many others (these documents were repudiated in open court). On March 1, 1936, the preliminary examination commenced, and on October 3 sixty-one defendants were formally charged; the leadership was accused with plotting to overturn the *kokutai*. The Kyoto District Court trial went on from August 10, 1938, to February 19, 1940. Deguchi was sentenced to from five years to life. The Osaka Appeals Court, which handled the case from October 16, 1940, to July 23, 1942, overturned the lower court's decision, ruling that the peace law did not apply. Consequently, charges against forty-one defendants were dropped and the others, found guilty of lèse majesté offenses, were freed. Deguchi and his wife were released on bond while an appeal motion was made to the Supreme Court. The motion was accepted on January 10 and the decision issued on September 8, 1945. The lesè majesté conviction stood, but on a reduced number of counts.[34]

While the lower court's stiff sentence for Deguchi must have pleased the prosecution and the Justice Ministry, the refusal of the Appeals Court to uphold the government's attempt to stretch the peace law illustrates three judges of independent mind. Moreover, the highest court, while it upheld the Appeals Court ruling, did reduce the number of counts. Here, then, is another example of judges refusing to be bullied by procurators.

There was erosion of judicial independence during the period between 1933 and 1945, especially in connection with trials involving rightists who claimed to kill in defense of the *kokutai*. Some scholars point to the trial of the Ketsumeidan (Blood Pact Group) as a turning point, since it was during this trial that savage rightist propaganda drove the chief judge off the bench and forced the Justice Ministry to replace him with a judge more to the defendants' liking.[35] Judges in this trial, as in others involving rightists, found themselves, along with the legal system, being "tried" in their own courtrooms by the lawyers and suspects lined up below them. When the assassins of Prime Minister Inukai Tsuyoshi (the May 15 Incident), came to trial, one defense attorney, after first attacking the proclivity of judicial authorities toward Western judicial theories, declared that the nation was more important than the law. Therefore, since the defendants acted to protect the nation, they should be freed.[36] The courts' continued withdrawal in the face of rightist pressure is also well illustrated by the trial of civilians involved in the Shinpeitai Jiken (Divine Soldiers Incident). Police apprehended the conspirators on July 10, 1933, just one day before their plan to liquidate the entire cabinet and replace it with a military government. At first the procurators saw this as an armed rebellion, and the trial was moved to the Supreme Court, but the Justice Ministry's zeal to push this case lagged as the public attack upon Professor Minobe Tatsukichi's Organ Theory heightened. Supreme Court judges attempted to duck this problem, but the defendants' lawyers made it the centerpiece of the trial, quizzing the judges and procurators about their personal views on the *kokutai*. By the end of this long trial (completed on March 15, 1941), the court was willing to accept the defendants' argument that they acted from pure motives in order to save the nation from corrupt politicians under the influence of the defunct Organ Theory. The defendants received short prison terms, with immediate remission of sentence.[37] The *Japan Times* viewed this judgment as "a triumph of law in Japan and a brilliant piece of political adjustment."[38]

Despite some adjustment of law to fit the times, judges did feel they were independent and were determined to protect their courts from interference. Vice-Minister of Justice Miyake Shō-tarō, speaking on the eve of the Pacific War, warned judges about following Professor Makino Eiichi's flexible interpretation of the law. In brief, Miyake was telling judges that they must protect the independence of the bench from the influence of the military and from civilian rightist pressure.[39] Nevertheless, government pressure on the courts continued. In February 1944, Prime Minister Tōjō Hideki and Justice Minister Iwamura Michio called on judges to aid the war effort with harsher sentences. Judge Hosono Nagayo, Hiroshima Appeals Court, said that this request violated judicial independence; Judge Okai Tōshirō, Yokohama, urged Tōjō to resign.[40] This attitude ensured defendants in so-called thought cases some hope of a fair trial.

Even the new peace law, which extended the powers of procurators, evinced concern for the procedural rights of people under investigation. The system of preventive detention, for example, worried people who were concerned over human rights abuses. Hence, seven-member committees were appointed to act as watchdogs in the application of the law.[41] This matter of protecting procedural rights also came up at a conference in July 1941. Judge Nagao Misao, Tokyo District Court, said that since one purpose of law was to protect human rights, judges should be in a position to determine whether a proposed arrest was reasonable. Therefore, he urged procurators to prepare a document in which the purpose of the arrest was clearly outlined and attach it to the arrest warrant.[42] Furthermore, justice officials not only did battle with the police but even took on Prime Minister Tōjō over matters of constitutional and procedural rights. Tōjō, worried about the activities of extreme rightists, instigated the arrest of Diet members Nakano Seigō and Mitamura Takeo. On October 25, 1943, when police asked Judge Kobayashi Kenji to extend their arrest period, he refused, citing the fact that the extraordinary Diet session was scheduled to open the next day. Article 53 of the constitution, Kobayashi said, made it mandatory that they be freed to attend the session.[43] Procurator General Matsuzaka Hiromasa, angry about these arrests, had a harsh confrontation with Tōjō.

The prime minister ordered Matsuzaka and Justice Minister Iwamura to silence Nakano one way or the other. Matsuzaka, who accused police of deliberately waiting until he was out of Tokyo on an official business trip, refused to take illegal action. He told Tōjō: "About the arrest, the procurator bureau was not anxious to do it from the beginning. Not only this time, but also in the prior arrest of Diet member Mitamura, who was arrested in violation of the Publication Law, the procurator bureau's thought section was against it."[44]

Courts continued to maintain a scrupulous regard for the letter of the law. Tsuda Sōkichi, the distinguished scholar of ancient Japan, was loudly attacked by rightists, who wanted his books prohibited. Eventually, this tactic worked, and in February 1940 four books were prohibited for sale or distribution. Authorities, however, were not content with an administrative punishment, so in March he was charged with lesè majesté (violation of Article 26 of the Publication Law). The Tokyo District Court trial (November 1, 1941, to May 21, 1942) sentenced Tsuda to three months in prison, with a stay of execution for two years. Both sides appealed the case, but somehow the court did not review the case within the one-year prescribed time (a violation of Article 33 of the Publication Law). Because of this mistake, charges were dropped.[45]

Conclusion

One scholar sees torture used during interrogations as a special characteristic of the Yokohama Incident; a research group agrees, but adds that the torture was induced by a kind of "paranoia."[46] Torture certainly played a major part in the manufacturing of criminal charges against the suspects, but its use was not a novelty. The label of "paranoia," which implies a mental disorder and abnormal reactions to surroundings, also distorts the situation. Actually, the Yokohama Incident was the logical outcome of the state's long-term policy toward leftist dissidents and the fruit of Home Ministry superiors consistently allowing Tokkō to operate outside legal norms. The only important difference between this incident and earlier ones was that animosity toward "Reds" increased with military reverses from late 1942. Members of the directive elite were caught up in the same anticommunist obsession as the Kanagawa prefecture Tokkō, which was a result of the state's all-too-successful anticommunist campaign. Indeed, Prince

Konoe Fumimaro and others, from early 1943, saw "Reds" in the background of Prime Minister Tōjō's plan for a centrally coordinated war effort. The following year in July at a conference of senior statesmen, Konoe acknowledged that defeat would be terrible but declared that a leftist revolution would be much worse. "Defeat is temporary and can be redressed, but if we have a leftist revolution, *kokutai* and everything will be gone to the winds. Thus, the most profound attention concerning leftist revolution is necessary. It is not only those who operate openly on the surface who are left-wing."[47] In an imperial audience in February 1945, Konoe directed the emperor's attention to the danger of communist revolution.[48]

Under wartime pressures procedural rights for criminal suspects and prisoners decreased. In fact, this bleak situation makes the action by lawyer Masaki Hiroshi to obtain justice for a murdered coal miner stand out as a singular event. Examples of brutality and torture, however, must not lure the historian into the trap of oversimplification, because the response of law enforcement officials was complex. Therefore, views such as the following must not be taken unreservedly as truth: "During the air raids the warders would sometimes unlock the doors of the cells of ordinary prisoners, but political prisoners were not granted that privilege and many of them perished in their cells."[49] It is doubtful that this statement is based on a close survey of conditions in more than fifty prisons and one hundred branches. One example of a different situation, of course, is also insufficient, but it does help restore perspective. The state's most worrisome political criminals were held in the Tokyo Preventive Detention Center in a section of Toyotama Prison until near the war's end, when they were moved to Fuchū Prison to escape the air raids. These unconverted communists were not kept locked in cells during air raids. Moreover, Director Yamada Noboru permitted inmates to dig a number of small shelters to supplement the large air raid shelter. Furthermore, he purchased a hand pump with which to fight fires. When the center caught fire during the air raid on the night of May 25, 1945, Tokuda Kyūichi led prisoners in fighting the blaze. It is reasonable to suppose that this information is accurate, since it is based on a postwar memoir by former prisoner Matsumoto Kazumi, who would hardly whitewash actions by authorities.[50]

6

Conclusion

THIS STUDY of the treatment of political criminal suspects concludes that their procedural rights were as often violated as they
were protected. These long-term and widespread violations of
procedural rights, including the rights of regular criminals, under-
mine the thesis that rule-by-law fully operated in pre-1945 Japan.
Ironically, the harsh revision of the peace law in 1941, which legal-
ized some previously illegal actions, brought the state one step
closer to rule-by-law.

The most serious procedural violations were committed by
police, with procurators and preliminary judges abetting illegal
actions by looking the other way. Procurator Abe Haruo sums it
up neatly: "In effect the blueprint of the machinery of criminal
justice under the new system [the Meiji Constitution and the various codes] was fairly satisfactory. Unfortunately, the application of
that machinery took an altogether different course from what had
been intended. The practice of forcing confession became rather
common among police; prisoners were often kept incommuni-
cado; the preliminary examination, which was kept secret from
the public, became a sort of Star Chamber Affair."[1] As demonstrated, the pattern of police-people relations inherited from Tokugawa and reinforced by Meiji practices was not amenable to
change despite repeated exhortations by Justice and Home Ministry officials and other high authorities. The police, who were
alienated from the people, simply refused to change their ways.
Two articles appearing on the same page of a newspaper in 1932
vividly illustrate the problem and the dilemma faced by the state:

rule-by-law in theory versus rule-by-illegal-police-actions in fact. Wakatsuki Reijirō, former prime minister and head of the Min-seitō, said at a meeting of party officials: "Some big nations have taken to despotic rule in recent years, and administration in these countries is marked by espionage and repression. Nothing presents a more pitiable sight than a nation deprived of freedom. The Japanese people are fortunately in full enjoyment of freedom as a constitutionally governed people."[2] The other article is about a policeman who beat a Korean to death with a wooden sword because the officer was dissatisfied with answers to his questions about two fugitives.[3]

Justice officials, too, broke procedural rules, as demonstrated in the Teijin affair, the secret report by Kawakami Kan, and numerous admissions by various officials. Certainly, the breaking of the law by these men of the law was several degrees more serious than illegal actions by low-ranking policemen. Preliminary judges, as Kokuryō aptly noted at the Tokyo trial of communists, remained silent as they looked at the bruised faces and broken heads of criminal suspects lined up below them. Unno Shinkichi, a defense lawyer in the Yokohama Incident, privately excoriated the preliminary judges for not criticizing police and procurators.[4]

On the positive side, prison conditions improved dramatically after 1900, and although examples of brutality and torture appear, the situation was not comparable to that in police jails. Moreover, the court system continued to function in a nearly normal manner in the face of increasingly severe rightist and wartime emergency pressures, with judges proudly maintaining a considerable degree of independence. Fortunately for defendants, the independent logic of the law exerted its own pressure for justice, setting limits to repression. The historian E. P. Thompson repudiates the oversimple Marxist view of law as a weapon used by the rulers to control the ruled by noting that law may be seen "in terms of its own logic, rules and procedures—that is simply *as law*."[5] And as law, with its own criteria of equity and logic, it can not only be just but can also inhibit the desires of the rulers.[6] Therefore, even harsh laws, like the Peace Preservation Law, develop a kind of autonomy, which power holders must respect. Add to this the tradition of autonomy within the court system and the results of some political trials appear less surprising. Furthermore, the state's *tenkō* policy, which fit in so snugly with traditional values, was a humane method of handling communist political criminals when compared with long prison terms and executions. Concern over human rights (i.e., procedural rights) was evidenced by lawyers in both the Radical Bar and the Civil Libertarian group, with the various bar associations also singling out abuses by authorities. Government officials, especially those in the Justice Ministry, also showed concern for the rights of suspects. Indeed, it is difficult not to be impressed by the commitment to human rights displayed by justice officials. Kawakami Kan, for instance, censured violent and illegal acts against criminal suspects: "This kind of act goes against humanity and it debases the dignity of the law." Moreover, "difficulty [of an investigation] does not justify illegal treatment" by justice police, he wrote. "For a procurator to not absolutely censure this kind of crime [i.e., abuse of human rights] caused by police officials, and [for a procurator] to protect his men [to cover up police mistakes] for petty selfish reasons, is not to defend the Constitution, which is a procurator's life." "Therefore, it is," he concluded, "a national duty to use national power to correct it [i.e., wrongdoing] and as much as possible search out the causes of it, in order to exterminate so-called abuses of human rights."[7] Another example is Motoji Shinkuma, who was procurator general from December 1936 and head of the Supreme Court from February 1939. Instructions given to procurators in 1938 emphasized that the human rights of criminal suspects had to be protected.[8] One only has to recall similar comments by Procurator General Koyama Matsukichi in the late 1920s and the many pronouncements by other justice officials to realize that Kawakami and Motoji were not alone. Therefore, if we add the various bar associations, legal scholars, newspapers, and concerned Diet members to these justice officials, we must reassess the common view that the human rights movement began with the institutional reforms of the Occupation era. It should be noted that it was during the difficult 1930s and early 1940s, the very "nadir for human rights,"[9] that the earlier human rights movement reached its peak. True, the Radical Bar was silenced by the mid-1930s, but lawyers aided by Justice Ministry officials and others continued to promote procedural rights under the law, and this during an era of semiwar from 1931 and full-scale war from 1937.

George M. Beckmann and Okubo Genji, in their classic *The Japanese Communist Party, 1922–1945,* state: "The absolute power

of the state, especially in its rawest form—the police and the military—was something that the communists could not combat effectively. *They had no civil liberties* with which to protect themselves,
either as individuals or as members of a political organization
[italics added]."[10] This is a puzzling viewpoint. "Civil liberty"
means the various immunities that protect an individual from government oppression; basic to this idea is the right to a fair trial by
a judicial system relatively independent of administrative control.
Freedom from illegal police practices such as excessive brutality
and torture are also usually included in the term *civil liberty*.[11] The
importance of a fair trial in the conception of civil liberty is underscored by Amendment 5 of the Bill of Rights in the United States
Constitution: "No person shall be held to answer for a capital
. . . crime unless on a presentment or indictment of a Grand
Jury . . . nor be deprived of life, liberty, or property, without due
process of law."[12] Viewing police actions, one must concede that
communist criminal suspects' civil liberties were often violated;
conversely, looking at the political trials covered in this book, one
must also concede that normally those rights were protected—
hardly the black-or-white picture portrayed by Beckmann and
Okubo.

There is no doubt that illegal police actions helped break the
Communist Party, but bureaucratic leaders in the Home and Justice ministries preferred the legal route and did, in fact, destroy
the party in a legal manner. The law, however, was a two-edged
sword that was also employed by the communists and their allies
against the government, as has been documented. That government foes had some faith in the law's protection and that they felt
there were civil liberties to protect is suggested by the publication
in 1931 of *Musansha Undō Torishimari Hōki Suchi*, by Irokawa
Kōtarō, and *Musansha Hōritsu Hikkei*, edited by Dōjin Sha, the following year. The former is a treatise on the various regulations
and laws aimed at control of the left-wing movements, including
legal recourse in case of illegal official actions; the latter is a six
hundred–page legal handbook for workers.[13] Moreover, the proletariat had access to some police material in which legal restrictions
on police actions were clearly outlined. For example, *Shihō Keisatsu
Shitsumu Yōten* (1924; Inoue Enzō, chief editor) was a handbook for
justice police. The general regulations for a criminal investigation
ordered justice police not to be too severe, to follow the law, and

not to use illegal force (Articles 51 and 52).[14] This pocket-sized volume was carried by a friend of mine, who referred to it many times between 1924 and 1945. Doubtless, he felt that laws and regulations did protect his civil liberties, however limited in scope they were. Finally, a Japanese Communist Party document written before March 15, 1928, which was seized when Ichikawa Shōichi was arrested in April 1929, discusses the confusion over what was "legal" and "illegal" and urges party members to use the law as a shield against police. If caught in the act of posting a party leaflet, for instance, the party member was to tell police that it had been merely picked up somewhere and was being posted as a joke. Faced with this situation, states the document, police would have no legal reason for an arrest.[15]

The previous chapters have recounted in great and grisly detail the widespread brutality and torture inflicted by police on both regular and political criminal suspects. Although these illegal actions were seldom officially blessed, they were unofficially encouraged by authorities who did not forcefully stop such practices. Kawakami Kan's in-house report, which shows that only 6 percent of the suspected cases of human rights abuses were prosecuted, tells us much more about official attitudes than the many private and public government pronouncements on the subject of following regulations and obeying laws. Besides that, as noted, police and others, in a continuing cover-up, destroyed evidence and denied wrongdoing. Even among the less informed members of the public, these illegal actions and the subsequent cover-ups were an open secret. While it would be an exaggeration to say that torture was a systematic policy, or that all police forced confessions by torture, or that the government was based on torture, the use of torture was pervasive and was accepted or tolerated by many procurators and preliminary judges.

One clue to widespread police abuse of procedural rights is supplied by the nature of the Meiji Constitution, in which the principle of legality was narrowly limited, with the subordination of administration to laws produced by the Diet unachieved. Moreover, administrators often disregarded the theoretical limitations of delegated legislative power; as a result, there were many instances of illegal administrative action. Remedies against illegal official action, whether by a highly placed bureaucrat or a policeman on the beat, were extremely limited.[16] This inadequacy of redress against infringement of rights stimulated police abuses. Illegal police actions were also stimulated by the 1908 Prison Law, which permitted police stations to hold criminal suspects in police station jails for long periods. Consequently, these "substitute prison" cells became hotbeds for brutality, torture, and forced confessions, especially after the enactment of the 1925 peace law. Another clue to widespread police abuse is found in Tokugawa techniques designed to produce a docile population, willing to accept authoritarian injustice. Most people, it appears, accepted the rule-by-status system and other parts of the system of social control and regarded this system as natural as the rising and setting of the sun. Motoori Norinaga, a leading figure in the national revival movement, wrote in 1786 that the people should obey all government regulations and perform their duty, since "[t]his is the true Way which has been handed down since the age of kami."[17] This equation of the orders from *okami* (authorities) with the will of the *kami* (the deities and other awe-inspiring human and nonhuman objects) was an enduring legacy from the Tokugawa to its Meiji successor. Modern police-state techniques cultivated by the new regime reinforced older methods of control and, to the extent that this amalgamation was successful, the general public's ability to protest illegal official actions was inhibited.

Another factor that may have contributed to police abuses was the impact of police practices in the colonies upon the metropole, especially in the case of Korea, where the Japanese brutally crushed the nationalist resistance and maintained control until 1919 via the army and gendarmes. Reforms after 1919 created a new police force, incorporating many former Japanese gendarmes; in 1930, 60 percent of the police force of 18,811 officers was Japanese. By the late 1920s the turnover in this force averaged 10 percent, and by the mid-1930s it had dropped to about 7 percent.[18] The question is, how many former officers in Korea took on police duties in the home islands? This would be significant information, because Koreans did not enjoy as many rights, and Japanese serving in Korea could easily transfer attitudes absorbed in the peninsula to the homeland. Policemen who were used to giving rough instant justice to Koreans, whom they considered inferior, could find adjustment to higher standards difficult. One student of this process elsewhere writes: "It is clear that law enforcement in England was to a significant extent, shaped by events and experiments in social control which occurred in Ireland, India, and other parts of Empire."[19] A possible link between the Korean colony and the home islands appears in Procurator Kawakami Kan's account of police brutality and torture in February 1936, when interrogators referred to water torture as the "Korean Criminal Code, Article No. 2" ("Infringement of Human Rights," Chapter 4). Certainly, torture was not legally practiced by police in Korea, but this remark does suggest feelings about a rougher sort of justice for an "inferior" people, and it may be an illustration of the application of such justice at home.

The state, in promoting the severe "Red scare," bears responsibility for illegal treatment of communist suspects, but the root cause of parts of the Tokkō apparatus running amuck lay in the fact that even though the highly centralized police structure was created as a watchdog for the state, it did not always obey its master. The police, like the army, was often disobedient, marching off to the beat of its own drum. Since the interwar years are replete with examples of army disobedience, examples of similar attitudes among policemen who exercised so much power should not come as a surprise. Like the military, the police represented the imperial mandate, and they justified each action accordingly. As we have seen, not even orders from the top of the Home Ministry could stop illegal police practices. The growing emergency in the late 1920s and 1930s, then, merely made a bad situation worse.

Linked to the above factors promoting police violence was the level of violence in the general society and in the military, in which many policemen had served. Both the army and the navy used systematic brutality and meted out cruel physical punishments. Like the police, petty officers beat their victims with a thick oak stick, a punishment that sometimes caused death. Beating with fists was common, as was slapping, which was universal in the military.[20] Former Tokkō officer Miyashita Hiroshi recalled that physical punishment was common in families and in the school system. When he entered the police he was hit by colleagues many of whom had earlier experienced army life. Thus, violence was a comparatively common occurrence among policemen, and it was easy to transfer this violence to interrogations. Itō Takashi agrees with Miyashita, saying that violence was common during the pre-1945 period except at the level of intellectual society.[21] Moreover, corporal punishment was commonly employed in schools as a major device for forcing compliance.[22] Mikiso Hane's research on coal miners supports this view of widespread brutality and physical violence. In 1888, following a riot at the Takashima mines, a journalist sent to investigate working conditions reported: "If a miner asks permission to rest . . . or if he disobeys the crew boss . . . [h]is hands are tied behind him and he is strung up by the beam, with his feet slightly above the ground. Then he is clubbed."[23] Suspension from a beam, a favorite method used by both regular police and Tokkō as a punishment and to force confessions, was also a Tokugawa method of torture. A woman miner, recalling events during the early years of this century, said that the crew boss's enforcer beat even those too ill to work. Another miner recalled a woman and man tied naked to crosses as punishment for adultery, with miners forced to hit their sexual organs. Stories of miners being burned with hot pokers and hung upside down over fires were common.[24] Considerable evidence, then, illustrates that cruelty and violence were inescapably present in the life of the common people, and against this background the brutality and torture by police seem less strange. This same evidence of violence in the general society coupled with police brutality and torture suggests that the generalization about "soft rule" (i.e., in Japan the tendency was to employ ideology and persuasion in contrast to the use of force in the West) rests in large measure on contradictory evidence. Even the *tenkō* policy, which superficially qualifies as "soft rule," is rife with contradictions (e.g., if force was used).

The Peace Preservation Law played a prominent role in the suppression of leftist political criminal suspects between 1925 and 1945. When compared with the number of suspects arrested (about seventy thousand), however, the number who reached the trial level was small (about seven thousand; includes the preliminary examination). Therefore, 90 percent of those suspected of peace law violations never reached the trial level but were handled by police and procurators.[25] Thus, this criminal law was not in fact mainly employed as such but instead was captured by Justice and Home Ministry bureaucrats and employed in an administrative fashion to pressure suspects into renouncing harmful ideologies.

A long-standing myth circulates among Japan specialists that one Japanese (Ozaki Hotsumi) and one foreigner (Richard Sorge) were executed in *naichi* (Japan proper) under the provisions of the

Peace Preservation Law.[26] The accusatory finger points at this author as well, because of an earlier acceptance of this myth.[27] While it is true that police and justice officials employed the peace law in the investigation of Ozaki and Sorge, the death penalty was not based on provisions of this law. Okudaira Yasuhiro, the leading authority on the peace law, states that there were no executions under this law in the home country.[28] He points out that the peace law was only marginal in the cases of Ozaki and Sorge; the serious charges against the defendants stemmed from the *Kokubō Hoan Hō* (National Defense Security Law: Law No. 49, promulgated on March 6 and enforced from May 10, 1941) and the *Gunyō Shigen Himitsu Hogo Hō* (Military Resources Secrets Protection Law: Law No. 25, March 24, 1939).[29] Another scholar also brushes away the peace law and points at violations of Article 4, Section 2 of the National Defense Security Law as the key to understanding the executions on November 7, 1944, of Ozaki and Sorge.[30] These political prisoners, then, were executed as spies who leaked military secrets to a foreign power. Odanaka Toshiki supports these views that no one was executed in Japan proper under the provisions of the peace law.[31] In the investigation's early stages it is understandable why police and justice officials employed the peace law, because Ozaki and Sorge were helping the international communist movement and undermining the Japanese state. It is also understandable why the Home Ministry's police force, which was engaged in a fierce power struggle with the Military Police, would wish to use the peace law to maintain control of the investigation. Moreover, police felt more comfortable using the provisions of the time-tested peace law rather than the new National Defense Security Law. Furthermore, suspects charged with a peace law violation could be held for longer periods.[32] Nevertheless, neither defendant was attempting to organize an association with the purpose of changing the *kokutai,* so the death penalty in Articles 1 to 3 of the 1941 peace law was not applicable.[33] On the other hand, Article 4, Section 2, National Defense Security Law states: "Persons who have for the purpose mentioned in the preceding paragraph obtained or collected State secrets, and who divulged them to foreign countries or made them public, shall be condemned to death, or punished with penal servitude for life or not less than three years."[34]

The provisions of the peace law applied to the Korean nationalist movement, according to the Supreme Court, because "to advocate the independence of Korea from Japan means to snatch away a part of the state under Imperial rule, thus constituting the grave crime of attempting to change Japan's national polity [*kokutai*] as defined in the Peace Preservation Law."[35] At first glance, it appears that the administrative use of the peace law was of less importance in the colony, where officials were more interested in using its harsh provisions to put down the independence movement. The decision of a court in Pyongyang in December 1933 seems vividly to illustrate the difference in punishment levels between the peninsula and the islands: "Twenty-three more 'Communists' have been sentenced to death in connection with the Chientao case. . . . Another twenty prisoners have received life sentences, and 302 have been sentenced to various terms. . . . Sixteen others have been liberated."[36] At least one scholar argues that these death sentences (cited as twenty-two rather than twenty-three) were given because of peace law violations. It should be noted, however, that each death sentence reads *"Chian Iji Hō Ihan sono ta"* (violation of the Peace Preservation Law and others).[37] Okudaira Yasuhiro regards "and others" as crucial, pointing out that other laws involved in the cases also carried a death penalty. Therefore, it is incorrect to conclude that these people were executed under the provisions of the peace law.[38] Mizuno Naoki agrees that in cases such as the above Okudaira is correct; these people were executed for murder, arson, and other capital crimes, and not for violating the provisions of the peace law. Indeed, he writes, an examination of the remaining court records shows not even one verdict of death based on the peace law.[39] It appears, then, that courts in Korea, like those in Japan proper, never employed the death penalty provision of the Peace Preservation Law.

A proper analysis of Japan's treatment of political criminals demands comparison with other states' handling of political prisoners. Such a comparison is a risky exercise given different social and political atmospheres, but the risk must be accepted to clarify what is typical and atypical in the Japanese experience.

Prior to the European Enlightenment, political crime was regarded as a breach of loyalty against a personal lord or monarch rather than ideologically stimulated political opposition to a regime. Punishments for this shameful and dishonorable crime were severe. Attitudes toward political crime, however, began to change during the late eighteenth and nineteenth centuries as the object of protection shifted from a monarch or a ruling group to an abstract entity called the state. While political criminals were considered misguided and deserving of punishment, the highest motives were seen behind their acts, and the severity of punishment declined. An expanding policy of leniency toward political offenders continued during the mid-nineteenth century in the face of revolutionary upheavals. During the late nineteenth century, Great Britain, France, and Germany, influenced by liberal ideology, employed selective and limited repression against political criminals, with only one major exception: the anarchists. Moreover, another qualification must be added: leniency was extended mainly to internal political crimes and not external (i.e., betrayal of the nation to another power). Following World War I, views began to change, as internal political crime began to lose its aura of respectability. This change may be attributed to the growth of nationalism, the Russian Revolution, the growth of antiliberal thought such as positivism, and the general material changes after the war. Great Britain, France, and Germany were caught up in the postwar years in a desperate power struggle that blurred the distinction between internal and external political offender and cast the former in the role of betrayer of national unity. Increasingly harsh penalties were the result.[40]

In France a law of November 1918 reestablished confiscation of property as punishment for those who betrayed the nation to another power; this penalty ran counter to the nineteenth-century liberal doctrine that punishment should not extend beyond the wrongdoer. A more severe espionage law was enacted in January 1934. Two years later the government was empowered to dissolve by decree all organizations that provoked armed demonstrations; imprisonment from six months to two years was ordered for those supporting such groups. In July 1939 parts of the Penal Code were revised: the death penalty was reintroduced for the crime of treason; harsher forms of imprisonment were provided; the 1918 provision for the confiscation of property was inserted; the nondisclosure of acts involving the internal and external security of the state became criminal for the first time since 1832; crimes against the external security of the state were to be treated like ordinary crimes. Moreover, court decisions of the 1920s applied to commu-

nist political offenders the laws enacted in the 1890s to cover anarchist propaganda crimes, converting communist criminal acts into
not merely attacks on the state's political organization but into
attacks on the general organization of society (i.e., turning a political crime into a common crime). Furthermore, these developments accelerated the blurring of the distinction between external
and internal political crimes.[41] The jurist Alec Mellor, whose *La
Torture* surveys the growth of torture in modern states, finds no
record of police torture in France until after World War I. "He
sees it as beginning around 1929 and increasing until after the
Second World War. From this period seems to date the infamous
passage à tabac, the French equivalent of the American 'Third
Degree', translatable approximately as 'rough handling' or
beating."[42]

As in France, in England World War I marked a change in the
attitude of the directive elite toward political offenders. The return
to the use of the death penalty for serious political offenses and
harsher punishment for lesser crimes is the most obvious reflection
of this change in attitude. New laws also reflected this change,
with an emphasis put on prevention of political crime and avoid-
ance of embarrassing court battles. Hence, the state resorted to
managing political crime behind the scenes, using the police for
surveillance and control. While maintaining a liberal facade, the
government cracked down hard on the communists in 1925, jail-
ing most of the party's leaders. Facing the first general strike in
1926, the government reacted as if revolution were at hand, prosecuting more than thirty-one hundred people for incitement to
sedition and violence.[43] The Incitement to Disaffection Act of
1934 (popularly known as the Sedition Act) empowered police
with a warrant to search any place or person for seditious literature. Mere possession was sufficient for prosecution. The Public
Order Act of 1936 extended police powers to regulate political
meetings and processions.[44] The liberal influences of the nineteenth century were reflected in the fact that no one was executed
for treason between 1820 and 1914 and that imprisoned political
criminals received special consideration. These policies began to
reverse during World War I with the return of executions. After
the war, the government used various legal maneuvers to apply
the harshest parts of laws to communists charged with sedition
and seditious libel.[45]

In Germany World War I also marked a great change in attitude toward political offenders. Caught between the revolutionaries of the right and the left, the Weimar Republic favored the former over the latter, since the communists were seen as tools of the old Russian enemy.[46] Nazi Germany under the leadership of Adolf Hitler is the paradigm of political repression in this century. "During his regime liberalism was completely rejected; and, with liberal restraints removed, the preventive tendency of all governmental measures against political crime was allowed to extend itself to its logical limits. Hitler started with legal, or at least quasilegal measures of repression, and ended with extralegal or illegal measures." This same tendency was present in France and Great Britain as well, but "[n]ever, however, in the West was the process carried as far as in Hitler's Germany."[47] Nazi contempt for law is illustrated by Hermann Göring's comment made early in Hitler's regime: "We deprive the enemies of the people of legal defense. . . . We National Socialists wittingly oppose false gentleness and false humanitarianism. . . . We do not recognize the fallacious quibbles of lawyers or the monkey tricks of judicial subtleties."[48]

The Emergency Decree to Protect the German People (February 1933) targeted the formerly legal left and anyone else suspected of certain antistate offenses. Protective custody could be maintained for up to three months. One part of this law was employed to start the concentration camps for people placed in custody. Later these camps, under Gestapo administration, were used to hold enemies of the people. That same month Göring officially sanctioned terror by ordering police to use firearms freely. Following decrees cleared the way for the removal of constitutional guarantees to protect individual rights; finally, the Reichstag passed a law suspending the constitution and giving the government the right to legislate on its own authority. Under the Nazi regime the National Socialist Party's needs took precedence over the state and the law. Strict interpretation of law was abandoned in order to punish enemies of the people. Numerous new laws were passed to cover all possible aspects of political crime, with the death penalty included in many provisions. A People's Court was created to deal with major political criminals (the Gestapo also worked at this task in an illegal manner). Since these courts were loyal to Hitler and designed to bypass the regular court system, defendants could not expect justice. Preventive detention was unlimited, defense counsel chosen by a defendant could be rejected, and there was no appeal.[49] Infamous before the outbreak of World War II, this court, during the war, "initiated a reign of terror in which defendants were sentenced to death in batches after hearings conducted amid the incredible ravings of the presiding judge."[50] For lesser political crimes, there were special six-man courts throughout the nation; army officers and members of the SS (Schutzstaffel; Nazi special police) dominated them. These courts, however, were not capable of eliminating all the state's potential enemies as well as ridding the nation of impure elements, since the question of "guilt" was usually not in question. The Nazi answer was the Gestapo and the concentration camps.[51] "The decision as to who was 'objectively dangerous' to the State could be made administratively and then measures could be taken directly by the secret police."[52] The task of the Gestapo was to suppress all criticism of the Nazi Party and the state and to employ any means to eliminate opposition. In January 1938 the Gestapo cut the last bonds of restraint when a decree empowered it to take into protective custody anyone who appeared to endanger the people or the state. Internment orders were unchallengeable by any judicial or administrative court.[53] Concentration camps under the SS were not designed for political reeducation but were employed as instruments of terror to frighten opponents of the regime; during the war some became factories manned by prisoners.[54]

Following the outbreak of war in September 1939, the state tightened up the criminal law, making many more offenses punishable by death. The Nazi leadership, however, was not content to employ harsh laws: "At the beginning of the war [Heinrich] Himmler was given instructions to use police against all subversive elements and to use them for the purpose not only of protective custody but in serious cases to liquidate the persons concerned without having recourse to the machinery of the law."[55] On the basis of this order and others many people were shot without trial, including persons seized from the prisons of judicial authorities. Concentration camps were the places where the illegal executions took place. Justice officials, who had been cowed earlier by Hitler's illegal executions of party leaders in 1934 and his pardoning of political police torturers in 1935, refused to challenge this newest manifestation of Hitler's will.[56]

Torture was deliberately and consciously employed by the

Third Reich, which even transformed it into a medical speciality. Indeed, torture "was ultimately institutionalized, and recognized by the Ministry of Justice in a formal agreement with the police, under the name 'intensified interrogation' . . . which included deprivation of sleep, exhausting exercises, and beating. . . . [Such brutality] not infrequently resulted in the prisoner's death from 'heart failure.' "[57] The use of the third degree was specifically approved by Himmler to force confessions: "The Third Degree in this case may be used only against communists, Marxists, Jehovah's Witnesses, saboteurs, terrorists, members of resistance movements, antisocial elements, refractory elements, or Polish or Soviet vagabonds. In all other cases, preliminary authorization is necessary."[58] Typical of Gestapo methods in France were the following: Suspects were "forced to kneel on a triangular bench while a torturer climbed on their shoulders; they were suspended with the arms tied behind their backs . . . ; they were kicked, thrashed with knouts, or struck with the fist. . . . Their teeth were filed, their nails torn out, and they were burned with cigarette stubs and on occasions with a soldering lamp. The electric torture was also practiced . . . [on] the most sensitive parts of the anatomy." On women "the torturers used their most odious refinements."[59] Traditionally, interrogators in various countries have employed torture to force a confession, or to obtain information about colleagues, or even to punish, but the Nazis sometimes used torture in a surprisingly "modern" manner—to intimidate potential opponents of the regime and thus keep them from expressing any dissent. For this kind of "terroristic torture," selection of victims could be random.[60]

Although the Nazis made liberal use of amnesties, they almost always limited this reward to rightists or minor common criminals. Amnesties were not extended to others because nothing would be accomplished through such a policy: "political opponents because of their beliefs could not be reintegrated into the national community; their existence in it could only detract from the facade of unity that had been created."[61]

Fascist Italy developed differently. The political police, for instance, was never fully captured by the party and maintained a resistance to more extreme party elements. No Himmler appeared in Italy, and the treatment of political criminals was, while sometimes harsh, unlike that of Germany. Still, the machinery of terror did produce beatings, torture, and executions. An Italian version of protective custody could confine a politically dangerous individual to an isolated village or island. This punishment was imposed administratively, without normal recourse to the courts.[62]

The Defense of the State Act (November 1926) reinstated the death penalty for political offenders, outlawed the communist movement, and created a Special Tribunal. All six members of this court were required to be members of the Fascist Party. The tribunal operated under rules similar to those of the Nazi People's Court.[63] To be considered "dangerous to the national order of the state" (Article 166 of the 1926 law), one needed not actually commit a crime; an assertion or insinuation from a Fascist source was adequate. Moreover, suspects acquitted in court were sometimes rearrested immediately afterwards. In the main, the judiciary surrendered its independence and served the interests of Benito Mussolini and the Fascist Party.[64]

From 1929 the Voluntary Organization for the Repression of Antifascism (i.e., the political police), "used torture regularly upon suspected enemies of state, party, and people."[65] Common torture methods in the early 1930s included placing a scorpion on the suspect's navel, burning with hot iron or boiling water, hitting over the heart with a rubber-covered hammer, tearing out nails, beating the soles of feet with steel strips, choking, and pressing testicles.[66]

Deportation to penal islands such as Lipari, Ustica, Favignana, Lampedusa, and Pantelleria was the harshest administrative measure against political offenders, with deportation for terms of one to five years. While appeals were permitted under the law, in practice they were futile. Life on the penal islands was carefully regulated and harsh: mail censored, reading censored, gifts restricted, and public places off limits. In addition, prisoners were subjected to brutality and torture.[67]

The Soviet Union's treatment of political criminals parallels that of the Third Reich, especially in the legitimation of torture. One of the first acts of the new regime was to establish the Extraordinary Commission to Fight Counterrevolution (the Cheka) in December 1917. Besides acting as a secret police, this organization played a key role in the civil war.[68] Counterrevolutionary "justice" was by late 1918 based on this Cheka procedure:

"Do not ask for incriminating evidence to prove that the prisoner opposed the Soviets either by arms or by words. Your first duty is to ask him to what class he belongs, what were his origins, education, and occupation. These questions should decide the fate of the prisoner."[69] Since organized terror was a watchword, legal safeguards were ignored in interrogating suspects and operating prisons. Besides beatings, the various Cheka groups devised novel forms of torture: rolling suspects around in internally nail-studded barrels, hand-flaying and scalping, branding with a five-pointed star, and crowning with barbed wire.[70] "The Kiev Cheka was said to have devised a method of interrogation which consisted of placing one open end of a metal cylinder against the prisoner's chest, placing a rat in the other end and sealing the outer end with wire mesh. When the tube was heated, the rat, in a frenzy to escape, ate its way into the prisoner's flesh."[71] Police torture, especially in political cases, continued to be widespread, particularly after 1936. Extraordinary procedures between 1917 and 1922, then, became routine after 1936.[72] In 1922 the State Political Administration (GPU.) replaced the Cheka. Over the following decades political surveillance was expanded to the point that the 1920s in retrospect appeared as a golden age of freedom. Among the multitudinous duties of the secret police were discovering enemies of the people, eliminating Stalin's rivals, and running the labor camps.[73]

Chapter three of *The Gulag Archipelago* surveys secret police methods of interrogation over a period of several decades. Methods of torture included loud sounds, burning with a cigarette, bright light, confinement in a dark box, standing four or five days, water deprivation, sleeplessness, continuous interrogation (three or four days), bedbug-infested box, punishment cell (icy cold), starvation, and beating. For beatings when they wished to leave no marks, interrogators used rubber truncheons and small sandbags. Other techniques were blows to the solar plexus or a hard kick to the genitals.[74] Nikolay Zabolotsky was arrested on March 19, 1938, in Leningrad and interrogated for four days by police trying to build a case against a counterrevolutionary writers' group about which the poet knew nothing. Protesting innocence, Zabolotsky pointed out his constitutional rights. "The Constitution stops operating at our front door," replied one interrogator.[75]

Over the days Zabolotsky was deprived of food and sleep and nearly beaten to death by tormentors working in shifts. In October he was sentenced without trial to five years in a labor camp.[76]

Labor camps were officially established in September 1918 when the Cheka was empowered to imprison certain categories of people. During the 1920s, the camps were limited in size and extent (e.g., in 1929 fewer than two hundred thousand including both political and regular criminals). Prisoners were not properly clothed, housed, or protected from disease, and executions were common. Those the government wanted quietly eliminated were sent to the killing climate of places like the Solovietsky Islands in the White Sea. The multicamp gulag, forcefully brought to the world's attention by Aleksandr Solzhenitsyn, was organized from 1930 as a result of an enormous increase in the number of political criminals. By 1936 the camps held six million inmates. While Solzhenitsyn experienced the gulag a few years later, his comment on mortality rates is no doubt accurate. Soon after arrival at Krasnaya Presnya he discovered that 80 percent of the prisoners given "general assignment" work died; those who managed to get "special assignment" orders stood a much better chance of survival.[77]

This brief survey indicates that police brutality and torture were ubiquitous, whether blessed by officials or illegal, and that the worldwide employment of state torture today rests on a broad and firm foundation. That brutality and torture flourished in America as well is amply documented in *Report on Lawlessness in Law Enforcement* (1931; the so-called Wickersham Report), written by the U.S. National Commission on Law Observance and Enforcement. Only one conclusion is possible: brutality and torture can flourish under any form of government. However, there are differences in degree and in the public response when brutal practices are exposed. In Japan, Kawakami Kan's Wickersham-style report was kept classified; in the United States, this sensational revelation spurred police reforms. In Nazi Germany and Communist Russia, justice officials were cowed, and torture was legitimatized and institutionalized. Illegal executions were commonplace in Germany. While the situation was not so extreme in Fascist Italy, courts surrendered their independence, and torture was widespread.

As for methods of torture, Japanese police were hardly on the cutting edge of new techniques, preferring time-tested methods and improvising torture implements. A 1986 United Nations report on torture presents the following list of methods of physical torture, which is not considered exhaustive: beating, burning, extracting (teeth, nails, etc.), suspending, suffocating, exposing to excessive light or noise, denying sleep or food, assaulting sexually, administering drugs, and electric shocks.[78] Cases of Japanese police torture presented in this book fall into all categories except the use of drugs, and only one example of electrical shock was discovered. Also, in place of extraction, police appear to have favored insertion: small needles under nails and larger tatami mat makers' needles for stabbing. Modern Japanese torture practices, when compared to the Tokugawa methods, do illustrate some continuities. What Ishii Ryōnosuke terms "true torture" (suspension with the arms tightly bound behind the back; the fourth stage of official torture) was a police favorite. Forcing suspects to kneel on sharp edges with heavy weights on their thighs also appears to be a Tokugawa carry-over. Perhaps the modern ubiquitous technique of beating suspects' thighs is derived from this kneeling torture. Tokugawa continuities, however, do not necessarily imply uniqueness, since Nazi torturers also employed suspension with arms tied behind the victim's back. Suspension of this type can also be documented in Surinam in the late eighteenth century and South Africa in the late twentieth, so it appears to be widespread over space and time.[79] Thus, only Japanese police fixation on victims' thighs stands out as unusual, but more research is required to determine if this method was truly "unique." Two methods were either little used or even undiscovered by the Japanese police: *falaga* or *falanga* (beating the soles of the feet) and *chevalet* (forcing the naked prisoner to ride an iron bar, thus causing tearing of the perineum).[80] As for mental torture, even though there is disagreement over a precise definition of what constitutes psychological torture, verbal abuse, threats of physical violence, prolonged interrogation, and being forced to strip naked (all of which were illegal police methods in pre-1945 Japan) certainly fall into this category.

The Japanese used the regular court system to handle political criminal suspects even though some streamlining of the process went into effect after the enactment of the 1941 peace law. Also, there were no concentration camps or penal islands; all political prisoners were housed in the regular prison system (even the

handful under preventive detention after 1941 were in one corner
of Toyotama Prison and then Fuchū Prison). No political prisoner
was executed under the provisions of the Peace Preservation Law.
Why was the treatment of political prisoners in Japan so different
from what it was in Nazi Germany, Soviet Russia, and Fascist
Italy? In the first place, no superparty rose above the state, and
the political system and laws fashioned during the Meiji era continued to function, even during the war. Moreover, the widely
accepted idea that the Japanese nation was an extended family,
making even political criminals children of the emperor, protected
political criminal suspects to a degree.

As Ingraham points out, nineteenth-century leniency toward
political criminals shifted to harsher policies during this century.
Basically, Japan followed this same pattern influenced by nineteenth-century liberalism: official torture was dropped, the prison
system improved by 1900, and more humane laws and regulations
introduced. Then, as the Europeans adopted harsher measures,
the Japanese seemed to again follow suit (e.g., the 1925 peace
law). Here, however, the Japanese case diverges from the increasingly harsh measures taken in some European nations: no executions under the peace law and the use of *tenkō,* which resulted in a
somewhat paradoxical policy of illegal brutality and torture and
official leniency. Viewed in this manner the Japanese response to
political crime appears to be a copy of the European example (i.e.,
harsher laws), but with a softer official policy in the enforcement
of such laws. However, a close examination suggests that the Japanese government was not just a follower but was the vanguard in
at least one respect: viewing leftist political criminals as people in
need of correction and rehabilitation rather than as deviates to be
imprisoned or killed. Thus, Japan's *tenkō* policy anticipated a post-
1945 change in the treatment of political criminals in some European nations.[81]

Recent scholarship in the field of modern Japanese history has
emphasized that one major political party (Kenseikai/Minseitō)
was more liberal than the other (Seiyūkai) and that the former
advanced progressive social policies while the latter preferred suppression to reform. Moreover, a view has emerged of a Home
Ministry more liberal than the Justice Ministry, with the former in
support of progressive social policies and the latter ever willing to
turn to harsh laws harshly applied.[82] While this viewpoint has

merit, it must not be permitted to obscure other important factors: the attitudes of political parties and the limitations of Taisho democracy. In their weak defense of the rights of criminal suspects, the two major parties were hardly distinguishable, with neither displaying much zeal in this area unless illegal actions by authorities hit their personal or political interests. For suspected communists, a bipartisan approach was adopted, with harsh laws for those who defied the *kokutai*. As for the Home Ministry, this study concludes that despite so-called liberal cliques among the ranking officials, police abuses of the constitution, laws, and regulations were ceaseless and that the leading officials were either unwilling or unable to impose their will on the rank and file, who simply refused to obey. The Justice Ministry, too, called for correction of illegal police actions and took steps to better train justice police, but orders from on high were defied. Nevertheless, as this study illustrates, it was within the independent court system that both regular and political criminal suspects came closest to receiving a fair measure of justice. Therefore, those who see only the harsh side of the Justice Ministry are guilty of minimizing internal differentiation within this section of the bureaucracy. Furthermore, justice officials, despite lapses in the application of law, together with lawyers and politicians played an important role in promoting a human rights movement.

Outstanding in an overview of the period investigated are the Tokugawa-inspired continuities, despite the wholesale introduction of Western legal forms: the transcendental administrative state; inadequate redress against authority; lack of individual rights outside the group; officials lording it over the masses; near total dependence upon confessions coupled with a willingness to use brutality and torture; harsh conditions in police jails. Indeed, illegal police actions, growing out of the legacy of suppression inherited from the Tokugawa regime, illustrate one line of continuity in the state's treatment of the people during the Meiji, Taisho, and Showa eras. Another line of continuity, which somewhat tempers the bleak view of illegal police actions, is the development of a human rights movement and the passage of humane laws. At first glance, these lines of continuity may appear paradoxical, but together they represent the conflicting realities of the pre-1945 era. Reviewing this era, one is struck by apparent contradictions: harsh laws versus humane laws; illegal forced confes-

sions versus compensation for victims of official abuse; a narrowing of the range of legal dissent in the 1930s versus the humane
conversion solution; filthy jails versus well-run prisons; a harsh
peace law versus no executions; and so on. These contradictions
are better understood, however, if Japan is viewed as a paternalistic police state, in which brutality was the other side of benevolence and, like yin and yang, together formed a whole. Looked at
this way, torturers treating victims to a meal seems less incongru-
ous, and various examples of the "soft rule" theory, too, blend
better into the record.

Notes

ABBREVIATIONS

The following abbreviations are used throughout the notes.

GSS: *Gendai Shi Shiryō*

TK: Kazahaya Yasoji (ed.), *Gokuchū no Showa Shi: Toyotama Keimusho*

JWC: *Japan Weekly Chronicle*

Kawakami Kan: Kawakami Kan, *Iwayuru Jinken Jūrin Mondai ni Tsuite*

KES: Shihōshō, Shihō Daijin Kanbō Hishoka, *Kunji Enjutsu Shū*

KHS: Wagatsuma Sakae (ed.) *Kyū Hōritsu Shū*

Kokusho: "Tokkō Keisatsu Kokusho" Henshū Iinkai (ed.), *Tokkō Keisatsu Kokusho*

SK: Japan, Shihōshō Keijikyoko, *Shisō Kenkyū*

SKST: Japan, Shihōshō Keijikyoku, *Shisō Kenkyū Shiryō Tokushū*

INTRODUCTION

1. Alan F. Sewell, "Political Crime: A Psychologist's Perspective," in M. Cherif Bassiouni (ed.), *International Terrorism and Political Crimes,* 13.

2. Max Lerner, "Political Offenders," in Edwin R. A. Seligman (ed.), *Encyclopedia of the Social Sciences,* 11–12:199.

3. Barton L. Ingraham, *Political Crime in Europe,* 19.

4. Ienaga Saburō, *The Pacific War,* 115–116.
5. Lawrence W. Beer, "Japan," in Jack Donnelly and Rhoda E. Howard (eds.), *International Handbook of Human Rights,* 214.
6. Ishida Takeshi, "The Introduction of Western Political Concepts into Japan: Non-Western Societies' Response to the Impact of the West," Nissan Occasional Paper Series, no. 2 (1986): 20–21.
7. Lawrence Beer and C. G. Weeramantry, "Human Rights in Japan: Some Protections and Problems," *Universal Human Rights* 1 (July–September 1979): 2–3.
8. Elise K. Tipton, "The Civil Police in the Suppression of the Prewar Japanese Left," Ph.D. diss., 46.
9. Ōno Tatsuzō, *Nihon no Seiji Keisatsu,* 28.
10. Ibid.
11. Asahi Jānaru (ed.), *Showa Shi no Shunkan* 1:43–44, 48.
12. Yamabe Kentarō (ed.), *Gendai Shi Shiryō* 16:viii.
13. Tsurumi Kazuko, *Social Change and the Individual: Japan Before and After Defeat in World War II,* 41.
14. Mikiso Hane, *Modern Japan: A Historical Survey,* 217.
15. Ralph J. D. Braibanti, "Japan's New Police Law," *Far Eastern Survey* 18 (January 24, 1949): 18.
16. J. Victor Koschmann, "Introduction: Soft Rule and Expressive Protest," in J. Victor Koschmann (ed.), *Authority and the Individual in Japan: Citizen Protest in Historical Perspective,* 12–13, 19.
17. David H. Bayley, *Forces of Order: Police Behavior in Japan and the United States,* 150, 156.

CHAPTER 1

1. Dan F. Henderson, "Law and Political Modernization in Japan," in Robert E. Ward (ed.), *Political Development in Modern Japan,* 393, 400–401, 403–404, 412; John W. Hall, "Rule by Status in Tokugawa Japan," *Journal of Japanese Studies* 1 (Autumn 1974): 43–45, 48–49.
2. Taikakai (ed.), *Naimushō Shi* 2:568.
3. D. Eleanor Westney, "The Emulation of Western Organizations in Meiji Japan: The Case of the Paris Prefecture of Police and the Keishichō," *Journal of Japanese Studies* 8 (Summer 1982): 311–317; Taikakai (ed.), *Naimushō Shi* 2:570.
4. Taikakai (ed.), *Naimushō Shi* 2:584, 588.
5. Ibid., 586; Ishii Ryōsuke, *Japanese Legislation in the Meiji Era,* 250, 252.
6. Nobutaka Ike, *The Beginnings of Political Democracy in Japan,* 91–92.
7. Ishii, *Japanese Legislation,* 461–462; Taikakai (ed.), *Naimushō Shi* 2:747; James B. Leavell, "The Development of the Modern Japanese Police System: Transition from Tokugawa to Meiji," Ph.D. diss., 150.

8. Paul Heng-chao Ch'en, *The Formation of the Early Meiji Legal Order: The Japanese Code of 1871 and Its Chinese Foundation*, 4–9, 16–20; Hiramatsu Yoshirō, "History of Penal Institutions: Japan," *Law in Japan: An Annual* (1973): 22.

9. Takayanagi Kenzo, "A Century of Innovation: The Development of Japanese Law, 1868–1961," in Arthur T. von Mehren (ed.), *Law in Japan: The Legal Order in a Changing Society*, 20, 20 n. 22.

10. Articles 1 and 2 of the section on "Trial and Imprisonment" in Ch'en, 179–180.

11. Anne Walthall, "Japanese *Gimin:* Peasant Martyrs in Popular Memory," *American Historical Review* 91 (December 1986): 1076–1077.

12. James W. White, "State Growth and Popular Protest in Tokugawa Japan," *Journal of Japanese Studies* 14 (Winter 1988): 17, 20.

13. Ch'en, 34 n. 7.

14. Robert N. Bellah, "Intellectual and Society in Japan," *Daedalus* 101 (Spring 1972): 94.

15. Ibid., 106.

16. Ch'en, 33–34.

17. Ibid., 62.

18. Ishii Ryōsuke, "The History of Evidence in Japan," *La Preuve* 19, pt. 3:531–532.

19. J. C. Hall, "The Tokugawa Legislation, IV," *Transactions of the Asiatic Society of Japan* 41 (1913), unnumbered pages after 804; also see Sasama Yoshihiko, *Zusetsu Edo no Keisatsu Shihō Jiten*, 203–212.

20. Ishii, "History of Evidence," 532.

21. W. Allyn Rickett, "Voluntary Surrender and Confession in Chinese Law: The Problem of Continuity," *Journal of Asian Studies* 30 (August 1971): 797; Judy F. Harrison, "Wrongful Treatment of Prisoners: A Case Study of Ch'ing Legal Practice," *Journal of Asian Studies* 23 (February 1964): 234; Dando Shigemitsu, *Japanese Criminal Procedure*, 12–14; Ishii Ryōsuke, *A History of Political Institutions in Japan*, 79; Ishii Ryōsuke, "Dan Fenno Henderson, Conciliation and Japanese Law—Tokugawa and Modern," *Law in Japan: An Annual* (1968): 223.

22. Harrison, *"Wrongful Treatment,"* 243.

23. J. R. McEwan, *The Political Writings of Ogyū Sorai*, 113.

24. Dan F. Henderson, "Chinese Legal Studies in Early 18th-Century Japan: Scholars and Sources," *Journal of Asian Studies* 30 (November 1970): 26.

25. Ch'en, 65–67.

26. Tezuka Yutaka, *Meiji Shoki Keihō Shi no Kenkyū*, 139–140.

27. David Huish, "The Meirokusha: Some Grounds for Reassessment," *Harvard Journal of Asiatic Studies* 32 (1972): 218.

28. William R. Braisted (trans.), *Meiroku Zasshi: Journal of the Japanese Enlightenment*, 94–96.

29. Ibid., 127–130.

30. Ch'en, 67.

31. Ibid., 67, 70.

32. Abe Haruo, "Criminal Justice in Japan: Its Historical Background and Modern Problems," *American Bar Association Journal* 47 (1961): 557.

33. Ch'en, 67–68.

34. Ibid., 68–70.

35. Sandra T. W. Davis, *Intellectual Change and Political Development in Early Modern Japan: Ono Azusa, A Case Study*, 81.

36. Ch'en, 70; Takayanagi, 20 n. 21. Ono Azusa must have suspected that the old habit of using torture to force confessions would be difficult to break, because his *Kokken henron* (Outline of the national constitution), completed on September 21, 1885, stated: "Prisoners, especially political prisoners, should not be subject to torture." Davis, 266, 294 n. 6.

37. Ishida Takeshi, *The Introduction of Western Political Concepts into Japan: Non-Western Societies' Response to the Impact of the West*, Nissan Occasional Paper Series, no. 2 (1986): 12.

38. Robert Epp, "The Challenge from Tradition: Attempts to Compile a Civil Code in Japan, 1866–78," *Monumenta Nipponica* 22, 1–2 (1967): 17–20; Mukai Ken and Toshitani Nobuyoshi, "The Progress and Problems of Compiling the Civil Code in the Early Meiji Era," *Law in Japan: An Annual* (1967): 35 n. 15.

39. Takayanagi, 24; Ishida, *Western Political Concepts*, 12–13.

40. Mukai and Toshitani, 38 n. 23.

41. Ibid., 36–37.

42. Walthall, 1076, 1084, 1088–1089.

43. Quoted in Ike, 61.

44. Ibid., 130–137; Janet Hunter (comp.), *Concise Dictionary of Modern Japanese History*, 237.

45. Quoted in Margaret B. Dardess, "The Thought and Politics of Nakae Chōmin (1847–1901)," Ph.D. diss., 81.

46. Quoted in ibid., 57.

47. Davis, 55–56.

48. Ibid., 266.

49. Ishida Takeshi, "Fundamental Human Rights and the Development of Legal Thought in Japan," *Law in Japan: An Annual* (1975): 49–50; Richard H. Mitchell, *Censorship in Imperial Japan*, 72.

50. Ishida, "Fundamental Human Rights," 52–53.

51. Quoted in ibid., 53.

52. Ibid., 54; Ienaga Saburō, *Ueki Emori Kenkyū*, 648; Ishida, *Western Political Concepts*, 14; Joseph Pittau, *Political Thought in Early Meiji Japan*, 101–104; Mikiso Hane, "Early Meiji Liberalism: An Assessment," *Monumenta Nipponica* 24, 4 (1969): 371.

53. Bob T. Wakabayashi, "Katō Hiroyuki and Confucian Natural Rights, 1861–1870," *Harvard Journal of Asiatic Studies* 44 (December 1984): 486–490.

54. Wagatsuma Sakae (ed.), *Kyū Hōrei Shū*, 431–447; Takayanagi, 17–19.

55. Wagatsuma (ed.), *KHS*, 13.

56. George M. Beckmann, *The Making of the Meiji Constitution: The Oligarchs and the Constitutional Development of Japan, 1868–1891*, 150, 152.

57. Henderson, "Law and Political Modernization," 422.

58. Ide Yoshinori, "Administrative Culture in Japan: Image of the *Kan* or Public Administration," *Annals of the Institute of Social Science*, no. 22 (1981): 154.

59. Quoted in Richard H. Minear, *Japanese Tradition and Western Law: Emperor, State, and Law in the Thought of Hozumi Yatsuka*, 79, 81–82.

60. Hashimoto Kiminobu, "The Rule of Law: Some Aspects of Judicial Review of Administrative Action," in von Mehren (ed.), 240; Henderson, "Law and Political Modernization," 427.

61. Takayanagi, 38.

62. J. E. de Becker (trans.), *Japanese Code of Criminal Procedure*, 1, 19–20, 25–26, 32.

63. Takayanagi, 18.

64. William J. Sebald (trans.), *The Criminal Code of Japan*, 142.

65. Takayanagi, 22; Hirano Ryuichi, "The Accused and Society: Some Aspects of Japanese Criminal Law," in von Mehren (ed.), 294; Nagashima Atsushi, "The Accused and Society: The Administration of Criminal Justice in Japan," in von Mehren (ed.), 299.

66. Japan, Shihōshō, *Kangoku Hō* (authorized Justice Ministry translation, undated).

67. Ibid.

68. Wagatsuma Sakae (ed.), *Shin Hōritsugaku Jiten*, 159; Japan Federation of Bar Associations, *The Documents Concerning the Daiyo-Kangoku (Japan Substitute Prison System)*, 2; Ono Takashi, "Bills on Treatment of Prisoners, Suspects Arouse Concern," *Japan Times* (National ed.), June 1, 1988, 3.

69. Mikiso Hane, *Modern Japan*, 114–115; Hunter, 117, 184, 191.

70. Roger F. Hackett, *Yamagata Aritomo in the Rise of Modern Japan, 1838–1922*, 97–98.

71. Quoted in Beckmann, 126, 128.

72. Roger W. Bowen, *Rebellion and Democracy in Meiji Japan: A Study of Commoners in the Popular Rights Movement*, 289–290.

73. Hane, *Modern Japan*, 125; Shigematsu Kazuyoshi, *Hokkaido Gyōkei Shi*, 222.

74. Bowen, 292, 294.

75. Ibid., 297.

76. Itagaki Taisuke (ed.), *Jiyūtō Shi* 2:332–337; Ike, 166–167; Sanseidō Henshūjo (ed.), *Konsaisu Jinmei Jiten,* 240, 439.

77. Hiramatsu, "Penal Institutions," 31–32; Hiramatsu Yoshirō, "Kindaiteki Jiyūkei no Tenkai," in Ōtsuka Hiroshi and Hiramatsu Yoshirō (eds.), *Gyōkei no Gendaiteki Shiten,* 110.

78. John A. Harrison, *Japan's Northern Frontier,* 4, 75–76, 76 n. 12.

79. Ibid., 76–77, 80–81.

80. Shigematsu, 121–122, 150–151.

81. Ibid., 130, 151, 159, 162, 189, 219, 233, 245–246, 237–238; Itagaki, 250, 317, 337; Hiramatsu, "Kindaiteki Jiyūkei no Tenkai," 11–12.

82. Robert M. Spaulding, *Imperial Japan's Higher Civil Service Examinations,* 65–66.

83. Shigematsu, 173–174.

84. Ibid., 174.

85. Ibid., 181, 186–187.

86. Hiramatsu, "Penal Institutions," 33–35.

87. Ibid., 41 n. 55.

88. Ibid., 36; Shigematsu, 189.

89. Quoted in Shigematsu, 176.

90. Ibid., 288; Hiramatsu, "Penal Institutions," 38.

91. Shigematsu, 153, 162, 216, 218, 238, 233–234.

92. Ibid., 159, 234, 247; Hiramatsu, "Kindaiteki Jiyūkei no Tenkai," 12.

93. Hiramatsu, "Penal Institutions," 38.

94. Shigematsu, 237–238.

95. Hiramatsu, "Penal Institutions," 40–43, 45; Hiramatsu, "Kindaiteki Jiyūkei no Tenkai," 11.

96. Shigematsu, 271–273; Hiramatsu, "Penal Institutions," 42; Bowen, 291, 295, 297.

97. Yoshino Sakuzō (ed.), *Meiji Bunka Zenshū* 18:575–606. Another source is Midoro Masaichi, *Meiji Taisho Shi: Genron Hen* 1:72–77, who lists two hundred journalists imprisoned from 1875 to 1889.

98. Gregory J. Kasza, *The State and the Mass Media in Japan, 1918–1945,* 5–6.

99. Nakamura Kikuo, *Hoshi Tooru,* 73–77.

100. Sharlie C. Ushioda, "Fukuda Hideko and the Woman's World of Meiji Japan," in Hilary Conroy, Sandra T. W. Davis, and Wayne Patterson (eds.), *Japan in Transition: Thought and Action in the Meiji Era, 1868–1912,* 281, 283, 287–288. The first woman to be executed for a political crime was one of the three women killed in 1876 by decapitation with exhibition of the head, a punishment used only for political offenses until exhibition was prohibited in 1879. Ch'en, 62.

101. Eugene Soviak, "Baba Tatsui: A Study of Intellectual Acculturation in the Early Meiji Period," Ph.D. diss., 294–296, 309–310.

102. Wagatsuma (ed.), *KHS,* 60–61; Taira Koji, *Economic Development and the Labor Market in Japan,* 134, 255 n. 13.

103. Quoted in Hyman Kublin, *Asian Revolutionary: The Life of Sen Katayama,* 139.

104. George O. Totten, *The Social Democratic Movement in Prewar Japan,* 26.

105. Wagatsuma (ed.), *KHS,* 63, 520, 459–460.

106. Quoted in Elise K. Tipton, "The Civil Police in the Suppression of the Prewar Japanese Left," Ph.D. diss., 46.

107. Morinaga Eizaburō, *Yamazaki Kesaya,* 155–157.

108. Taikakai (ed.), *Naimushō Shi* 2:710; Okudaira Yasuhiro, "Some Preparatory Notes for the Study of the Peace Preservation Law in Prewar Japan," *Annals of the Institute of Social Science,* no. 14 (1973): 55; Ishii, *Japanese Legislation in the Meiji Era,* 557.

109. Leavell, 156.

110. Takahashi Yūsai, *Meiji Keisatsu Shi Kenkyū* 2:17.

111. Nihon Kindai Shiryō Kenkyū Kai (ed.), *Taisho Kōki Keihokyoku Kankō Shakai Undō Shiryō,* 4.

112. Quoted in ibid., 4–5.

113. Ibid., 1, 4.

114. F. G. Notehelfer, *Kōtoku Shūsui: Portrait of a Japanese Radical,* 162, 174 n. 1.

115. Koyama Matsukichi, "Meiji Jidai no Shakaishugi Undō ni Tsuite," in *SKST* 59 (March 1939): 32.

116. Ibid., 11–13.

117. Ibid., 8.

118. John Crump, *The Origins of Socialist Thought in Japan,* 302.

119. Ibid., 305–306; Thomas A. Stanley, *Ōsugi Sakae—Anarchist in Taishō Japan: The Creativity of the Ego,* 44.

120. Notehelfer, 188–189, 200.

121. Nihon Kindai Shiryō Kenkyū Kai (ed.), 1–2; Okudaira, "Preparatory Notes," 56; Tipton, 91–96; Kyoto Daigaku Bungakubu Kokushi Kenkyūshitsu (ed.), *Nihon Kindai Shi Jiten,* 177.

122. Stanley, 80–81, 83, 87–89.

123. Nihon Kindai Shiryō Kenkyū Kai (ed.), 10–11.

124. Henry D. Smith, *Japan's First Student Radicals,* 83, 83 n. 68.

125. Notehelfer, 109–110.

126. George Elison, "Kōtoku Shūsui: The Change in Thought," *Monumenta Nipponica* 22, 3–4 (1967): 446.

127. Notehelfer, 116.

128. Stanley, 43, 47–48, 53.

129. Quoted in Ibid., 50.

130. Ibid., 47, 51.

131. Crump, 301.

132. Kublin, 210–211; *Konsaisu Jinmei Jiten,* 296.

133. Akamatsu Katsumaro, "The Russian Influence on the Early Japanese Social Movement," in Nobori Shomu and Akamatsu Katsumaro, *The Russian Impact on Japan: Literature and Social Thought,* 104.

134. Crump, 247.

135. Notehelfer, 113, 116; Stanley, 51.

136. Kenneth Strong, *Ox Against the Storm: A Biography of Tanaka Shozo: Japan's Conservationist Pioneer,* 124 n. 1, 182 n. 1.

137. Taikakai (ed.), *Naimushō Shi* 4:364–365, 369–370.

138. Quoted in Spaulding, 147.

139. Kawakami Kan, in *SK* 24 (14) (February 1938): 12–15.

140. Takayanagi, 34; Gail L. Bernstein, *Japanese Marxist: A Portrait of Kawakami Hajime, 1879–1946,* 87; Morinaga Eizaburō, *Nihon Bengoshi Retsuden,* 201–202.

141. Yoshikawa Mitsusada, "Iwayuru Kome Sōdō Jiken no Kenkyū," in *SKST* 51 (1938): 58–59.

142. Morinaga, *Nihon Bengoshi Retsuden,* 230–231.

143. Yoshikawa, 99; Watanabe Tooru and Inoue Kiyoshi, *Kome Sōdō no Kenkyū* 5:156.

144. Watanabe and Inoue, 156–158.

145. Hirano Yoshitarō, "Jinken o Mamotta Hitobito: Fuse Tatsuji o Chūshin ni," *Hōgaku Seminā,* November 1959, 57–58; Morinaga Eizaburō, "Fuse Tatsuji (Jinken Yōgo Undō Shijō no Ni Sendachi)," *Hōgaku Seminā,* December 1956, 44; Fuse Kanji, *Aru Bengoshi no Shōgai: Fuse Tatsuji,* 35–36; Morinaga, *Nihon Bengoshi Retsuden,* 60, 62.

146. Iwao F. Ayusawa, *A History of Labor in Modern Japan,* 85, 140–141; Jiyū Hōsō Dan (ed.), *Jiyū Hōsō Dan Monogatari: Senzenhen,* 13.

147. Jiyū Hōsō Dan (ed.), 17, 19–20.

148. Ibid., i, 20; Hirano Yoshitarō, 61.

149. The Ōtsu Incident began with the attempted assassination of Russian Crown Prince Nicholas by a Japanese policeman on May 11, 1891, and developed into a power struggle between the cabinet and the judges handling the case. See Barbara Teters, "The Otsu Affair," in David Wurfel (ed.), *Meiji Japan's Centennial.* For the High Treason Incident, see Koyama, *SKST* 59:42.

150. Strong, 124 n. 1.

151. Taikakai (ed.), *Naimushō Shi* 4:364–365, 369–370.

CHAPTER 2

1. Wagatsuma (ed.), *KHS,* 451; for an English translation of the law, see Richard H. Mitchell, "Peace Preservation Law of 1925," *Encyclopedia of Japan* 6 (1983): 168–169; *Kokutai* is explained in Richard H. Mitchell, *Thought Control in Prewar Japan,* 20; the best book on the law is Okudaira Yasuhiro, *Chian Iji Hō Shōshi.*

2. Matsuo Takayoshi, "The Development of Democracy in Japan— Taishō Democracy: Its Flowering and Breakdown," *Developing Economies* 4 (December 1966): 629; Elise K. Tipton, "The Civil Police in the Suppression of the Prewar Japanese Left," Ph.D. diss., 183–184.

3. Odanaka Toshiki, "Daiichiji Kyōsantō Jiken: Nihon Kyōsantō Sōritsu to Chian Iji Hō Jidai Zenya no Saiban," in Wagatsuma Sakae (ed.), *Nihon Seiji Saiban Shiroku, Taisho,* 350–353; George M. Beckmann and Okubo Genji, *The Japanese Communist Party, 1922–1945,* 59, 64–65.

4. Odanaka, 354–355; Kikukawa Tadao, *Gakusei Shakai Undō Shi,* 212–213.

5. Kikukawa, 212.

6. Odanaka, 350.

7. Ibid., 355, 362–363.

8. Ibid., 356.

9. Quoted in ibid.

10. Quoted in ibid., 357.

11. Ibid., 357–358.

12. Ibid., 358.

13. Ibid., 358–360.

14. Quoted in ibid., 361.

15. Ibid., 361–362.

16. Beckmann and Okubo, 68–69.

17. Imai Seiichi, *Nihon no Rekishi* 23:381, 392.

18. Tamiya Hiroshi, "Amakasu Jiken: Kenpei ni Gyakusatsu Sareta Museifushugisha Ōsugi Sakae," in Wagatsuma Sakae (ed.), *Nihon Seiji Saiban Shiroku, Taisho,* 415–416; Shinobu Seizaburō, *Taisho Seiji Shi,* 1128–1129.

19. Shinobu, 1129.

20. Minami Kiichi, "Kameido Jiken no Giseisha: Watakushi wa Jikeidanchō to shite Chōsenjin no Inochi o Mamotta. Sono Yokujitsu Nankatsu Rōdōkai ni Ita Otōto wa Gyakusatsu Sareta," *Chūō Kōron,* no. 923 (September 1, 1964): 224–227.

21. Tamiya, 415–416; Hirano Yoshitarō, "Jinken o Mamotta Hitobito: Fuse Tatsuji o Chūshin ni," *Hōgaku Seminā,* November 1959, 59–60.

22. Tamiya, 417; Miyake Shōichi, *Gekidōki no Nihon Shakai Undō Shi,* 98, 100.

23. Miyake, 99.

24. Ibid.

25. Tamiya, 420–421.

26. Naimushō Keihokyoku, *Showa Shichinenchū ni okeru Shakai Undō no Jōkyō,* 1517; Naimushō Keihokyoku Hoanka, *Taisho Jūyonenchū ni okeru Zairyū Chōsenjin no Jōkyō,* 74; Hŏ Se-ke, "Pak Yŏl Jiken: Shiitagerareta mono no Hangyaku," *Nihon Seiji Saiban Shiroku, Taisho,* 381, 383; Michael Weiner, *The Origins of the Korean Community in Japan,* 107, 149–152; Robert A. Scalapino and Chong-sik Lee, *Communism in Korea* 1:57 n. 118.

27. Imai, 382, 389.

28. Hŏ, 385–386; Matsuo Takayoshi, *Chian Iji Hō: Dan'atsu to Teikō no Rekishi*, 110.

29. Shiono Suehiko Kaikoroku Kankōkai, *Shiono Suehiko Kaikoroku*, 24.

30. Quoted in Hŏ, 381, 383.

31. Ibid., 401–402; Nomura Masao, *Hōsō Fūunroku: Anohito Konohito Hōmonki* 2:224–225; Shiono, 232.

32. Hŏ, 379, 390, 395, 407–411; Matsuo, *Chian Iji Hō*, 111; Procurator Shiono states that Wakatsuki asked for a sentence reduction; it was granted (on April 15) because the crime had not been fully carried out. Shiono, 231 n. 2.

33. Hŏ, 404.

34. Tamiya, 419–421; Shinobu, *Taisho Seiji Shi*, 1131–1132; Thomas A. Stanley, *Ōsugi Sakae, Anarchist in Taishō Japan: The Creativity of the Ego*, 159–160.

35. "Ōsugi Jiken," in Takahashi Masae (ed.), *Zoku, GSS* 6:491–492.

36. Quoted in ibid., 491.

37. Ibid., 492.

38. Tamiya, 419, 422–426, 433–434.

39. "Ōsugi Jiken," in Takahashi (ed.), *GSS*, 492.

40. *KES*, 233.

41. Imai, 381, 385.

42. Tamiya Hiroshi, "Fukuda Taishō Sogeki Jiken: Ōsugi Sakae Gyakusatsu ni Taisuru Hōfukutero no Shippai," in Wagatsuma Sakae (ed.), *Nihon Seiji Saiban Shiroku, Taisho*, 487–493.

43. Ibid., 490.

44. Quoted in Tanaka Tokihiko, "Toranomon Jiken: Kōtaishi o Sogeki Shita Nanba Daisuke," in Wagatsuma Sakae (ed.), *Nihon Seiji Saiban Shiroku, Taisho*, 439.

45. Imai, 415; *SKST* 7 (October 1933): 239.

46. Tanaka, 442–448, 450, 452–454, 456, 462, 464, 469; *SKST* 7:239.

47. Tanaka, 464–472, 475–477.

48. Ibid., 468, 471, 476–477.

49. Henry D. Smith, *Japan's First Student Radicals*, 110–119.

50. Quoted in ibid., 124.

51. Kikukawa, 432; Kawasaki Takukichi Denki Hensankai, *Kawasaki Takukichi*, 304; Smith, 191–192.

52. Kikukawa, 439, 441; Matsuo, *Chian Iji Hō*, 72, 74; *SKST* 12 (May 1934): 211–213; Smith, 192–193; Okudaira Yasuhiro, *Chian Iji Hō Shōshi*, 66.

53. Smith, 193.

54. Matsuo, *Chian Iji Hō*, 75–77; Kikukawa, 441–444, 449–450.

55. Kikukawa, 450–451; "Gakuren Jiken Dainishin Hanketsubun (1929)," in Okudaira Yasuhiro (ed.), *GSS* 45:540–542.

56. Smith, 193.

57. Quoted in Kikukawa, 445.

58. Matsuo, *Chian Iji Hō*, 73, 75, 77.

59. Yamabe Kentarō (ed.), *GSS* 16:vii, xii–xiii; Itō Miyoji, "Himitsu Kessha Nihon Kyōsantō Jiken no Gaiyō," in ibid., 1–2, 5–6; Kita Kazuo, *Nihon Kyōsantō Shimatsuki*, 14, 18, 20–21; Asahi Jānaru (ed.), *Showa Shi no Shunkan* 1:46–47; Beckmann and Okubo, 94, 105, 111–112, 153.

60. Matsuzaka Hiromasa, "San'ichigo, Yon'ichiroku Jiken Kaiko," in Yamabe (ed.), *GSS* 6:49.

61. Ibid., 49–51.

62. Ibid., 50.

63. Ibid., 53–54; Odanaka Toshiki, "San'ichigo, Yon'ichiroku Jiken: Chian Iji Hō Saiban to Hōtei Tōsō," in Wagatsuma Sakae (ed.), *Nihon Seiji Saiban Shiroku, Showazen*, 130.

64. Matsuzaka, 54.

65. Okudaira (ed.), *GSS* 45:646.

66. Beckmann and Okubo, 176, 180–181; Kita, 164–166, 179; Okudaira (ed.), *GSS* 45:647.

67. Tokuda Kyūichi and Shiga Yoshio, *Gokuchū Jūhachinen*, 115–116.

68. Ibid., 53–55.

69. Hijikata Tetsu, *Hisabetsu Buraku no Tatakai: Ningen ni Hikari Are*, 116–117, 122.

70. Quoted in ibid., 117–118.

71. Ibid., 118–121.

72. Matsuo, *Chian Iji Hō*, 147–148.

73. Ueda Seikichi, *Showa Saiban Shiron: Chian Iji Hō to Hōritsukatachi*, 18.

74. Ishioka Matsugorō, "Toyotama Keimusho no Omoide," in *TK*, 5, 7.

75. Kita, 67–70; Matsuoka Hideo, *Jinken Yōgo Rokujūnen: Bengoshi Unno Shinkichi*, 60–61.

76. Mori Tadashi, *Chian Iji Hō Saiban to Bengoshi*, 116, 164–167; Kita, 122–128.

77. Kita, 35–36; Itō Miyoji, "Himitsu Kessha Nihon Kyōsantō Jiken no Gaiyō," in Yamabe (ed.), *GSS* 16:7.

78. Mitchell, *Thought Control*, 88–91; Wagatsuma (ed.), *KHS*, 451.

79. Fuse Tatsuji, *Kyōsantō Jiken ni Taisuru Hihan to Kōgi*, 4.

80. Ibid., 5, 7, 12.

81. Ibid., 15, 26–45.

82. Kobayashi Takiji, *Senkyūhyakunijūhachinen Sangatsu Jūgonichi, Kanikōsen, Tō Seikatsusha*, 222–224.

83. Ibid., 47–51, 55–56, 65.

84. Quoted in ibid., 65.

85. Matsuo, *Chian Iji Hō,* 149.
86. Ichikawa Yoshio (ed.), *Rōdōsha Nōmin Daigishi: Yamamoto Senji wa Gikai de Ikani Tatakattaka,* 55–62.
87. Quoted in ibid., 62.
88. Ibid., 63–64, 70.
89. Ibid., 89, 93, 100, 105–106.
90. Quoted in ibid., 106.
91. *SKST* 7:445, 489, 495.
92. *KES,* 263, 266–268.
93. Ibid., 298–299.
94. Ibid., 301–302.
95. *Kokusho,* 116; Nanba Hideo, *Ichi Shakai Undōka no Kaisō,* 75–76.
96. *KES,* 318–319.
97. Ibid., 321–322.
98. Sakamoto Hideo, *Shisōteki Hanzai ni Taisuru Kenkyū,* in *SK* 8 (6) (December 1928): 659.
99. Frank O. Miller, *Minobe Tatsukichi: Interpreter of Constitutionalism in Japan,* 153.
100. Quoted in ibid., 148.
101. *Ibid.,* 149.
102. Harry E. Wildes, "The Japanese Police," *Journal of Criminal Law, Criminology and Police Science* 19 (November 1928): 393–394.
103. Ishihara Masajirō, *Shisō Keisatsu Gairon,* 3, 35, 110.
104. Ibid., 35.
105. Nosaka Sanzō Shiryō Hensan Iinkai (ed.), *Nosaka Sanzō no Ayunda Michi,* 45–47.
106. Beckmann and Okubo, 389.
107. Yamashiro Tomoe and Makise Kikue (eds.), *Tanno Setsu Kakumei Undō ni Ikiru,* 137.
108. Quoted in Igarashi Motosaburō, "Toyotama Keimusho de," in *TK,* 31.
109. Ibid., 32–34.
110. Matsumoto Tomone, "From Marxism to Japanism: A Study of Kamei Katsuichirō," Ph.D. diss., 94–95.
111. Tipton, 172, 174, 183–185. Obinata Sumio, *Tennōsei Keisatsu to Minshū,* has a good summary of people-police relations, 119–120, 125, 141–143. For a brief summary of the debate within the Home Ministry over changing the police image, see Sheldon Garon, *The State and Labor in Modern Japan,* 87–89.
112. Garon, 174–175.
113. Yamashiro and Makise (eds.), 18, 53.
114. Ibid., 18, 53, 167–168.
115. Beckmann and Okubo, 156.
116. Quoted in Maezawa Hiroaki (ed.), *Nihon Kokkai Nanajūnen Shi,* 763.

117. Beckmann and Okubo, 156.
118. Quoted in Maezawa (ed.), 525.

CHAPTER 3

1. Richard H. Mitchell, *Thought Control in Prewar Japan*, 93–94, 119, 170–172, 196.
2. Patricia G. Steinhoff, "Tenkō," *Encyclopedia of Japan* 8:6–7.
3. B. J. George, "The Impact of the Past upon the Rights of the Accused in Japan," *Civil Law and Military Journal* 5.3–4 (July–December 1969): 63, 74; Nagashima Atsushi, "The Accused and Society: The Administration of Criminal Justice in Japan," in Arthur T. von Mehren (ed.), *Law in Japan: The Legal Order in a Changing Society*, 304–305.
4. Ueda Seikichi, *Showa Saiban Shiron: Chian Iji Hō to Hōritsukatachi*, 109–111; Morinaga Eizaburō, "Fuse Tatsuji (Jinken Yōgo Undō Shijō no Ni Sendachi)," *Hōgaku Seminā*, December 1956, 47.
5. "Bengoshi Unno Shinkichi" Kankō Iinkai (ed.), *Bengoshi Unno Shinkichi*, 713–714; Matsuoka Hideo, *Jinken Yōgo Rokujūnen: Bengoshi Unno Shinkichi*, 208; Hirai Atsuko, *Individualism and Socialism: The Life and Thought of Kawai Eijirō (1891–1944)*, 182–194.
6. Matsuoka, 67.
7. Morinaga, "Fuse," 47; Mori Tadashi, *Chian Iji Hō Saiban to Bengoshi*, 53–54, 56, 67, 81, 84.
8. Mori, 40, 99, 102–103.
9. Odanaka Toshiki, "San'ichigo, Yon'ichiroku Jiken: Chian Iji Hō Saiban to Hōtei Tōsō," in Wagatsuma Sakae (ed.), *Nihon Seiji Saiban Shiroku, Showazen*, 190–194; for a complete list of defense lawyers, see Mori, 102–103.
10. Miyagi Minoru, "Watakushi no Keiken Yori Mitaru Kyōsantō Jiken no Shinri ni Tsuite," in Yamabe (ed.), *GSS* 16:603; *SKST* 57 (February 1939): 49, 51–54, 57; Odanaka, "San'ichigo, Yon'ichiroku Jiken," 203–204.
11. *SKST* 57:65–66.
12. *JWC*, July 9, 1931, 54.
13. Ibid., July 16, 1931, 80; *SKST* 57:65.
14. Odanaka, "San'ichigo, Yon'ichiroku Jiken," 209, 211–212.
15. Ibid., 208–209; for the 1932 Thesis, see George M. Beckmann and Okubo Genji, *The Japanese Communist Party, 1922–1945*, 332–351.
16. *JWC*, July 14, 1932, 55.
17. Ueda, 114; Mori, 189, 193, 196, 198, 223, 244–245.
18. Nabeyama Sadachika, *Watakushi wa Kyōsantō o Suteta: Jiyū to Sokoku o Motomete*, 141.
19. *JWC*, October 8, 1931, 431.
20. Tokyo Bengoshikai ni okeru Keimu Iinkai, "Ichigaya Keimusho ni

okeru Ryōgyaku Bōkō Jiken no Kōkoku (1931)," in Yamabe Kentarō (ed.), *GSS* 18:339.

21. "Yon'ichiroku Jiken Kōhan Daihyō Chinjutsu (1932)," in ibid., 326–328.

22. Odanaka, "San'ichigo, Yon'ichiroku Jiken," 210, 217.

23. Tokuda Kyūichi and Shiga Yoshio, *Gokuchū Jūhachinen*, 130.

24. Quoted in Mori, 194.

25. Ibid., 198, 209; Morinaga, "Fuse," 47.

26. Odanaka, "San'ichigo, Yon'ichiroku Jiken," 215–218.

27. Ibid., 200; *SKST* 57:72.

28. Mitchell, *Thought Control*, 110–111.

29. Sone Chūichi, *Tokkō Keisatsu to Shakai Undō no Gaisetsu*, 53.

30. Beckmann and Okubo, 245–251.

31. Hasebe Kingo, *Shisōhan no Hogo ni Tsuite*, SK 21 (10) (March 1937): 54, 56.

32. Odanaka, "San'ichigo, Yon'ichiroku Jiken," 221, 225–227.

33. Mori, 103, 330; *JWC*, September 21, 1933, 371; *JWC*, November 23, 1933, 641.

34. Quoted in Mori, 342.

35. Ibid.

36. Quoted in ibid., 343.

37. Ibid.

38. Ueda, 109; "Hikokunin Fuse Tatsuji ni Taisuru Chian Iji Hō Ihan Jiken Daiisshin Hanketsu," in Shihōshō Keijikyoku, *Shisō Geppō* 23 (May 1936): 284–290, 319, 348.

39. Ueda, 111.

40. Okudaira Yasuhiro (ed.), *GSS* 45:646–648.

41. William J. Sebald (trans.), *The Criminal Code of Japan*, v.

42. Hoshino Yoshiki, *Kyōsanshugi Sotsugyō no Ki: Shisō no Henreki to Waga Hansei*, 30–33, 39, 41.

43. Kokusho, 115–116.

44. Matsuo Takayoshi, *Chian Iji Hō: Dan'atsu to Teikō no Rekishi*, 148.

45. Yamabe (ed.), *GSS*, 14:xix; Beckmann and Okubo, 387.

46. Kokusho, 113–114.

47. Ibid., 124–125, 129.

48. Donald Keene, *Dawn to the West: Japanese Literature of the Modern Era: Fiction* 1:671–618, 621, 623.

49. *JWC*, March 2, 1933, 284.

50. Frank Motofuji (trans.), *"The Factory Ship" and "The Absentee Landlord"* (Kobayashi Takiji), xxxi.

51. Kokusho, 134–136.

52. Ibid., 137, 198.

53. Quoted in ibid., 198.

54. Ibid., 225.

55. Ueda, 90.
56. Kokusho, 117–118.
57. Beckmann and Okubo, 379; Yamabe (ed.), *GSS* 14:xix.
58. Kokusho, 140; Kawakami Kan, 100.
59. Keene, 873–874.
60. *JWC,* May 28, 1931, 590.
61. Ibid., June 11, 1931, 649.
62. Ibid., January 21, 1932, 72.
63. Ibid., July 28, 1932, 110.
64. Ibid., August 4, 1932, 139.
65. Ibid., April 20, 1933, 550.
66. Ibid., May 11, 1933, 655, 657.
67. Kawakami Kan, 138.
68. *JWC,* May 24, 1934, 690.
69. Ibid., May 9, 1935, 600–601.
70. Ibid., August 15, 1935, 211.
71. Ibid., May 21, 1931, 556.
72. Ibid., June 30, 1932, 869.
73. Ibid., August 4, 1932, 150.
74. Ibid., May 11, 1933, 650.
75. Ibid., November 16, 1933, 615.
76. Ibid., May 16, 1935, 634.
77. Ibid., May 30, 1935, 708.
78. Ibid., August 22, 1935, 243.
79. Sone, 8.
80. Ibid., 52–54.
81. Ishihara Masajirō, *Shisō Keisatsu Gairon,* 57.
82. Ibid., 43–44, 58–60, 104.
83. Keisatsu Kenkyū Kai (ed.), *Shakai Undō ni Chokumen Shite,* 77, 80, 111.
84. Ibid., 91, 93.
85. Ibid., 78–79, 126, 177.
86. Sasaki Yoshizō, *Tokkō Zensho,* 5.
87. Ibid., 6, 168, 247, 249, 251–252.
88. Ibid., 5.
89. Nakagawa Norikata, *Shisō Hanzai Sōsa Teiyō,* i.
90. Aoki Sadao, *Tokkō Kyōtei,* 6–7, 165.
91. Quoted in Elise K. Tipton, "The Civil Police in the Suppression of the Prewar Japanese Left," Ph.D. diss., 196.
92. Ibid., 205.
93. Quoted in Kokusho, 225.
94. Hiramatsu Yoshirō, "History of Penal Institutions: Japan," *Law in Japan: An Annual* (1973): 46–47; Masaki Akira, *Reminiscences of a Japanese Penologist,* 24, 70, 131.

95. Masaki, 62–63, 65, 69, 71; Shiono Suehiko Kaikoroku Kankōkai, *Shiono Suehiko Kaikoroku,* 900; Hiramatsu, 48; *JWC,* November 9, 1933, 588; *JWC,* April 14, 1938, 469–470.

96. *JWC,* November 16, 1933, 611.

97. Ibid., October 27, 1938, 489.

98. Ibid., June 11, 1931, 649.

99. Ibid., December 28, 1939, 732.

100. Ibid., April 14, 1938, 470.

101. Ibid., January 31, 1935, 134.

102. Matsumoto Tomone, "From Marxism to Japanism: A Study of Kamei Katsuichirō," Ph.D. diss., 96.

103. Roger Swearingen and Paul Langer, *Red Flag in Japan: International Communism in Action, 1919–1951,* 32.

104. Igarashi Motosaburō, "Toyotama Keimusho de," in *TK* 30–32; Sano Hidehiko, "Gokusha Seikatsu no Kiroku," in *TK,* 26.

105. Akita Ujaku, *Gojūnen Seikatsu Nenpu,* 199, 210.

106. Suzuki Mosaburō, *Aru Shakai Shugisha no Hansei,* 226, 231, 237.

107. *SKST* 88 (October 1941): 134–137.

108. Kishi Seiji, "Watakushi to Toyotama Keimusho," in *TK,* 41–43; Igarashi Motosaburō, 30, 32.

109. Tokuda and Shiga, 99–100, 144, 148, 152.

110. Nabeyama, 170; Nabeyama Sadachika and Sano Manabu, *Tenkō Jūgonen,* 135–136.

111. Tokuda and Shiga, 92, 144–145; Nabeyama and Sano, 110, 119.

112. Quoted in Matsumoto, 107.

113. Kawakami Hajime, *Gokuchū Nikki,* 3, 13, 22, 42, 44.

114. Keene, 886.

115. Fujita Toshitsugu, "Dokubō no Kaiwa," in *TK,* 65; Yahata Saburō, "Toyotama: Watakushi no Daigaku," in *TK,* 72–73.

116. Beckmann and Okubo, 264.

117. Patricia G. Steinhoff, "Tenkō: Ideology and Social Integration in Prewar Japan," Ph.D. diss., 128–129.

118. Tokuda and Shiga, 152.

119. Ibid., 92–93.

120. Keene, 850–851.

121. Thomas R. Havens, *Valley of Darkness: The Japanese People and World War Two,* 125, 132.

122. Quoted in ibid., 118.

123. *JWC,* February 17, 1938, 201.

124. Nabeyama and Sano, 147; Nabeyama, 188.

125. Beckmann and Okubo, 362–389.

126. *SKST* 34 (December 1936): 25.

127. Mitchell, *Thought Control,* 156.

128. Beckmann and Okubo, 260, 262; George O. Totten, *The Social*

Democratic Movement in Prewar Japan, 167, 171, 419; William D. Wray, "The Japanese Popular Front Movement, July 1936–February 1938," in Papers on Japan from Seminars at Harvard University 5:129.

129. Suzuki, 231–232, 236–237.

130. SKST 34:26.

131. Ibid., 26–27.

132. SKST 37 (July 1937): 21.

133. Totten, 167; Wray, 129.

134. SKST 45 (August 1938): 40, 49–50, 52–53, 71.

135. Okudaira (ed.), GSS 45:646–648.

136. SKST 45:201, 215, 217, 244, 248–251, 253.

137. JWC, March 26, 1936, 382.

138. Ibid., June 18, 1936, 783.

139. Ibid., June 25, 1936, 804.

140. SKST 37:22.

141. JWC, February 17, 1938, 201.

142. Matsuzaka Hiromasa, "San'ichigo, Yon'ichiroku Jiken Kaiko," in Yamabe (ed.), GSS 16:55.

143. Quoted in Iwagiri Noboru (ed.), Motoji Shinkuma Den, 121.

144. Quoted in ibid.

145. Quoted in ibid., 121–122.

146. Quoted in ibid., 123–124.

147. JWC, July 2, 1936, 31.

148. Ibid., June 2, 1938, 681.

149. Ibid., October 26, 1939, 455.

150. Japan, Naimushō Keihokyoku, Tokkō Keisatsu Reikishū, sec. 3 (1939): 7, 9.

151. Ibid., 10, 14.

152. Ibid., 14.

153. JWC, February 10, 1938, 171.

154. Gordon Mark Berger, Parties Out of Power in Japan, 1931–1941, 141–144, 147–148, 169.

155. Shiono Suehiko Kaikoroku Kankōkai, Shiono Suehiko Kaikoroku, 592.

156. Hasebe, 56.

157. Beckmann and Okubo, 183–187.

158. Hasebe, 54; Yamabe (ed.), GSS 16:xiv.

159. SK 16 (August 1932): 114, 116, 119–120.

160. Tozawa Shigeo, "Shisō Hanzai no Kensatsu Jitsumu ni Tsuite," in Yamabe (ed.), GSS 16:26–27.

161. SKST 16 (October 1934): 135–138.

162. SKST 22 (September 1935): 34–37, 42–43, 47, 49–51, 54, 57–59, 62–64, 66–67, 69, 76, 79, 86.

163. "Shisōhan Hogo Kansatsu Hō Kankei Shiryō (1936)," in Okudaira (ed.), GSS 45:273.

164. Shihōshō Hogokyoku, *Shihō Hogo Jigyō Hōkirui Shū,* 327–328; Hasebe, 77–78.

165. *SKST* 34:26.

166. Moriyama Takeichirō, *Shisōhan Hogo Kansatsu Hō Kaisetsu,* 21.

167. Ibid., 1–3.

168. Moriyama Takeichirō, "Rescuing Radicals by Law," *Contemporary Japan: A Review of Japanese Affairs* 6, 2 (September 1937): 277–278.

169. Ibid., 279.

170. *SKST* 34:32–33, 35.

171. *SKST* 86 (May 1941): 151.

172. Ibid., 361; *SKST* 57:43.

173. Suekawa Hiroshi (ed.), *Roppō Zensho,* 76–78.

174. Hattori Takaaki, "The Legal Profession in Japan: Its Historical Development and Present State," in von Mehren (ed.), 129 n. 67.

175. Yokoyama Shōichirō, "Keiji Hoshō: Hō no Enkaku to Unyō no Mondaiten," *Hōritsu Jihō,* November 1959, 94.

176. Yokoyama Shōichirō, "Keiji Hoshō," in Takioka Takahisa and Yokoyama Shōichirō, *Sōgō Hanrei Kenkyū Sōsho,* 125, 127; Ōkubo Shūhachi (ed.), *Kyojin Shinjin Fusen Daigishi Meienzetsu Shū,* 441, 462.

177. Suekawa (ed.), 76–78.

178. Yokoyama, "Keiji Hoshō," in Takioka and Yokoyama (eds.), 137–138; Ōkubo (ed.), 435.

179. *JWC,* March 5, 1931, 238.

180. Ibid.

181. Yokoyama, "Keiji Hoshō: Hō no Enkaku to Unyō no Mondaiten," 95, 97.

182. Ibid., 95.

183. These figures are drawn from ibid., 96; Yokoyama, "Keiji Hoshō," in Takioka and Yokoyama, 144; Yokoi Daizō, *Shin Keiji Hoshō Hō Taii,* 30–31.

184. *JWC,* July 21, 1932, 86.

185. Yokoyama, "Keiji Hoshō," in Takioka and Yokoyama, 131.

186. Ibid., 133–134.

187. Yokoi, 31.

188. Yokoyama, "Keiji Hoshō," in Takioka and Yokoyama, 130, 139.

189. Ibid., 133–134; Yokoyama, "Keiji Hoshō: Hō no Enkaku to Unyō no Mondaiten," 96.

190. Yokoyama, "Keiji Hoshō," in Takioka and Yokoyama, 138.

191. Tozawa, 35.

192. *SKST* 22:37–38, 50, 58, 70.

193. *SKST* 34:26–27; 37:22, 45.

194. *SKST* 47:52, 116, 119.

195. *SKST* 64:225; 79:195–196.

196. *SKST* 86:338.

197. *SKST* 88:144, 200.
198. Kawakami Kan, 88–89, 102, 127, 132.
199. *JWC,* May 30, 1935, 708.
200. Kawakami Kan, 117–118; *SKST* 37:22.
201. Kawakami Kan, 148.
202. Japan, Shihōshō Keijikyoku, *Keiji Tōkei Nenpyō:* 1926, 310, 746, 756; 1927, 338, 764, 774; 1928, 348, 782, 792; 1929, 348, 780, 792; 1930, 358–361, 792, 802; 1931, 400, 844, 856; 1932, 398, 816, 826; 1933, 422, 886, 898; 1934, 422, 886, 898; 1935, 420, 884, 896; 1936, 426, 892, 904; 1937, 426, 892, 904; 1938, 428, 876, 888; 1939; 420, 786, 798; 1940, 416, 744, 756.
203. Ibid.

CHAPTER 4

1. Miyashita Hiroshi, Itō Takashi, and Nakamura Tomoko, *Tokkō no Kaisō: Aru Jidai no Shōgen,* 123, 249.
2. *JWC,* February 5, 1931, 139.
3. Ibid., March 12, 1931, 278.
4. Ibid., December 31, 1931, 856.
5. Ibid.
6. Ibid., January 14, 1932, 52.
7. Quoted in ibid., February 18, 1931, 219.
8. Ibid., September 29, 1932, 429.
9. Ibid., June 8, 1933, 781.
10. Ibid., June 15, 1933, 837.
11. Ibid., July 5, 1934, 29; July 12, 1934, 67.
12. Ibid., January 31, 1935, 135.
13. Ibid., February 21, 1935, 251.
14. Ibid., April 25, 1935, 551.
15. Ibid., 553.
16. Quoted in ibid., May 23, 1935, 682.
17. Ibid., September 19, 1935, 375.
18. Ibid., October 3, 1935, 424.
19. Ibid., June 30, 1936, 159.
20. Ibid., September 17, 1936, 377.
21. Ibid., October 8, 1936, 471.
22. Quoted in ibid., February 4, 1937, 134.
23. Ibid., February 11, 1937, 174.
24. Ibid., March 4, 1937, 274.
25. Quoted in ibid., March 10, 1938, 309.
26. Ibid., February 10, 1938, 179.
27. Quoted in ibid., December 22, 1938, 746.
28. Arthur E. Tiedemann, "Big Business and Politics in Prewar

Japan," in James W. Morley (ed.), *Dilemmas of Growth in Prewar Japan,* 294–295; Matsuo Takayoshi, "Teijin Incident," *Encyclopedia of Japan* (1983), 7:375; *JWC,* December 23, 1937, 835.

29. *JWC,* January 10, 1935, 31.
30. Ibid., January 31, 1935, 125.
31. Ibid., 126.
32. Quoted in ibid., 134.
33. Ibid., 118.
34. Ibid., December 23, 1937, 818.
35. Ibid., 836.
36. Ibid., February 7, 1935, 161.
37. Ibid., February 14, 1935, 196.
38. Ibid., February 28, 1935, 272.
39. Ibid., May 14, 1936, 600.
40. Ibid., February 25, 1937, 237.
41. Ibid., March 4, 1937, 259.
42. Ibid., March 11, 1937, 293.
43. Ibid., April 1, 1937, 396.
44. Ibid., February 10, 1938, 170; February 24, 1938, 238; March 10, 1938, 303.
45. Ibid., January 21, 1937, 65.
46. Ibid., March 5, 1931, 238–239.
47. Ibid., July 14, 1932, 54.
48. Kawakami Kan, iv, 139, 150.
49. Quoted in ibid., 116.
50. Ibid., 9, 56.
51. Ibid., 71–72.
52. Ibid., 73–82.
53. Ibid., 84–86, 90–96, 99–101.
54. Ibid., 97, 101–102.
55. Ibid., 103, 107–109.
56. Quoted in ibid., 110.
57. Ibid., 150–151.
58. Ibid., 122, 127–132.
59. Ibid., 112.
60. *JWC,* March 4, 1937, 259.
61. Ibid., 251.
62. Ōno Masao, "Shokugyō Shi to shite no Bengoshi oyobi Bengoshi-kai no Rekishi," in Ōno Masao (ed.), *Kōza Gendai no Bengoshi, 2: Bengoshi no Dantai,* 104–105, 107–108.
63. Morinaga Eizaburō, *Nihon Bengoshi Retsuden,* 210.
64. Miyashita, 96–97, 202.
65. Ogino Fujio, *Tokkō Keisatsu Taisei Shi: Shakai Undō Yokuatsu Torishimari no Kōzō to Jittai,* 215.
66. *JWC,* February 21, 1935, 226.

67. Ibid., January 8, 1931, 25.

68. For attitudes toward communists, see Sheldon Garon, *The State and Labor in Modern Japan,* 150; and Gregory J. Kasza, *The State and the Mass Media in Japan, 1918–1945,* 42–44, 54.

69. Japan, Naimushō Keihokyoku, *Dai 65-kai Teikoku Gikai Chian Iji Hō Kaisei Hōritsuan,* 160; *JWC,* February 15, 1934, 201–202.

70. Kasza, 137 n. 53.

71. Japan, Naimushō Keihokyoku, *Dai 65-kai,* 17–21, 23.

72. Quoted in Mishima Yukio, *Runaway Horses,* 349–351.

73. Frank Miller, *Minobe Tatsukichi: Interpreter of Constitutionalism in Japan,* 154.

74. *JWC,* January 31, 1935, 126.

75. Miller, 153–154; *JWC* March 5, 1931, 250.

76. Makino Eiichi, *Hijōji Rippō Kō,* 199.

77. Andrew E. Barshay, *State and Intellectual in Imperial Japan: The Public Man in Crisis,* 44.

78. Miyashita, 123–124, 253.

79. Quoted in ibid., 128.

80. Ibid., 313.

81. Maruyama Masao, *Thought and Behavior in Modern Japanese Politics,* 12–13, 18.

82. Elise K. Tipton, "The Civil Police in the Suppression of the Prewar Japanese Left," Ph.D. diss., 177, 192, 197.

83. Kawakami Kan, 102.

84. Quoted in *JWC* March 19, 1931, 311.

85. Kawakami Kan, 113–116, 127, 132.

86. Japan, Naimushō Keihokyoku, *Kyokusa Bunshi no Buki Shiyō ni yoru Shōgai Teido Narabi ni sono Bukibetsu Shirabe. Kyokusa Bunshi no Buki Shiyō ni yoru Keisatsukan Shōgai Shirabe,* 1–6.

87. George M. Beckmann and Okubo Genji, *The Japanese Communist Party, 1922–1945,* 192–193, 236–237.

CHAPTER 5

1. *SKST* 79 (August 1940): 101.

2. Ibid., 197.

3. Ibid., 430.

4. Miyashita Hiroshi, Itō Takashi, and Nakamura Tomoko, *Tokkō no Kaisō: Aru Jidai no Shōgen,* 156–158; Ben-Ami Shillony, *Politics and Culture in Wartime Japan,* 14–15; Edward J. Drea, "The Japanese General Election of 1942: A Study of Political Institutions in Wartime," Ph.D. diss., 343–344.

5. Shōkadō Henshūbu (comp.), *Chian Keisatsu Kyōhon,* 74, 141-1. This peculiar numbering system (i.e., "141-1") is correct.

6. Kuroda Hidetoshi, *Chishikijin Genron Dan'atsu no Kiroku,* 146.

7. Richard H. Mitchell, *Thought Control in Prewar Japan,* 166–170; for the complete text, see Domei Tsushin Sha (trans. and comp.), *Wartime Legislation in Japan: A Selection of Important Laws Enacted or Revised in 1941,* 69–103; or Wagatsuma (ed.), *KHS,* 451–454.

8. *SKST* 79:158–159.

9. Ibid., 166–167.

10. Kyōsei Kyōkai (ed.), *Senji Gyōkei Jitsuroku,* 354.

11. Articles 39–64 of the peace law; Domei Tsushin Sha, 88–101; Abe Haruo "The Former Japanese System of Preventive Detention," *International Commission of Jurists Journal* 3, 1 (1961): 100–102.

12. *SKST* 91 (June 1942): 1, 25.

13. Matsumoto Kazumi, "Tokyo Yobō Kōkinjo no Kaisō," in *TK,* 166, 179, 181–182, 193.

14. Tsuchiya Shukurō, *Yobō Kōkinjo,* 8, 21–24, 205.

15. Matsumoto, 175–177, 191–194.

16. Kuroda Hidetoshi, *Yokohama Jiken,* 211–231; Hatanaka Shigeo, "Kaikon, soshite Kaikon kara no Dasshutsu," in *Yokohama Jiken: Genron Dan'atsu no Kōzu,* 62, 65–66; Jay Rubin, *Injurious to Public Morals: Writers and the Meiji State,* 267–269; Richard H. Mitchell, *Censorship in Imperial Japan,* 329–330; Kokusho, 119; Shillony, 125–126; Tsurumi Shunsuke, *An Intellectual History of Wartime Japan, 1931–1945,* 90–93.

17. Quoted in Okudaira Yasuhiro, "Yokohama Jiken to Chian Iji Hō," in *Yokohama Jiken: Genron Dan'atsu no Kōzu,* 50.

18. "Bengoshi Unno Shinkichi" Kankō Iinkai (ed.), *Bengoshi Unno Shinkichi,* 110–111.

19. Katō Keiji (ed.), *Zoku GSS* 7:xxxvi–xxxviii; "Yokohama Jiken Hikoku Aikawa Hiroshi Shuki (1943)," in ibid., 677–722.

20. Miyashita, 242.

21. Kokusho, 28–29, 72–73.

22. Ienaga Saburō, *The Pacific War,* 212–213; Shillony, 133.

23. Muroga Sadanobu, *Showa Juku: Dan'atsu no Arashi no nakademo Jiyū no Akari o Mamori Tsuzuketa Hitotsu no Juku ga Atta,* 145–146; Gino K. Piovesana, "Miki Kiyoshi: Representative Thinker of an Anguished Generation," in Joseph Roggendorf (ed.), *Studies in Japanese Culture,* 159.

24. Nakanishi Mitsuhiro, "Miki Kiyoshi no Gokushi," in *TK,* 255–256.

25. Kuroda, *Yokohama Jiken,* 220–222.

26. Nagao Ryuichi, "Richard H. Minear, Japanese Tradition and Western Law: Emperor, State, and Law in the Thought of Yatsuka Hozumi," *Law in Japan: An Annual* (1972), 188, 190.

27. Okudaira Yasuhiro, "Chian Iji Hō ni okeru Yobō Kōkin: Sono Seiritsu ni tsuite no Junbiteki Kōsatsu," in Tokyo Daigaku Shakai Kagaku Kenkyūjo (ed.), *Fashizumuki no Kokka to Shakai, 4, Senji Nihon no Hōtaisei,* 224–225.

28. "Bengoshi Unno Shinkichi," 68.

29. Ibid.

30. Ibid., 69-79.

31. George M. Beckmann, and Okubo Genji, *The Japanese Communist Party, 1922-1945,* 76, 107-108, 110.

32. "Bengoshi Unno Shinkichi," 71-72; Odanaka Toshiki, "Jinmin Sensen Jiken: Hansen, Hanfashizumu Seiryoku e no Dan'atsu," in Wagatsuma Sakae (ed.), *Nihon Seiji Saiban Shiroku, Showakō,* 295.

33. Minobe Ryōkichi, *Kumon suru Demokurashii,* 135-140, 155, 158, 160, 168-179, 172-173; Odanaka, "Jinmin Sensen Jiken," 297; Matsuo Takayoshi, *Chian Iji Hō: Dan'atsu to Teikō no Rekishi,* 196, 198.

34. Thomas P. Nadolski, "The Socio-Political Background of the 1921 and 1935 Ōmoto Suppression in Japan," Ph.D. diss., 255-258, 265-268.

35. "Kanketsu ni Atatte (Zadankai)," in Wagatsuma Sakae (ed.), *Nihon Seiji Saiban Shiroku, Showakō,* 594-595; Amamiya Shōichi, "Ketsumeidan Jiken: 'Shihōken Dokuritsu' no Kijakusei no Rotei," in Wagatsuma Sakae (ed.), *Nihon Seiji Saiban Shiroku, Showazen,* 400-461. The Blood Pact Group, which carried out the assassinations of Inoue Junnosuke and Dan Takuma, was organized by Inoue Nisshō. Janet Hunter (comp.), *Concise Dictionary of Modern Japanese History,* 15.

36. *JWC,* August 31, 1933, 281.

37. "Kanketsu ni Atatte (Zadankai)," 576; Hunter, 201; for the "Organ Theory," see Frank O. Miller, *Minobe Tatsukichi: Interpreter of Constitutionalism in Japan,* 27.

38. Quoted in Richard Storry, *A History of Modern Japan,* 196.

39. "Kanketsu ni Atatte (Zadankai)," 589-591.

40. Shillony, 34-35.

41. Abe, "Preventive Detention," 102.

42. *SKST* 90 (January 1942): 203.

43. Shillony, 48-49.

44. Quoted in Matsuzaka Hiromasa Den Kankō Kai (ed.), *Matsuzaka Hiromasa Den,* 222.

45. Mitchell, *Censorship,* 298-299.

46. Okudaira, "Yokohama Jiken to Chian Iji Hō," 49; "Bengoshi Unno Shinkichi," 110.

47. Quoted in J. W. Dower, *Empire and Aftermath: Yoshida Shigeru and the Japanese Experience, 1878-1954,* 258-259.

48. Ibid., 260-264.

49. Shillony, 84-85.

50. Matsumoto, 191-193.

CHAPTER 6

1. Abe Haruo, "Criminal Justice in Japan: Its Historical Background and Modern Problems," *American Bar Association Journal* 47 (June 1961): 558.

2. *JWC,* July 28, 1932, 127.

3. Ibid.

4. Hatanaka Shigeo, "Kaikon, soshite Kaikon kara no Dasshutsu," in *Yokohama Jiken: Genron Dan'atsu no Kōzu,* 64.

5. E. P. Thompson, *Whigs and Hunters: The Origins of the Black Act,* 260.

6. Ibid., 263–264.

7. Kawakami Kan, 87–88, 110, 112.

8. Iwagiri Noboru (ed.), *Motoji Shinkuma Den,* 120–124.

9. Lawrence W. Beer, "Japan," in Jack Donnelly and Rhoda E. Howard (eds.), *International Handbook of Human Rights,* 214.

10. George M. Beckmann and Okubo Genji, *The Japanese Communist Party, 1922–1945,* 270.

11. Raymond D. Gastil, *Freedom in the World: Political Rights and Civil Liberties, 1978,* 18.

12. Milton R. Konvitz, *Bill of Rights Reader: Leading Constitutional Cases,* 1.

13. Cecil H. Uyehara, *Leftwing Social Movements in Japan: An Annotated Bibliography,* 371, 373.

14. Inoue Enzō (ed.), *Shihō Keisatsu Shitsumu Yōten,* 33.

15. "Soshikijō ni kansuru Shirei (1926–1929)," in Yamabe Kentarō (ed.), *GSS* 14:178–179.

16. Hashimoto Kiminobu, "The Rule of Law: Some Aspects of Judicial Review of Administration Action," in Arthur T. von Mehren (ed.), *Law in Japan: The Legal Order in a Changing Society,* 239–240.

17. Matsumoto Shigeru, *Motoori Norinaga 1730–1801,* 142.

18. Ching-chih Chen, "Police and Community Control Systems in the Empire," in Ramon H. Myers and Mark R. Peattie (eds.), *The Japanese Colonial Empire, 1895–1945,* 221, 223, 225; Michael E. Robinson, "Colonial Publication Policy and the Korean Nationalist Movement," in ibid., 313.

19. Quoted in Mike Brogden, "An Act to Colonise the Internal Lands of the Island: Empire and the Origins of the Professional Police," *International Journal of the Sociology of Law* 15, 2 (May 1987): 183.

20. Alvin D. Coox, "Evidences of Antimilitarism in Prewar and Wartime Japan," *Pacific Affairs* 46, 3 (Fall 1973): 505, 507.

21. Miyashita Hiroshi, Itō Takashi, and Nakamura Tomoko, *Tokkō Kaisō: Aru Jidai no Shōgen,* 123–124, 313.

22. Ross Mouer and Yoshio Sugimoto, *Images of Japanese Society: A Study in the Social Construction of Reality,* 248.

23. Quoted in Mikiso Hane, *Peasants, Rebels, and Outcasts: The Underside of Modern Japan,* 228–229.

24. Ibid., 231–232.

25. Ueda Seikichi, *Showa Saiban Shiron: Chian Iji Hō to Hōritsukatachi,* 146.

26. Chalmers Johnson, *An Instance of Treason: Ozaki Hotsumi and the Sorge Spy Ring*, 8, 17, 170; Ben-Ami Shillony, *Politics and Culture in Wartime Japan*, 13.

27. Richard H. Mitchell, *Thought Control in Prewar Japan*, 191.

28. Okudaira Yasuhiro, "Some Preparatory Notes for the Study of the Peace Preservation Law in Pre-war Japan," *Annals of the Institute of Social Science*, no. 14 (1973): 50.

29. Letter to the author, December 15, 1988.

30. Hŏ Se-ke, "Zoruge Jiken: Kokusai Seiji no Urakata," in Wagatsuma Sakae (ed.), *Nihon Seiji Saiban Shiroku, Showakō*, 448, 452.

31. "Kanketsu ni Atatte (Zadankai)," in ibid., 569.

32. Miyashita, 194–195, 238; Hŏ, "Zoruge Jiken," 453.

33. Domei Tsushin Sha (trans. and comp.), *Wartime Legislation in Japan: A Selection of Important Laws Enacted or Revised in 1941*, 70–72.

34. Ibid., 5.

35. Quoted in Yamabe Kentarō, "A Note on *The Korean Communist Movement* of Dae-Sook Suh, With Special Reference to Source Materials Used," *Developing Economies* 5, 2 (June 1967): 410.

36. *JWC*, December 28, 1933, 799.

37. Pak Kyŏng-sik, "Chian Iji Hō ni yoru Chōsenjin Dan'atsu," *Kikan Gendai Shi*, no. 7 (June 1976): 123.

38. Okudaira Yasuhiro, "Chian Iji Hō o Ronzuru: Shimizu Ikutarō 'Sengo o Utagau' o Utagau," *Sekai*, no. 396 (November 1978): 112.

39. Mizuno Naoki, "Chian Iji Hō to Chōsen Oboegaki," *Chōsen Kenkyū*, no. 188 (April 1979): 50.

40. Barton L. Ingraham, *Political Crime in Europe: A Comparative Study of France, Germany, and England*, 47, 56–58, 84, 117, 119, 219–221, 318.

41. Ibid., 229–233, 245.

42. Edward Peters, *Torture*, 112.

43. Ingraham, 288–291.

44. Robert Graves and Alan Hodge, *The Long Week-end: A Social History of Great Britain, 1918–1939*, 312–313.

45. Ingraham, 304–308.

46. Ibid., 252–253, 284–285.

47. Ibid., 256–257.

48. Jacques Delarue, *The Gestapo: A History of Horror*, 34.

49. Ingraham, 257–264.

50. Ibid., 264.

51. Ibid., 264–265.

52. Ibid., 265.

53. Delarue, 77, 179.

54. Heinz Höhne, *The Order of the Death's Head: The Story of Hitler's S.S.*, 201.

55. Helmut Krausnick and Martin Broszat, *Anatomy of the SS State*, 209.

56. Ibid., 166-167; 209-211.

57. Alan Merson, *Communist Resistance in Nazi Germany,* 53-54.

58. Quoted in Peters, 125.

59. Delarue, 234.

60. Henry Shue, "Torture," *Philosophy and Public Affairs* 7, 2 (Winter 1978): 130-133.

61. Ingraham, 266.

62. Carl J. Friedrich and Zbigniew K. Brzezinski, *Totalitarian Dictatorship and Autocracy,* 144-146; Philip V. Cannistraro, *Historical Dictionary of Fascist Italy,* 431.

63. Nathaniel Cantor, "The Fascist Political Prisoners," *Journal of the American Institute of Criminal Law and Criminology* 27 (1936-1937): 173-174.

64. William Ebenstein, *Fascist Italy,* 72, 79, 84; Cantor, 177.

65. Peters, 122.

66. Cantor, 178.

67. Ibid., 171-173; Ebenstein, 73-77; E. K. Branstedt, *Dictatorship and Political Police: The Technique of Control by Fear,* 63-64.

68. Friedrich and Brzezinski, 141; Jonathan R. Adelman, "Soviet Secret Police," in Jonathan R. Adelman (ed.), *Terror and Communist Politics,* 87.

69. Quoted in ibid., 84.

70. Peters, 128-129.

71. Ibid., 129.

72. Peters, 129-130; Friedrich and Brzezinski, 158.

73. Adelman, 90, 98, 100-101.

74. Aleksandr I. Solzhenitsyn, *The Gulag Archipelago, 1918-1956: An Experiment in Literary Investigation,* parts 1 and 2, 108-116.

75. N. A. Zabolotsky, "The Story of My Imprisonment," *Times Literary Supplement,* October 9, 1981, 1179.

76. Ibid., 1179-1180.

77. Stefan T. Possony, "From Gulag to Guitk: Political Prisons in the USSR Today," in Willem A. Veenhoven (ed.), *Case Studies on Human Rights and Fundamental Freedoms: A World Survey* 1:5, 12, 15; Adelman, 91, 98-99; Solzhenitsyn, 563-564.

78. United Nations, Economic and Social Council, Commission on Human Rights (42d Session), P. Kooijmans (Special Rapporteur), *Torture and Other Cruel, Inhuman or Degrading Treatment or Punishment,* February 19, 1986, 28-29.

79. David B. Davis, "The Ends of Slavery," *New York Review of Books* 36, (March 30, 1989): 31; D. H. Foster, D. Sandler, and D. M. Davis, "Detention, Torture and the Criminal Justice Process in South Africa," *Journal of the Sociology of Law* 14, 2 (May 1987): 111.

80. United Nations, *Torture,* 29.

81. Ingraham, 35.

82. Sheldon Garon, *The State and Labor in Modern Japan,* 2, 4–6, 35–36, 47, 54–65, 133–134, 150–151, 178–185; Andrew Gordon, *The Evolution of Labor Relations in Japan: Heavy Industry, 1853–1955,* 208–210; Elise K. Tipton, "The Civil Police in the Suppression of the Prewar Japanese Left," Ph.D. diss., 218–219, 263.

Bibliography

OFFICIAL PUBLICATIONS AND DOCUMENTS

de Becker, J. E. (trans.). *Japanese Code of Criminal Procedure*. Yokohama: Kelley & Walsh, 1918.

Domei Tsushin Sha (trans. and comp.). *Wartime Legislation in Japan: A Selection of Important Laws Enacted or Revised in 1941*. Tokyo: Nippon shogyo tsushin sha, 1941.

"Gakuren Jiken dainishin hanketsubun (1929)" (Second trial verdict for the Gakuren Incident, 1929). In Okudaira Yasuhiro (ed.), *Gendai shi shiryō* (Materials on contemporary history). 45. Tokyo: Misuzu shobō, 1973.

Hasebe Kingo. *Shisōhan no hogo ni tsuite* (On the protection of thought offenders). Shihōshō Chōsaka (Justice Ministry, Research Section), *Shihō kenkyū* (hōkokusho) (Justice research, report). 21 (10). (March 1937).

"Hikokunin Fuse Tatsuji ni taisuru Chian Iji Hō ihan jiken daiisshin hanketsu (Tokyo Keiji Chihō Saibansho hōkoku)" (The first trial verdict for suspect Fuse Tatsuji's Peace Preservation Law violation incident [Tokyo Criminal Affairs District Court's report]). Shihōshō Keijikyoku (Justice Ministry, Criminal Affairs Bureau), *Shisō geppō* (Monthly report on thought). 23 (May 1936).

Itō Miyoji. "Himitsu kessha Nihon Kyōsantō Jiken no gaiyō" (A summary of a secret society: The Japanese Communist Party Incident). In Yamabe Kentarō (ed.), *Gendai shi shiryō* (Materials on contemporary history). 16 Tokyo: Misuzu shobō, 1965.

Japan Federation of Bar Associations. *The Documents Concerning the Daiyo-Kangoku (Japan Substitute Prison System)*. Tokyo: Japan Federation of Bar Associations, 1981.

Japan, Naimushō Keihokyoku (Home Ministry, Police Bureau). *Dai 65-kai Teikoku Gikai Chian Iji Hō Kaisei Hōritsuan* (The Sixty-fifth Imperial Diet and the Peace Preservation Law Revision Bill). 1934.

———. *Kyokusa bunshi no buki shiyō ni yoru shōgai teido narabi ni sono bukibetsu shirabe. Kyokusa bunshi no buki shiyō ni yoru keisatsukan shōgai shirabe* (Seriousness of injuries caused by weapons used by extreme leftists and a survey of the weapons. A survey of injuries of policemen caused by weapons used by extreme leftists). 1935.

———. *Showa shichinenchū ni okeru shakai undō no jōkyō* (The present state of the social movement). 1932.

———. *Taisho jūyonenchū ni okeru zairyū Chōsenjin no jōkyō* (The condition of resident Koreans during 1925). 1926. Library of Congress, Reel SP47. Special Studies 155.

———. *Tokkō keisatsu reikishū* (Collection of regulations for the Special Higher Police). Section 3. 1939.

Japan, Shihōshō (Justice Ministry). *Kangoku Hō* (Prison law). Undated.

Japan, Shihōshō Chōsaka (Justice Ministry, Research Section). *Shihō kenkyū* (Justice research). 16 (August 1932). Dai jukkai Jitsumuka Kaidō (The tenth Conference of Administrators).

Japan, Shihōshō Chōsaka Hogokyoku (Justice Ministry, Research Section, Protection Bureau). *Shihō hogo jigyō hōkirui shū* (Collection of laws and regulations for justice protection affairs). 1942.

Japan, Shihōshō Keijikyoku (Justice Ministry, Criminal Affairs Bureau). *Keiji Tōkei nenpyō* (Annual criminal statistics). 1926–1940.

———. *Shisō kenkyū shiryō tokushū* (Thought research materials, special number). 7 (October 1933). *Daigojukkai Teikoku Gikai Chian Iji Hōan giji sokkiroku narabi iinkai giroku* (The Fiftieth Imperial Diet. Stenographic record of the deliberations on the Peace Preservation Law Bill and record of committee meetings). Reprint, ed. by Shakai mondai shiryō kenkyū kai. Kyoto: Tōyō bunka sha, 1972.

———. *Shisō kenkyū shiryō tokushū* (Thought research materials, special number). 16 (October 1934). *Showa 9-nen 5-gatsu Shisō Jimu Kaidō gijiroku* (Record of the proceedings at the May 1934 Conference on Thought Affairs).

———. *Shisō kenkyū shiryō tokushū* (Thought research materials, special number). 22 (September 1935). *Showa 10-nen 6-gatsu Shisō Jitsumuka Kaidō narabi ni Shihō Kenkyū Jitsumuka Kaidō giji sokkiroku* (Stenographic record of the proceedings at the Thought Administrators' Conference and the Justice Research Administrators' Conference in June, 1935).

———. *Shisō kenkyū shiryō tokushū* (Thought research materials, special number). 34 (December 1936). *Showa 11-nen 11-gatsu Shisō Jitsumuka Kaidō giji sokkiroku* (Stenographic record of the proceedings at the November 1936 Conference of Thought Administrators).

———. *Shisō kenkyū shiryō tokushū* (Thought research materials, special number). 37 (July 1937). *Showa 12-nen 6-gatsu Shisō Jitsumuka Kaidō giji sokkiroku* (Stenographic record of the proceedings at the June 1937 Conference of Thought Administrators).

———. *Shisō kenkyū shiryō tokushū* (Thought research materials, special number). 45 (August 1938). *Showa 13-nendo 6-gatsu Shisō Jitsumuka Kaidō giji sokkiroku* (Stenographic record of the proceedings at the June 1938 Conference of Thought Administrators).

———. *Shisō kenkyū shiryō tokushū* (Thought research materials, special number). 57 (February 1939). *Showa 13-nen 10-gatsu Shisō Jitsumuka Kaidō kōenshū (sono I)* (Collection of lectures at the October 1938 Conference of Thought Administrators, part 1).

———. *Shisō kenkyū shiryō tokushū* (Thought research materials, special number). 64 (September 1939). *Showa 14-nen 6-gatsu Shisō Jitsumuka Kaidō giji sokkiroku* (Stenographic record of the proceedings at the June 1939 Conference of Thought Administrators).

———. *Shisō kenkyū shiryō tokushū* (Thought research materials, special number). 79 (August 1940). *Showa 15-nen 5-gatsu Shisō Jitsumuka Kaidō gijiroku* (Record of the proceedings at the May 1940 Conference of Thought Administrators).

———. *Shisō kenkyū shiryō tokushū* (Thought research materials, special number). 86 (May 1941). *Showa 15-nendo kōsoin kannai Shisō Jitsumuka Kaidō gijiroku* (Record of the proceedings at the 1940 Conference of Thought Administrators within the jurisdiction of appeals courts).

———. *Shisō kenkyū shiryō tokushū* (Thought research materials, special number). 88 (October 1941). *Showa 16-nen 4-gatsu rinji Shisō Jitsumuka Kaidō gijiroku* (Record of the proceedings at the April 1941 extraordinary Conference of Thought Administrators).

———. *Shisō kenkyū shiryō tokushū* (Thought research materials, special number). 90 (January 1942). *Showa 16-nen 7-gatsu Shisō Jitsumuka Kaidō gijiroku* (Record of the proceedings at the July 1941 Conference of Thought Administrators).

———. *Shisō kenkyū shiryō tokushū* (Thought research materials, special number). 91 (June 1942). *Showa 16-nendo kōsoin kannai Shisō Kensatsu Kaidō gijiroku* (Record of the proceedings at the 1941 Conference on Thought Prosecution within the jurisdiction of appeals courts).

———. Shihō Daijin Kanbō Hishoka (The Justice Minister's Secretariat). *Kunji enjutsu shū* (Collection of oral instructions). May 1909–May 1933.

Katō Keiji (ed.). *Zoku, gendai shi shiryō* (Materials on contemporary history, continued). 7. Tokyo: Misuzu shobō, 1982.

Kawakami Kan. *Iwayuru jinken jūrin mondai ni tsuite* (About the so-called infringement of human rights). In Shihōshō Chōsaka (Justice Ministry, Research Section), *Shihō kenkyū* (hōkokusho) (Justice research, report). 24 (14) (February 1938).

Koyama Matsukichi. "Meiji Jidai no shakaishugi undō ni tsuite" (Socialism and its movement during the Meiji Period). In Shihōshō Keijikyoku (Justice Ministry, Criminal Affairs Bureau). *Shisō kenkyū shiryō tokushū* (Thought research materials, special number). 59 (March 1939). *Showa 13-nen 10-gatsu Shisō Jitsumuka Kaidō kōenshū (sono II)* (Collection of lectures at the October 1938 Conference of Thought Administrators, part 2).

Matsuzaka Hiromasa. "San'ichigo, Yon'ichiroku Jiken kaiko" (Recollection of the March 15 and April 16 Incidents). In Yamabe Kentarō (ed.), *Gendai shi shiryō* (Materials on contemporary history). 16. Tokyo: Misuzu shobō, 1965.

Miyagi Minoru. "Watakushi no keiken yori mitaru Kyōsantō Jiken no shinri ni tsuite" (On the Communist Party Incident trial, from the standpoint of my experience). In Yamabe Kentarō (ed.), *Gendai shi shiryō* (Materials on contemporary history). 16. Tokyo: Misuzu shobō, 1965.

Nihon kindai shiryō kenkyūkai (Association for research on modern Japanese historical materials) (ed.). *Taisho kōki Keihokyoku kankō shakai undō shiryō* (Social movement materials published by the Police Bureau during the late Taisho period). Tokyo: Nihon kindai shiryō kenkyūkai, 1968.

Okudaira Yasuhiro (ed.). *Gendai shi shiryō* (Materials on contemporary history). 45. Tokyo: Misuzu shobō, 1973.

"Ōsugi Jiken" (Ōsugi Incident). In Takahashi Masae (ed.), *Zoku, gendai shi shiryō* (Materials on contemporary history, continued). 6. Tokyo: Misuzu shobō, 1982.

Sakamoto Hideo. *Shisōteki hanzai ni taisuru kenkyū* (Research on thought crimes). In Shihōshō Chōsaka (Justice Ministry, Research Section), *Shihō kenkyū* (hōkokushoshū) (Justice research, report). 8 (6) (December 1928).

Sebald, William J. (trans.). *The Criminal Code of Japan.* Kobe: Japan chronicle press, 1936.

"Shisōhan hogo kansatsu hō kankei shiryō (1936)" (Materials in connection with the Thought Criminals' Protection and Supervision Law, 1936). In Okudaira Yasuhiro (ed.), *Gendai shi shiryō* (Materials on contemporary history). 45. Tokyo: Misuzu shobō, 1973.

Sone, Chūichi. *Tokkō Keisatsu to shakai undō no gaisetsu* (An outline of the Special Higher Police and the social movement). Yamagata: Yamagata ken keisatsubu tokubetsu kōtōka, 1930.

"Soshikijō ni kansuru shirei (1926–1929)" (Instructions about the organization, 1926–1929). In Yamabe Kentarō (ed.), *Gendai shi shiryō* (Materials on contemporary history). 14. Tokyo: Misuzu shobō, 1964.

Suekawa Hiroshi (ed.). *Roppō zensho* (A compendium of the six codes). Tokyo: Iwanami shoten, 1944.

Takahashi Masae (ed.). *Zoku, gendai shi shiryō* (Materials on contemporary history, continued). 6. Tokyo: Misuzu shobō, 1982.

Tokyo Bengoshikai ni okeru Keimu Iinkai (Criminal Affairs Committee of the Tokyo Bar Association). "Ichigaya Keimusho ni okeru ryōgyaku bōkō jiken no hōkoku (1931)" (Report on the outrageous assault incident at Ichigaya Prison, 1931). In Yamabe Kentarō (ed.), *Gendai shi shiryō* (Materials on contemporary history). 18. Tokyo: Misuzu shobō, 1966.

Tozawa Shigeo. "Shisō hanzai no kensatsu jitsumu ni tsuite" (About the business of investigating thought crimes). In Yamabe Kentarō (ed.), *Gendai shi shiryō* (Materials on contemporary history). 16. Tokyo: Misuzu shobō, 1965.

United Nations. Economic and Social Council. Commission on Human Rights (42d Session). P. Kooijmans (Special Rapporteur). *Torture and Other Cruel, Inhuman or Degrading Treatment or Punishment.* February 19, 1986.

United States. National Commission on Law Observance and Enforcement. *Report on Lawlessness in Law Enforcement.* Washington, D.C.: U.S. Government Printing Office, 1931.

Yamabe Kentarō (ed.). *Gendai shi shiryō* (Materials on contemporary history). 14, 16, 18. Tokyo: Misuzu shobō, 1964, 1965, 1966.

"Yokohama Jiken hikoku Aikawa Hiroshi shuki (1943)" (The memoir of Yokohama Incident defendant Aikawa Hiroshi, 1943). In Katō Keiji (ed.), *Zoku, gendai shi shiryō* (Materials on contemporary history, continued). 7. Tokyo: Misuzu shobō, 1982.

"Yon'ichiroku Jiken kōhan daihyō chinjutsu (1932)" (Representatives' statements at the 4/16 Incident open trial, 1932). In Yamabe Kentarō (ed.), *Gendai shi shiryō* (Materials on contemporary history). 18. Tokyo: Misuzu shobō, 1966.

Yoshikawa Mitsusada. *Iwayuru Kome Sōdō Jiken no kenkyū* (Research on the so-called Rice Riots Incident). Shihōshō Keijikyoku (Justice Ministry, Criminal Affairs Bureau), *Shisō kenkyū shiryō tokushū* (Thought research materials, special number). 51 (1938). Reprinted by Hōmufu Kenmukyoku (Judicial Affairs Office, Investigative Affairs Bureau), *Kōan kankei shiryō daisanshū* (Materials on public safety), no. 3 (July 1952).

BOOKS

Adelman, Jonathan R. "Soviet Secret Police." In Jonathan R. Adelman (ed.), *Terror and Communist Politics.* Boulder, Colo.: Westview Press, 1984.

Akamatsu, Katsumaro. "The Russian Influence on the Early Japanese

210

Bibliography

Bibliography

Social Movement." In Peter Berton, Paul F. Langer, and George O. Totten (trans. and eds.), *The Russian Impact on Japan: Literature and Social Thought.* Los Angeles, Calif.: University of Southern California Press, 1981.

Akita Ujaku. *Gojūnen seikatsu nenpu* (A fifty-year history of my life). Tokyo: Naukasha, 1936.

Amamiya Shōichi. "Ketsumeidan Jiken: 'shihōken dokuritsu' no zeijakusei no rotei" (The Blood Pact Group Incident: exposing the fragility of 'judicial independence' "). In Wagatsuma Sakae (ed.), *Nihon seiji saiban shiroku, Showazen* (A history of political trials in Japan, early Showa). Tokyo: Daiichi hōki shuppan kabushikikaisha, 1970.

Aoki Sadao. *Tokkō kyōtei* (A textbook for the Special Higher Police). Tokyo: Shinkōkaku, 1937.

Asahi Jānaru (ed.). *Showa shi no shunkan* (Historical moments during Showa). 1. Tokyo: Asahi shinbun sha, 1966.

Ayusawa, Iwao R. *A History of Labor in Modern Japan.* Honolulu: East-West Center Press, 1966.

Barshay, Andrew E. *State and Intellectual in Imperial Japan: The Public Man in Crisis.* Berkeley, Calif.: University of California Press, 1988.

Bayley, David H. *Forces of Order: Police Behavior in Japan and the United States.* Berkeley, Calif.: University of California Press, 1976.

Beckmann, George M. *The Making of the Meiji Constitution: The Oligarchs and the Constitutional Development of Japan, 1868–1891.* Lawrence, Kan.: University of Kansas Press, 1957.

Beckmann, George M., and Okubo Genji. *The Japanese Communist Party, 1922–1945.* Stanford, Calif.: Stanford University Press, 1969.

Beer, Lawrence W. "Japan." In Jack Donnelly and Rhoda E. Howard (eds.), *International Handbook of Human Rights.* New York: Greenwood Press, 1987.

"Bengoshi Unno Shinkichi" kankō iinkai (ed.). *Bengoshi Unno Shinkichi* (Attorney Unno Shinkichi). Tokyo: "Bengoshi Unno Shinkichi" kankō iinkai, 1972.

Berger, Gordon M. *Parties Out of Power in Japan, 1931–1941.* Princeton, N.J.: Princeton University Press, 1977.

Bernstein, Gail L. *Japanese Marxist: A Portrait of Kawakami Hajime, 1879–1946.* Cambridge, Mass.: Harvard University Press, 1976.

Bowen, Roger W. *Rebellion and Democracy in Meiji Japan: A Study of Commoners in the Popular Rights Movement.* Berkeley, Calif.: University of California Press, 1980.

Braisted, William R. (trans.). *Meiroku Zasshi: Journal of the Japanese Enlightenment.* Tokyo: University of Tokyo Press, 1976.

Bramstedt, E. K. *Dictatorship and Political Police: The Technique of Control by Fear.* London: Kegan Paul, Trench, Trubner, 1945.

Chen, Ching-chih. "Police and Community Control Systems in the Empire." In Ramon H. Myers and Mark R. Peattie (eds.), *The Japanese Colonial Empire, 1895-1945.* Princeton, N.J.: Princeton University Press, 1984.

Ch'en, Paul Heng-chao. *The Formation of the Early Meiji Legal Order: The Japanese Code of 1871 and Its Chinese Foundation.* Oxford: Oxford University Press, 1981.

Crump, John. *The Origins of Socialist Thought in Japan.* London: Croom Helm, 1983.

Dando, Shigemitsu. *Japanese Criminal Procedure,* South Hackensack, N.J.: Fred B. Rothman, 1965.

Davis, Sandra T. W. *Intellectual Change and Political Development in Early Modern Japan: Ono Azusa, A Case Study.* Cranbury, N.J.: Associated University Presses, 1980.

Delarue, Jacques. *The Gestapo: A History of Horror.* New York: Paragon House, 1987.

Dōjin sha (ed.). *Musansha hōritsu hikkei* (Legal handbook for the proletariat). Tokyo(?): Dōjin sha, 1932.

Dower, J. W. *Empire and Aftermath: Yoshida Shigeru and the Japanese Experience, 1878-1954.* Cambridge, Mass.: Harvard University Press, 1979.

Eberstein, William. *Fascist Italy.* New York: Russell and Russell, 1939.

Friedrich, Carl J., and Zbigniew K. Brzezinski. *Totalitarian Dictatorship and Autocracy.* New York: Frederick A. Praeger, 1965.

Fujita Toshitsugu. "Dokubō no kaiwa" (Conversation in solitary confinement). In Kazahaya Yasoji (ed.), *Gokuchū no Showa shi: Toyotama Keimusho* (Showa history of imprisonment: Toyotama Prison). Tokyo: Aoki shoten, 1986.

Fuse Kanji. *Aru bengoshi no shōgai: Fuse Tatsuji* (The life of one lawyer: Fuse Tatsuji). Tokyo: Iwanami shinsho, 1963.

Fuse Tatsuji. *Kyōsantō jiken ni taisuru hihan to kōgi* (Critique and protest against the Communist Party Incident). Tokyo: Kyōseikaku, 1929.

Garon, Sheldon. *The State and Labor in Modern Japan.* Berkeley, Calif.: University of California Press, 1987.

Gastil, Raymond D. *Freedom in the World: Political Rights and Civil Liberties 1978.* Boston: G. K. Hall, 1978.

Gordon, Andrew. *The Evolution of Labor Relations in Japan: Heavy Industry, 1853-1955.* Cambridge, Mass.: Harvard University Press, 1985.

Hane, Mikiso. *Modern Japan: A Historical Survey.* Boulder, Colo.: Westview Press, 1986.

————. *Peasants, Rebels, and Outcasts: The Underside of Modern Japan.* New York: Pantheon Books, 1982.

Hackett, Roger F. *Yamagata Aritomo in the Rise of Modern Japan, 1838-1922.* Cambridge, Mass.: Harvard University Press, 1971.

Harrison, John A. *Japan's Northern Frontier: A Preliminary Study in Coloniza-
tion and Expansion with Special Reference to the Relations of Japan and
Russia.* Gainesville, Fla.: University of Florida Press, 1953.

Hashimoto, Kiminobu. "The Rule of Law: Some Aspects of Judicial
Review of Administrative Action." In Arthur T. von Mehren
(ed.), *Law in Japan: The Legal Order in a Changing Society.* Cambridge,
Mass.: Harvard University Press, 1963.

Hatanaka Shigeo. "Kaikon, soshite kaikon kara no dasshutsu" (Remorse, and escape from remorse). In *Yokohama Jiken: genron dan'atsu
no kōzu* (Yokohama Incident: illustration of the suppression of
speech). Tokyo: Iwanami shoten, 1987.

Havens, Thomas R. *Valley of Darkness: The Japanese People and World War
Two.* New York: W. W. Norton, 1978.

Henderson, Dan F. "Law and Political Modernization in Japan." In
Robert E. Ward (ed.), *Political Development in Modern Japan.* Princeton, N.J.: Princeton University Press, 1968.

Hijikata Tetsu. *Hisabetsu buraku no tatakai: ningen ni hikari are* (Struggle of
the unjustly discriminated community: light of hope for human
beings). Tokyo: Shinsensha, 1972.

Hirai, Atsuko. *Individualism and Socialism: The Life and Thought of Kawai
Eijirō (1891–1944).* Cambridge, Mass.: Harvard University Press,
1986.

Hiramatsu Yoshirō. "Kindaiteki jiyūkei no tenkai" (Development of the
modern flexible penalty). In Ōtsuka Hiroshi and Hiramatsu
Yoshirō (eds.), *Gyōkei no gendaiteki shiten* (Modern penal viewpoints).
Tokyo: Yūhikaku, 1981.

Hirano, Ryuichi. "The Accused and Society: Some Aspects of Japanese
Criminal Law." In Arthur T. von Mehren (ed.), *Law in Japan: The
Legal Order in a Changing Society.* Cambridge, Mass.: Harvard Uni-
versity Press, 1963.

Hŏ Se-ke. "Pak Yŏl Jiken: shiitagerareta mono no hangyaku" (Pak Yŏl
Incident: revolt by an oppressed people). In Wagatsuma Sakae
(ed.), *Nihon seiji saiban shiroku, Taisho* (A history of political trials in
Japan, Taisho). Tokyo: Daiichi hōki shuppan kabushikikaisha,
1969.

————. "Zoruge Jiken: kokusai seiji no urakata" (The Sorge Incident:
the hidden side of international politics). In Wagatsuma Sakae
(ed.), *Nihon seiji saiban shiroku, Showakō* (A history of political trials
in Japan, latter Showa). Tokyo: Daiichi hōki shuppan kabushikikaisha, 1970.

Hodge, Alan, and Robert Graves. *The Long Week-end: A Social History of
Great Britain, 1918–1939.* New York: W. W. Norton, 1963.

Höhne, Heinz. *The Order of the Death's Head: The Story of Hitler's S.S.* New
York: Coward-McCann, 1970.

Hoshino Yoshiki. *Kyōsanshugi sotsugyō no ki: shisō no henreki to waga hansei* (Chronicle of a graduate from communism: my half lifetime thought pilgrimage). Tokyo: Tosa shobō, 1948.

Ichikawa Yoshio (ed.). *Rōdōsha nōmin no daigishi: Yamamoto Senji wa gikai de ikani tatakatta ka* (Labor-Farmer parlimentary member: how did Yamamoto Senji fight in the diet?). Kyoto: San'ichi shobō, 1949.

Ienaga, Saburō. *The Pacific War: World War II and the Japanese, 1931–1945.* New York: Pantheon Books, 1978.

————. *Ueki Emori kenkyū* (Research on Ueki Emori). Tokyo: Iwanami shoten, 1970.

Igarashi Motosaburō. "Toyotama Keimusho de" (In Toyotama Prison). In Kazahaya Yasoji (ed.), *Gokuchū no Showa shi: Toyotama Keimusho* (Showa history of imprisonment: Toyotama Prison). Tokyo: Aoki shoten, 1986.

Ike, Nobutaka. *The Beginnings of Political Democracy in Japan.* Baltimore, Md.: Johns Hopkins Press, 1950.

Imai Seiichi. *Nihon no rekishi* (A history of Japan). 23. Tokyo: Chūō kōron sha, 1966.

Ingraham, Barton L. *Political Crime in Europe: A Comparative Study of France, Germany, and England.* Berkeley, Calif.: University of California Press, 1979.

Inoue Enzō (ed.). *Shihō Keisatsu shitsumu yōten* (Essentials for Justice Police official duties). Tokyo: Shimizu shoten, 1924.

Irokawa Kōtarō. *Musansha undō torishimari hōki suchi* (All laws and regulations to control the proletarian movement). Kyoto: Kyōseikaku, 1931.

Ishihara Masajirō. *Shisō Keisatsu gairon* (An introduction to the Thought Police). Tokyo: Shōkadō, 1930.

Ishii, Ryōsuke. "The History of Evidence in Japan." In *La Preuve.* 19 (Part 3). Brussels: Editions De La Librairie Encyclopedique, 1963.

————. *A History of Political Institutions in Japan.* Tokyo: University of Tokyo Press, 1980.

————. *Japanese Legislation in the Meiji Era.* Tokyo: Pan-Pacific, 1958.

Itagaki Taisuke (ed.). *Jiyūtō shi* (A history of the Liberal Party). 2. Tokyo: Gosharō, 1910.

Ishioka Matsugorō. "Toyotama Keimusho no omoide" (Reminiscences of Toyotama Prison). In Kazahaya Yasoji (ed.), *Gokuchū no Showa shi: Toyotama Keimusho* (Showa history of imprisonment: Toyotama Prison). Tokyo: Aoki shoten, 1986.

Iwagiri Noboru (ed.). *Motoji Shinkuma den* (A biography of Motoji Shinkuma). Tokyo: Chūō shuppan sha, 1955.

Jiyū Hōsō Dan (ed.). *Jiyū Hōsō Dan monogatari: senzenhen* (Story of the Liberal Legal Association: prewar compilation). Tokyo: Nippon hyōron sha, 1976.

214 Bibliography

Johnson, Chalmers. *An Instance of Treason: Ozaki Hotsumi and the Sorge Spy Ring.* Stanford, Calif.: Stanford University Press, 1964.

"Kanketsu ni atatte (zadankai)" (Toward a conclusion, a round-table talk). In Wagatsuma Sakae (ed.), *Nihon seiji saiban shiroku, Showakō* (A history of political trials in Japan, latter Showa). Tokyo: Daiichi hōki shuppan kabushikikaisha, 1970.

Kasza, Gregory J. *The State and the Mass Media in Japan, 1918–1945.* Berkeley, Calif.: University of California Press, 1988.

Kawakami Hajime. *Gokuchū nikki* (Prison diary). Tokyo: Sekai hyōron sha, 1949.

Kawasaki Takukichi denki hensankai. *Kawasaki Takukichi.* Tokyo: Kawasaki Takukichi denki hensankai, 1961.

Keene, Donald. *Dawn to the West: Japanese Literature of the Modern Era: Fiction.* 1. New York: Holt, Rinehart & Winston, 1984.

Keisatsu kenkyūkai (ed.). *Shakai undō ni chokumen shite* (Confronted by the social movement). Tokyo: Shōkadō, 1932.

Kikukawa Tadao. *Gakusei shakai undō shi* (A history of the student social movement). Tokyo: Chūō kōron sha, 1931.

Kishi Seiji. "Watakushi to Toyotama Keimusho" (Toyotama Prison and I). In Kazahaya Yasoji (ed.), *Gokuchū no Showa shi: Toyotama Keimusho* (Showa history of imprisonment: Toyotama Prison). Tokyo: Aoki shoten, 1986.

Kobayashi Takiji. *Senkyūhyakunijūhachinen Sangatsu Jūgonichi, Kanikōsen, Tō Seikatsusha* (The Fifteenth of March 1928, The Crab Factory Ship, Life of a Party Member). Tokyo: Shin Nihon shuppan sha, 1963.

Konvitz, Milton R. *Bill of Rights Reader: Leading Constitutional Cases.* Ithaca, N.Y.: Cornell University Press, 1973.

Koschmann, J. Victor. "Introduction: Soft Rule and Expressive Protest." In J. Victor Koschmann (ed.), *Authority and the Individual in Japan: Citizen Protest in Historical Perspective.* Tokyo: University of Tokyo Press, 1978.

Krausnick, Helmut, and Martin Broszat. *Anatomy of the SS State.* London: Granada, 1982.

Kublin, Hyman. *Asian Revolutionary: The Life of Sen Katayama.* Princeton, N.J.: Princeton University Press, 1964.

Kuroda Hidetoshi. *Chishikijin genron dan'atsu no kiroku* (A record of the suppression of intellectuals' speech). Tokyo: Shiraishi shoten, 1976.

———. *Yokohama Jiken* (Yokohama Incident). Tokyo: Gakugei shorin, 1975.

Kyōsei kyōkai (ed.). *Nihon kinsei gyōkei shikō* (A history of Japan's modern penal administration). 1. Tokyo: Kyōsei kyōkai, 1978.

————. *Senji gyōkei jitsuroku* (An authentic record of penal administration during wartime). Tokyo: Kyōsei kyōkai, 1966.

Maezawa Hiroaki (ed.). *Nihon Kokkai nanajūnen shi* (A seventy-year history of Japan's Diet). Tokyo: Shinbun gōdō tsūshin sha, 1953.

Makino Eiichi. *Hijōji rippō kō* (Consideration of emergency period legislation). Tokyo: Chūō kōron sha, 1943.

Masaki, Akira. *Reminiscences of a Japanese Penologist.* Tokyo: Japanese Criminal Policy Association, 1964.

Matsumoto Kazumi. "Tokyo Yobō Kōkinjo no kaisō" (Recollection of the Tokyo Preventive Detention Center). In Kazahaya Yasoji (ed.), *Gokuchū no Showa shi: Toyotama Keimusho* (Showa history of imprisonment: Toyotama Prison). Aoki shoten, 1986.

Matsumoto, Shigeru. *Motoori Norinaga, 1730–1801.* Cambridge, Mass.: Harvard University Press, 1970.

Matsuo Hiroya. "Kyoto Gakuren Jiken: hatsudō sareta Chian Iji Hō" (The Kyoto Gakuren Incident: putting the Peace Preservation Law into motion). In Wagatsuma Sakae (ed.), *Nihon seiji saiban shiroku, Showazen* (A history of political trials in Japan, early Showa). Tokyo: Daiichi hōki shuppan kabushikikaisha, 1970.

Matsuo Takayoshi. *Chian Iji Hō: dan'atsu to teikō no rekishi* (The Peace Preservation Law: a history of repression and resistance). Tokyo: Shin Nihon shuppan sha, 1971.

Matsuoka Hideo. *Jinken yōgo rokujūnen: bengoshi Unno Shinkichi* (Sixty years of defending human rights: attorney Unno Shinkichi). Tokyo: Chūō kōron sha, 1975.

Matsuzaka Hiromasa den kankō kai (ed.). *Matsuzaka Hiromasa den* (Biography of Matsuzaka Hiromasa). Osaka: Dai Nihon insatsu kabushikikaisha, 1969.

McEwan, J. R. *The Political Writings of Ogyū Sorai.* Cambridge: Cambridge University Press, 1962.

Merson, Allan. *Communist Resistance in Nazi Germany.* London: Lawrence and Wishart, 1985.

Midoro Masaichi. *Meiji Taisho shi: genron hen* (A history of Meiji and Taisho: public expression compilation). 1. Tokyo: Asahi shinbun sha, 1930.

Miller, Frank. *Minobe Tatsukichi: Interpreter of Constitutionalism in Japan.* Berkeley, Calif.: University of California Press, 1965.

Minear, Richard H. *Japanese Tradition and Western Law: Emperor, State, and Law in the Thought of Hozumi Yatsuka.* Cambridge, Mass.: Harvard University Press, 1970.

Minobe Ryōkichi. *Kumon suru demokurashii* (Democracy in agony). Tokyo: Bungei shunjū, 1959.

Mishima, Yukio. *Runaway Horses.* New York: Alfred A. Knopf, 1973.

Mitchell, Richard H. *Censorship in Imperial Japan.* Princeton, N.J.: Princeton University Press, 1983.
————. *Thought Control in Prewar Japan.* Ithaca, N.Y.: Cornell University Press, 1976.
Miyake Shōichi. *Gekidōki no Nihon shakai undō shi* (A history of Japan's social movement during a violent period). Tokyo: Gendai hyōron sha, 1973.
Miyashita Hiroshi, Itō Takashi, and Nakamura Tomoko. *Tokkō no kaisō: aru jidai no shōgen* (Special Higher Police reminiscences: testimony from a particular era). Tokyo: Tabata shoten, 1978.
Mori Tadashi. *Chian Iji Hō saiban to bengoshi* (Lawyers and the Peace Preservation Law trials). Tokyo: Nippon hyōron sha, 1985.
Morinaga Eizaburō. *Nihon bengoshi retsuden* (Biographies of Japanese lawyers). Tokyo: Shakai shisō sha, 1984.
————. *Yamazaki Kesaya.* Tokyo: Kinokuniya shoten, 1972.
Moriyama Takeichirō. *Shisōhan Hogo Kansatsu Hō kaisetsu* (An explanation of the Thought Criminals' Protection and Supervision Law). Tokyo: Shōtokukai, 1937.
Motofuji, Frank (trans.). *"The Factory Ship" and "The Absentee Landlord,"* by Kobayashi Takiji. Seattle, Wash.: University of Washington Press, 1973.
Mouer, Ross, and Yoshio Sugimoto. *Images of Japanese Society: A Study in the Social Construction of Reality.* London: KPI, 1986.
Muroga Sadanobu. *Showa Juku: dan'atsu no arashi no nakademo jiyū no akari o mamori tsuzuketa hitotsu no juku ga atta* (Showa School: there was one school protecting the light of liberty during the storm of suppression). Tokyo: Nihon keizai shinbun sha, 1978.
Nabeyama Sadachika. *Watakushi wa kyōsantō o suteta: jiyū to sokoku o motomete* (I discarded the Communist Party: my search for freedom and my homeland). Tokyo: Rōdō shuppan sha, 1950.
Nabeyama Sadachika and Sano Manabu. *Tenkō jūgonen* (Fifteen years since our conversion). Tokyo: Rōdō shuppan sha, 1949.
Nakagawa Norikata. *Shisō hanzai sōsa teiyō* (A summary for investigating thought crimes). Tokyo: Shinkōkaku, 1935.
Nakamura Kikuo. *Hoshi Tooru.* Tokyo: Yoshikawa kōbunkan, 1966.
Nakanishi Mitsuhiro. "Miki Kiyoshi no gokushi" (Miki Kiyoshi's prison death). In Kazahaya Yasoji (ed.), *Gokuchū no Showa shi: Toyotama Keimusho* (Showa history of imprisonment: Toyotama Prison). Tokyo: Aoki shoten, 1986.
Nagashima, Atsushi. "The Accused and Society: The Administration of Criminal Justice in Japan." In Arthur T. von Mehren (ed.), *Law in Japan: The Legal Order in a Changing Society.* Cambridge, Mass.: Harvard University Press, 1963.

Nanba Hideo. *Ichi shakai undōka no kaisō* (Reminiscences of one partici-
pant in the social movement). Tokyo: Shiraishi shoten, 1974.

Nomura Masao. *Hōsō fūunroku: anohito konohito hōmonki* (Record of affairs
in judicial circles: interviews of various people). 2. Tokyo: Asahi
shinbun sha, 1966.

Nosaka Sanzō shiryō hensan iinkai (ed.). *Nosaka Sanzō no ayunda michi*
(The path that Nosaka Sanzō walked). Shin Nihon shuppan sha,
1964.

Notehelfer, F. G. *Kōtoku Shūsui: Portrait of a Japanese Radical.* Cambridge:
Cambridge University Press, 1971.

Obinata Sumio. *Tennōsei keisatsu to minshū* (Emperor system police and the
people). Tokyo: Nippon hyōron sha, 1987.

Odanaka Toshiki. "Daiichiji Kyōsantō Jiken: Nihon Kyōsantō sōritsu to
Chian Iji Hō jidai zenya no saiban" (The First Communist Party
Incident: The establishment of the Japanese Communist Party and
the trial on the eve of the Peace Preservation Law era). In Wagatsuma Sakae (ed.), *Nihon seiji saiban shiroku, Taisho* (A history of
political trials in Japan, Taisho). Tokyo: Daiichi hōki shuppan kabushikikaisha, 1969.

―――. "Jinmin Sensen Jiken: hansen, hanfashizumu seiryoku e no
dan'atsu" (The Popular Front Incident: suppression of antiwar
and anti-Fascism influence). In Wagatsuma Sakae (ed.), *Nihon seiji
saiban shiroku, Showakō* (A history of political trials in Japan, latter
Showa). Tokyo: Daiichi hōki shuppan kabushikikaisha, 1970.

―――. "San'ichigo Yon'ichiroku Jiken: Chian Iji Hō saiban to hōtei
tōsō" (The March 15 and April 16 Incidents: The Peace Preservation Law trial and the court struggle). In Wagatsuma Sakae (ed.),
Nihon seiji saiban shiroku, Showazen (A history of political trials in
Japan, early Showa). Tokyo: Daiichi hōki shuppan kabushikikaisha, 1970.

Ogino Fujio. *Tokkō Keisatsu taisei shi: shakai undō yokuatsu torishimari no kōzō
to jittai* (An organizational history of the Special Higher Police:
structure and substance of the oppressive control of the social
movement). Tokyo: Sekita shobō, 1984.

Okudaira Yasuhiro. "Chian Iji Hō ni okeru yobō kōkin: sono seiritsu ni
tsuite no junbiteki kōsatsu (Preventive detention in the Peace Preservation Law: preparatory thoughts on its establishment). In
Tokyo daigaku shakai kagaku kenkyūjo (ed.), *Fashizumuki no kokka
to shakai, 4: senji Nihon no hōtaisei* (Nation and society during the Fascist era, 4: Japanese legal structure during wartime). Tokyo: Tokyo
daigaku shakai kagaku kenkyūjo, 1979.

―――. *Chian Iji Hō shōshi* (A short history of the Peace Preservation
Law). Tokyo: Chikuma shoten, 1977.

————. "Yokohama Jiken to Chian Iji Hō" (The Yokohama Incident and the Peace Preservation Law). In *Yokohama Jiken: genron dan'atsu no kōzu* (Yokohama Incident: illustration of the suppression of speech). Tokyo: Iwanami shoten, 1987.

Ōno Masao. "Shokugyō to shite no bengoshi oyobi bengoshikai no rekishi" (Occupational history of lawyers and lawyer associations). in Ōno Masao (ed.), *Kōza gendai no bengoshi 2: bengoshi no dantai* (Lectures on modern lawyers 2: lawyer groups). Tokyo: Nippon hyōron sha, 1970.

Ōno Tatsuzō. *Nihon no seiji keisatsu* (Japan's political police). Tokyo: Shin Nihon shuppan sha, 1985.

Peters, Edward. *Torture.* Oxford: Basil Blackwell, 1985.

Piovesana, Gino K. "Miki Kiyoshi: Representative Thinker of an Anguished Generation." In Joseph Roggendorf (ed.), *Studies in Japanese Culture.* Tokyo: Sophia University Press, 1963.

Pittau, Joseph. *Political Thought in Early Meiji Japan, 1868–1889.* Cambridge, Mass.: Harvard University Press, 1967.

Possony, Stefan T. "From Gulag to Guitk: Political Prisons in the USSR Today." In Willem A. Veenhoven (ed.), *Case Studies on Human Rights and Fundamental Freedoms: A World Survey.* The Hague: Martinus Nijhoff, 1975.

Robinson, Michael E. "Colonial Publication Policy and the Korean Nationalist Movement." In Ramon H. Myers and Mark R. Peattie (eds.), *The Japanese Colonial Empire, 1895–1945.* Princeton, N.J.: Princeton University Press, 1984.

Rubin, Jay. *Injurious to Public Morals: Writers and the Meiji State.* Seattle, Wash.: University of Washington Press, 1984.

Sano Hidehiko. "Gokusha seikatsu no kiroku" (Record of a prisoner's life). In Kazahaya Yasoji (ed.), *Gokuchū no Showa shi: Toyotama Keimusho* (Showa history of imprisonment: Toyotama Prison). Tokyo: Aoki shoten, 1986.

Sasaki Yoshizō. *Tokkō zensho* (A complete book on the Special Higher Police). Tokyo: Shōkadō, 1933.

Scalapino, Robert A., and Chong-sik Lee. *Communism in Korea.* 1. Berkeley, Calif.: University of California Press, 1972.

Sewell, Alan F. "Political Crime: A Psychologist's Perspective." In M. Cherif Bassiouni (ed.), *International Terrorism and Political Crimes.* Springfield, Ill.: Charles C. Thomas, 1975.

Shigematsu Kazuyoshi. *Hokkaido gyōkei shi* (A history of Hokkaido's penal system). Tokyo: Zufu shuppan, 1970.

Shillony, Ben-Ami. *Politics and Culture in Wartime Japan.* Oxford: Clarendon Press, 1981.

Shinobu Seizaburō. *Taisho demokurashii shi* (A history of Taisho democracy). 3. Tokyo: Nippon hyōron sha, 1964.

————. *Taisho seiji shi* (A political history of the Taisho period). Tokyo: Keisō shobō, 1968.

Shiono Suehiko kaikoroku kankōkai. *Shiono Suehiko kaikoroku* (The memoirs of Shiono Suehiko). Tokyo: Shiono Suehiko kaikoroku kankōkai, 1958.

Shōkadō henshūbu (comp.). *Chian keisatsu kyōhon* (Peace police textbook). Tokyo: Shōkadō, 1941.

Smith, Henry D. *Japan's First Student Radicals*. Cambridge, Mass.: Harvard University Press, 1972.

Solzhenitsyn, Aleksandr I. *The Gulag Archipelago, 1918–1956: An Experiment in Literary Investigation*. Parts 1 and 2. New York: Harper & Row, 1973.

Spaulding, Robert M. *Imperial Japan's Higher Civil Service Examinations*. Princeton, N.J.: Princeton University Press, 1967.

Stanley, Thomas A. *Ōsugi Sakae, Anarchist in Taishō Japan: The Creativity of the Ego*. Cambridge, Mass.: Harvard University Press, 1982.

Steinhoff, Patricia G. "Tenkō and Thought Control." In Gail L. Bernstein and Haruhiro Fukui (eds.), *Japan and the World: Essays on Japanese History and Politics in Honour of Ishida Takeshi*. New York: St. Martin's Press, 1988.

Storry, Richard. *A History of Modern Japan*. Harmondsworth, Eng.: Penguin Books, 1982.

Strong, Kenneth. *Ox Against the Storm: A Biography of Tanaka Shozo: Japan's Conservationist Pioneer*. Tenterden, Eng.: Paul Norbury, 1977.

Suzuki Mosaburō. *Aru shakaishugisha no hansei* (Half a lifetime of one socialist). Tokyo: Bungei shunjū shinsha, 1958.

Swearingen, Rodger, and Paul Langer. *Red Flag in Japan: International Communism in Action, 1919–1951*. New York: Greenwood Press, 1968.

Taikakai (ed.). *Naimushō Shi* (A history of the Home Ministry). 2 and 4. Tokyo: Chihō zaimu kyōkai, 1971.

Taira, Koji. *Economic Development and the Labor Market in Japan*. New York: Columbia University Press, 1970.

Takahashi Yūsai. *Meiji keisatsu shi kenkyū* (Research on the history of the Meiji police). Tokyo: Reibun sha, 1961.

Takayanagi, Kenzo. "A Century of Innovation: The Development of Japanese Law, 1868–1961." In Arthur T. von Mehren (ed.), *Law in Japan: The Legal Order in a Changing Society*. Cambridge, Mass.: Harvard University Press, 1963.

Tamiya Hiroshi. "Amakasu Jiken: Kenpei ni gyakusatsu sareta museifushugisha Ōsugi Sakae" (Amakasu Incident: the brutal killing of the anarchist Ōsugi Sakae by the Military Police). In Wagatsuma Sakae (ed.), *Nihon seiji saiban shiroku, Taisho* (A history of political trials in Japan, Taisho). Tokyo: Daiichi hōki shuppan kabushikikaisha, 1969.

220   *Bibliography*

————. "Fukuda Taishō Sogeki Jiken: Ōsugi Sakae gyakusatsu ni taisuru hōfukutero no shippai" (The General Fukuda Shooting Incident: the unsuccessful retaliation terrorism for the brutal killing of Ōsugi Sakae). In Wagatsuma Sakae (ed.), *Nihon seiji saiban shiroku, Taisho* (A history of political trials in Japan, Taisho). Tokyo: Daiichi hōki shuppan kabushikikaisha, 1969.

Tanaka Tokihiko. "Toranomon Jiken: kōtaishi o sogeki shita Nanba Daisuke" (The Toranomon Incident: Nanba Daisuke's shot at the crown prince). In Wagatsuma Sakae (ed.), *Nihon seiji saiban shiroku, Taisho* (A history of political trials in Japan, Taisho). Tokyo: Daiichi hōki shuppan kabushikikaisha, 1969.

Teters, Barbara. "The Otsu Affair: The Formation of Japan's Judicial Conscience." In David Wurfel (ed.), *Meiji Japan's Centennial: Aspects of Political Thought and Action.* Lawrence, Kans.: University of Kansas Press, 1971.

Tezuka Yutaka. *Meiji shoki keihō shi no kenkyū* (Research on the history of early Meiji penal law). Tokyo: Keiō tsūshin kabushikikaisha, 1956.

Tiedemann, Arthur E. "Big Business and Politics in Prewar Japan." In James W. Morley (ed.), *Dilemmas of Growth in Prewar Japan.* Princeton, N.J.: Princeton University Press, 1971.

Thompson, E. P. *Whigs and Hunters: The Origin of the Black Act.* New York: Pantheon Books, 1975.

"Tokkō Keisatsu kokusho iinkai" (ed.). *Tokkō Keisatsu kokusho* (Special Higher Police black paper). Tokyo: Shin Nihon shuppan sha, 1977.

Tokuda Kyūichi and Shiga Yoshio. *Gokuchū jūhachinen* (Eighteen years in prison). Tokyo: Jiji tsūshin sha, 1947.

Totten, George O. *The Social Democratic Movement in Prewar Japan.* New Haven, Conn.: Yale University Press, 1966.

Tsuchiya Shukurō. *Yobō kōkinjo* (Preventive detention center). Tokyo: Bansei sha, 1988.

Tsurumi, Kazuko. *Social Change and the Individual: Japan before and after Defeat in World War II.* Princeton, N.J.: Princeton University Press, 1970.

Tsurumi, Shunsuke. *An Intellectual History of Wartime Japan, 1931–1945.* London: KPI, 1986.

Ueda Seikichi. *Showa saiban shiron: Chian Iji Hō to hōritsukatachi* (A historical essay on Showa trials: The Peace Preservation Law and the legalists). Tokyo: Ōtsuka shoten, 1983.

Ushioda, Sharlie C. "Fukuda Hideko and the Woman's World of Meiji Japan." In Hilary Conroy, Sandra T. W. Davis, and Wayne Patterson (eds.), *Japan in Transition: Thought and Action in the Meiji Era, 1868–1912.* Rutherford, N.J.: Fairleigh Dickinson University Press, 1984.

Ushiomi Toshitaka (ed.). *Nihon no bengoshi* (Japanese lawyers). Tokyo: Nippon hyōron sha, 1972.
Watanabe Tooru and Inoue Kiyoshi. *Kome Sōdō no kenkyū* (A study of the Rice Riots). 5. Tokyo: Yūhikaku, 1959.
Weiner, Michael. *The Origins of the Korean Community in Japan.* Atlantic Highlands, N.J.: Humanities Press, 1989.
Wray, William D. "The Japanese Popular Front Movement, July 1936–February 1938." In vol. 5: *Papers on Japan From Seminars at Harvard University.* Cambridge, Mass.: East Asian Research Center, Harvard University, 1972.
Yahata Saburō. "Toyotama: watakushi no daigaku" (Toyotama: my university). In Kazahaya Yasoji (ed.), *Gokuchū no Showa shi: Toyotama Keimusho* (Showa history of imprisonment: Toyotama Prison). Tokyo: Aoki shoten, 1986.
Yamashiro Tomoe and Makise Kikue (eds.). *Tanno Setsu: kakumei undō ni ikiru* (Tanno Setsu: living the revolutionary movement). Tokyo: Keisō shobō, 1969.
Yamazaki Kesaya. *Jishin, Kenpei, kaji, junsa* (Earthquake, Military Police, fire, and police). Tokyo: Iwanami shoten, 1984.
Yokoi Daizō. *Shin Keiji Hoshō Hō taii* (An outline of the New Criminal Compensation Law). Tokyo: Tachibana shoten, 1950.
Yokoyama Shōichirō. "Keiji hoshō" (Criminal compensation). In Takioka Takahisa and Yokoyama Shōichirō, *Sōgō hanrei kenkyū sōsho* (A comprehensive collection of research on judicial precedents). Tokyo: Yūhikaku, 1962.
Yoshino Sakuzō (ed.). *Meiji bunka zenshū* (Collected works on Meiji culture). 18. Tokyo: Nippon hyōron sha, 1928.

ARTICLES

Abe, Haruo. "The Former Japanese System of Preventive Detention." *International Commission of Jurists Journal* 3, 1 (1961): 99–108.
———. "Criminal Justice in Japan: Its Historical Background and Modern Problems." *American Bar Association Journal* 97 (June 1961): 555–559.
Beer, Lawrence W., and C. G. Weeramantry. "Human Rights in Japan: Some Protections and Problems." *Universal Human Rights* 1, 3 (July–September 1979): 1–33.
Bellah, Robert N. "Intellectual and Society in Japan." *Daedalus* 101, 2 (1972): 89–115.
Braibanti, Ralph J. D. "Japan's New Police Law." *Far Eastern Survey* 18 (January 24, 1949): 17–22.
Brogden, Mike. "An Act to Colonise the Internal Lands of the Island:

Empire and the Origins of the Professional Police." *International Journal of the Sociology of Law,* no. 2 (May 1987): 179–208.

Cantor, Nathaniel. "The Fascist Political Prisoners." *Journal of the American Institute of Criminal Law and Criminology* 27 (1936–1937): 169–179.

Coox, Alvin D. "Evidences of Antimilitarism in Prewar and Wartime Japan." *Pacific Affairs* 46, 3 (Fall 1973): 502–514.

Davis, David B. "The Ends of Slavery." *New York Review of Books* 36 (March 30, 1989): 29–34.

Elison, George. "Kōtoku Shūsui: 'The Change in Thought.' " *Monumenta Nipponica* 22, 3–4 (1967): 437–467.

Epp, Robert. "The Challenge from Tradition: Attempts to Compile a Civil Code in Japan, 1866–78." *Monumenta Nipponica* 22, 1–2 (1967): 15–48.

Foster, D. H., D. Sandler, and D. M. Davis. "Detention, Torture and the Criminal Justice Process in South Africa." *Journal of the Sociology of Law* 15, 2 (May 1987): 105–120.

George, B. J. "The Impact of the Past upon the Rights of the Accused in Japan." *Civil Law and Military Journal* 5, 3–4 (July–December 1969): 57–76.

Hall, John W. "Rule by Status in Tokugawa Japan." *Journal of Japanese Studies* 1, 1 (Autumn 1974): 39–49.

Hall, J. C. "The Tokugawa Legislation, IV." *Transactions of the Asiatic Society of Japan* 41 (1913): 683–804 plus unnumbered pages.

Hane, Mikiso. "Early Meiji Liberalism: An Assessment." *Monumenta Nipponica* 24, 4 (1969): 353–371.

Harrison, Judy F. "Wrongful Treatment of Prisoners: A Case Study of Ch'ing Legal Practice." *Journal of Asian Studies* 23, 2 (February 1964): 227–244.

Henderson, Dan F. "Chinese Legal Studies in Early 18th-Century Japan: Scholars and Sources." *Journal of Asian Studies* 30, 1 (November 1970): 21–56.

Hiramatsu, Yoshirō. "History of Penal Institutions: Japan." *Law in Japan: An Annual* (1973): 1–48.

Hirano Yoshitarō. "Jinken o mamotta hitobito: Fuse Tatsuji o chūshin ni" (People who protected human rights: centered on Fuse Tatsuji). *Hōgaku seminā* (November 1959): 56–61.

Huish, David. "The Meirokusha: Some Grounds for Reassessment." *Harvard Journal of Asiatic Studies* 32 (1972): 208–229.

Ide, Yoshinori. "Administrative Culture in Japan: Image of the *Kan* or Public Administration." *Annals of the Institute of Social Science,* no. 22 (1981): 152–182.

Ishida, Takeshi. "Fundamental Human Rights and the Development of Legal Thought in Japan." *Law in Japan: An Anuual* (1975): 39–66.

————. "The Introduction of Western Political Concepts into Japan." Nissan Occasional Paper Series, no. 2. 1986. 1–26.

Ishii, Ryōsuke. "Dan Fenno Henderson, Conciliation and Japanese Law —Tokugawa and Modern." *Law in Japan: An Annual* (1968): 198–224.

Itoh, Hiroshi. "Frank O. Miller, Minobe Tatsukichi: Interpreter of Constitutionalism in Japan." *Law in Japan: An Annual* (1969): 200–206.

Matsuo, Takayoshi. "The Development of Democracy in Japan— Taishō Democracy: Its Flowering and Breakdown." *Developing Economies* 4 (December 1966): 612–637.

Minami Kiichi. "Kameido Jiken no giseisha: watakushi wa jikeidanchō to shite Chōsenjin no inochi o mamotta. Sono yokujitsu Nankatsu Rōdō Kai ni ita Otōto wa gyakusatsu sareta" (Victims of the Kameido Incident: as head of a vigilante committee, I protected the lives of Koreans. My younger brother, who was a member of the Nankatsu Labor Association, was brutally killed the following day). *Chūō kōron,* no. 923 (September 1, 1964): 224–227.

Mizuno Naoki. "Chian Iji Hō to Chōsen—oboegaki" (The Peace Preservation Law and Korea—a memorandum). *Chōsen kenkyū,* no. 4 (1979): 45–60.

Morinaga Eizaburō. "Fuse Tatsuji (jinken yōgo undō shijō no ni sen-dachi)" (Fuse Tatsuji [two pioneers in the history of the human rights movement]). *Hōgaku seminā,* December 1956, 44–48.

Moriyama, Takeichiro. "Rescuing Radicals By Law." *Contemporary Japan: A Review of Japanese Affairs* 6, 2 (September 1937): 277–281.

Mukai, Ken, and Toshitani Nobuyoshi. "The Progress and Problems of Compiling the Civil Code in the Early Meiji Era." *Law in Japan: An Annual* (1967): 25–59.

Nagao, Ryūichi. "The Legal Philosophy of Tatsukichi Minobe." *Law in Japan: An Annual* (1972): 165–191.

————. "Richard H. Minear, Japanese Tradition and Western Law: Emperor, State and Law in the Thought of Yatsuka Hozumi." *Law in Japan: An Annual* (1972): 209–225.

Okudaira Yasuhiro. "Chian Iji Hō o ronzuru: Shimizu Ikutarō 'sengo o utagau' o utagau" (Discussing the Peace Preservation Law: having doubts about Shimizu Ikutarō's 'postwar doubts' ") *Sekai,* no. 396 (November 1978): 103–117.

————. "Some Preparatory Notes for the Study of the Peace Preservation Law in Pre-war Japan." *Annals of the Institute of Social Science,* no. 14 (1973): 49–69.

Pak Kyŏng-sik. "Chian Iji Hō ni yoru Chōsenjin dan'atsu" (The suppression of Koreans based on the Peace Preservation Law). *Kikan gendai shi,* no. 7 (June 4, 1976): 114–134.

Rickett, W. Allyn. "Voluntary Surrender and Confession in Chinese

Law: The Problem of Continuity." *Journal of Asian Studies* 30, 4 (August 1971): 797–814.

Shue, Henry. "Torture." *Philosophy and Public Affairs* 7, 2 (Winter 1978): 124–143.

Wagatsuma, Sakae. "Guarantee of Fundamental Human Rights Under the Japanese Constitution." *Washington Law Review.* Special edition, reprint volume: "Legal Reforms in Japan During the Allied Occupation" (1977): 146–166.

Wakabayashi, Bob Tadashi. "Katō Hiroyuki and Confucian Natural Rights, 1861–1870." *Harvard Journal of Asiatic Studies* 44, 2 (December 1984): 469–492.

Walthall, Anne. "Japanese *Gimin:* Peasant Martyrs in Popular Memory." *American Historical Review* 91, 5 (December 1986): 1076–1102.

Westney, D. Eleanor. "The Emulation of Western Organizations in Meiji Japan: The Case of the Paris Prefecture of Police and the Keishi-chō." *Journal of Japanese Studies* 8, 2 (Summer 1982): 307–342.

White, James W. "State Growth and Popular Protest in Tokugawa Japan." *Journal of Japanese Studies* 14, 1 (Winter 1988): 1–25.

Wildes, Harry E. "The Japanese Police." *Journal of Criminal Law, Criminology and Police Science* 19 (November 1928): 390–398.

Yamabe, Kentarō. "A Note on *The Korean Communist Movement* by Daesook Suh, With Special Reference to Source Materials Used." *Developing Economies* 5, 2 (June 1967): 405–412.

Yokoyama Shōichirō. "Keiji hoshō: hō no enkaku to unyō no mondaiten" (Criminal compensation: the background of the law and problems of its enforcement). *Hōritsu jihō* 31, 356 (November 1959): 95–105.

BIBLIOGRAPHIES, COLLECTIONS, DICTIONARIES, AND ENCYCLOPEDIAS

Baldwin, Roger N. "Political Police." In Edwin R. A. Seligman (ed.), *Encyclopedia of the Social Sciences* 11–12: 203–207. New York: Macmillan, 1937.

Cannistraro, Philip V. (ed.). *Historical Dictionary of Fascist Italy.* Westport, Conn.: Greenwood Press, 1982.

Hunter, Janet E. (comp.). *Concise Dictionary of Modern Japanese History.* Berkeley, Calif.: University of California Press, 1984.

Kyoto daigaku bungakubu kokushi kenkyū shitsu (ed.). *Nihon kindai shi jiten* (A dictionary of modern Japanese history). Tokyo: Tōyō keizai shinpō sha, 1958.

Lerner, Max. "Political Offenders." In Edwin R. A. Seligman (ed.),

Encyclopedia of the Social Sciences 11–12: 199–203. New York: Macmillan, 1937.
Matsuo, Takayoshi. "Teijin Incident." In Itasaka Gen (ed.), *Encyclopedia of Japan* 7:375. Tokyo: Kodan sha, 1983.
Mitchell, Richard H. "Peace Preservation Law of 1925." In Itasaka Gen (ed.), *Encyclopedia of Japan* 6:168–169. Tokyo: Kodan sha, 1983.
Ōkubo Shūhachi (ed.). *Kyojin shinjin fusen daigishi meienzetsu* (Collected names and speeches: senior and newly elected representatives). Tokyo: Dai Nihon yūbenkai kōdan sha, 1928.
Sanseidō henshūjo (ed.). *Konsaisu jinmei jiten* (A concise biographical dictionary). Tokyo: Sanseidō kabushikikaisha, 1976.
Sasama, Yoshihiko. *Zusetsu Edo no keisatsu shihō jiten* (A dictionary explaining police and justice in Edo). Tokyo: Kashiwara shobō, 1980.
Steinhoff, Patricia G. "Tenkō." In Itasaka Gen (ed.), *Encyclopedia of Japan* 8:6–7. Tokyo: Kodan sha, 1983.
Uyehara, Cecil H. *Leftwing Social Movements in Japan: An Annotated Bibliography.* Tokyo: Charles Tuttle, 1959.
Wagatsuma Sakae (ed.). *Kyū hōrei shū* (A collection of old laws and regulations). Tokyo: Yūhikaku, 1968.
———. *Shin hōritsugaku jiten* (A new jurisprudence dictionary). Tokyo. Yūhikaku, 1967.

NEWSPAPERS

Japan Weekly Chronicle, 1931–1939.
Ono, Takashi. "Bills on Treatment of Prisoners, Suspects Arouse Concern." *Japan Times* (National edition), June 1, 1988, 3.
Zabolotsky, N. A. "The Story of My Imprisonment." *Times Literary Supplement,* October 9, 1981, 1179–1181.

UNPUBLISHED MATERIAL

Dardess, Margaret B. "The Thought and Politics of Nakae Chōmin (1847–1901)." Ph.D. dissertation, Columbia University, 1973.
Drea, Edward J. "The Japanese General Election of 1942: A Study of Political Institutions in Wartime." Ph.D. dissertation, University of Kansas, 1978.
Leavell, James B. "The Development of the Modern Japanese Police System: Transition from Tokugawa to Meiji." Ph.D. dissertation, Duke University, 1975.
Matsumoto, Tomone. "From Marxism to Japanism: A Study of Kamei Katsuichirō." Ph.D. dissertation, University of Arizona, 1979.
Nadolski, Thomas P. "The Socio-Political Background of the 1921 and

1935 Ōmoto Suppression in Japan." Ph.D. dissertation, University of Pennsylvania, 1975.

Soviak, Eugene. "Baba Tatsui: A Study of Intellectual Acculturation in the Early Meiji Period." Ph.D. dissertation, University of Michigan, 1962.

Steinhoff, Patricia G. "*Tenkō:* Ideology and Societal Integration in Prewar Japan." Ph.D. dissertation, Harvard University, 1969.

Tipton, Elise K. "The Civil Police in the Suppression of the Prewar Japanese Left." Ph.D. dissertation, Indiana University, 1977.

Index

About the Author

Richard H. Mitchell, who received his Ph.D. from the University of Wisconsin-Madison in 1963, is professor of modern Japanese history at the University of Missouri-St. Louis. He is the author of *The Korean Minority in Japan* (1967), *Thought Control in Prewar Japan* (1976), and *Censorship in Imperial Japan* (1983).

 Production Notes

Composition and paging were done on the
Quadex Composing System and typesetting
on the Compugraphic 8400 by the design
and production staff of University of
Hawaii Press.

The text typeface is Baskerville and the
display typeface is Trump.

Offset presswork and binding were done by
The Maple-Vail Book Manufacturing Group.
Text paper is Glatfelter Offset Vellum,
basis 50.